THE ARCHAEOLOGY OF A GREAT ESTATE:
CHATSWORTH AND BEYOND

The Archaeology of a Great Estate:
Chatsworth and Beyond

John Barnatt and Nicola Bannister

WIND*gather*
PRESS

Windgather Press
is an imprint of
Oxbow Books

ISBN 978-1-905119-27-1

A CIP record for this book is available from the British Library

This book is available direct from

Oxbow Books, Oxford, UK
(Phone: 01865-241249; Fax: 01865-794449)

and

The David Brown Book Company
PO Box 511, Oakville, CT 06779, USA
(Phone: 860-945-9329; Fax: 860-945-9468)

or from our website

www.oxbowbooks.com

Printed in Singapore by
KHL Printing Co Pte Ltd

Contents

List of Figures

Acknowledgements

....

This book would not have been possible without the enthusiastic support of the Late 11th Duke, the Dowager Duchess of Devonshire, and the Trustees of the Chatsworth Settlement, who commissioned the survey and allowed unlimited access to Estate land and archives. The 12th Duke and Duchess are thanked equally for their continued support which allowed this book to be produced. Amongst the many other people at Chatsworth who have helped over the years, particular thanks go to Roger Wardle, Ian Else, Peter Day, Charles Noble, Tom Askey, Stewart Band, Andrew Pepin, Simon Seligman, Diane Naylor, Sarah Sweetland, and to the tenant farmers and other Estate staff/workers for their forbearance and frequent displays of kindness.

Appreciation is also extended to Elise Percifull, Steven Thomas and Tom Williamson, who undertook the original designed landscape survey of the park and gardens, for their invaluable exchange of information. Tom is thanked particularly for his collaboration with *Chatsworth: A Landscape History* and for his inspirational approach plus great knowledge of designed landscapes.

Special thanks are extended to David Bannister for undertaking the field recording of the buildings and preparation of the draft Buildings Survey reports, and also to Angus Foad for his invaluable assistance throughout all the boundary and woodland fieldwork across the Estate. Frank Robinson kindly shared much of his local knowledge of Beeley and helped identify some of the features on the moors. Heidi Taylor and Alice Ullathorne carried out some of the archaeological survey fieldwork of the Chatsworth farmland. John Roberts helped with survey of parts of the parkland and New Piece Plantation. Jim Rieuwerts and Paul Smith provided information on mines.

The photographs are taken by John Barnatt. Exceptions are Figures 32–34, 37–38 and 45 which are from the Chatsworth Photo Library at the Devonshire Collection, Chatsworth, and are reproduced by permission of Chatsworth Settlement Trustees. The line drawings are by John Barnatt. Some of the survey information shown in Figure 93 is base on work undertaken jointly by the Peak District National Park Authority and RCHME. Similarly Figure 9 is partially based on a RCHME survey.

John Barnatt and Nicola Bannister were funded by English Heritage to prepare the manuscript. They also funded the initial archaeological surveys via the Trustees of the Chatsworth Settlement. Pete Wilson and Jonathan Last supervised this assessment for English Heritage. Ken Smith of the Peak District

National Park Authority was instrumental both in the setting up of the survey and in the publication of this book. Tom Williamson, Jonathan Last and Ken Smith kindly commented on the text.

   Last but not least, we would like to thank Richard Purslow of Windgather Press for agreeing to publish this book and to Oxbow Books for their continued support, with particular mention of Clare Litt and Val Lamb, and to thank our families for their forbearance.

CHAPTER ONE

Chatsworth in Context

....

Setting the scene: Chatsworth's place in the world

For those not intimately familiar with upland landscapes such as that around Chatsworth, and those in the Peak District more generally, it may come as a great surprise that the historic landscapes here are as rich as they are. Commonly, upstanding features such as a 4000 year old ritual monument can sit alongside a medieval earthwork of 1200 AD or a lead mine worked 300 years ago. The archaeological legacy is far more than a few scattered sites, the whole landscape has great time depth. Everywhere you look has a rich palimpsest of features creating a land imbued with the past and strongly evoking the many generations of people who have inhabited this place and helped shape what we see today.

At Chatsworth we see the Peak in microcosm. However, at this one special place, not only is survival of evidence particularly good, but the landscapes around the Estate are diverse and tell contrasting stories. Chatsworth House and its gardens, with the grand landscape park beyond, are the icing on the cake as they create an exceptional centrepiece. To pick out some highlights, in the park started in 1758–59 are some of the best archaeological earthworks of medieval open fields and later enclosure in Britain. On the Estate moorlands there are exceptional survivals of prehistoric stone circles, barrows, fields and settlements. In contrast, the Estate's enclosed farmland tells of continuous occupation and gradual changes made over the last thousand years.

While this book concentrates on the archaeology of this 'Great Estate', it also tells a broader story throughout, drawing on the links between Chatsworth-owned land and the wider landscape.

Chatsworth and the surrounding Estate villages and farms are different things to different people. For a few, their home and place of work is here. For many, Chatsworth is a place to visit, to wonder at the splendours of the House and gardens with their spectacular parkland backdrop. Most visitors appreciate the impressive classical architecture, and the antiques and paintings therein. The gardens, with their trees, plants, fountains, cascade and grottos are equally fascinating. The long history of the Cavendish family, here since 1549 and bearing the Duke of Devonshire title since 1694, draws people here. Some wander into the park to take the air and enjoy the views and the ancient oaks, or visit the model village of Edensor. Others are on missions to the garden centre

or the farm shop. Some visit the surrounding somewhat quaint Estate villages and follow footpaths through the farmland, woods and moorland to enjoy the wider countryside and its plants and animals.

However, there is a complementary side to Chatsworth Estate which is equally fascinating, and one that not many people have previously had access to detailed information about, namely the historic landscape and its archaeology. This book seeks to redress the balance.

Recently another book on Chatsworth's park and gardens has given an in-depth picture of their history and what went before.[1] The current offering is very different in scope and emphasis. Here the whole of the Estate landscape, including the extensive farmland and moorlands beyond the park, are included, and the book concentrates on the visible archaeology and what this can tell us about the past. Other books on Peak District archaeology are available, such as 'The Peak District: Landscapes Through Time', which gives an overview of the archaeology of the region.[2] The current Chatsworth book complements this overview, covering the same themes but looking at one place in more detail.

Beyond the House, gardens and landscape park at its heart, the Chatsworth Estate spreads over many acres of enclosed farmland in the valley of the River Derwent, around Edensor, Calton, Beeley, Baslow and Bubnell. To the east there are extensive bleak moorlands and scattered farmsteads. All these areas have rich and diverse stories to be told, derived from the many archaeological vestiges that remain.

Archaeology is about how people have lived and how they have affected the land in the past. It studies what they have left behind. This is not restricted to obvious archaeological monuments such as prehistoric barrows, ancient hillforts, churches and castles. It includes all the remains of human activity

FIGURE 1. Chatsworth House from the park, with Stand Wood behind.

FIGURE 2. The Peak District and the location of Chatsworth in relation to surrounding cities, towns and larger villages.

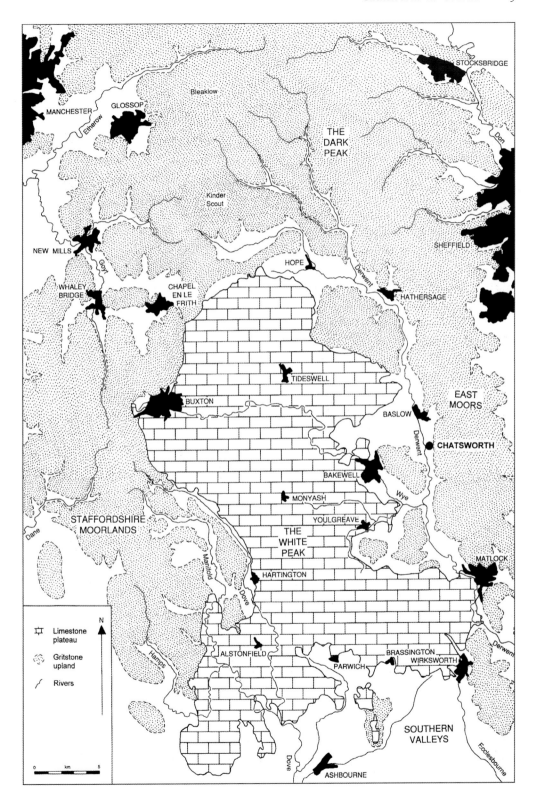

through time that have survived above or below ground to the present day, whether 5,000 or 50 years old. At Chatsworth, this includes the relics left by farmers, smallholders, labourers, millstone makers, quarrymen, and miners of coal and lead, as well as members of the landed aristocracy. Equally important is evidence for people crossing the land to and from the Derwent Valley around Chatsworth. They came and went from markets, workshops and factories, as well as farms, villages and towns. Meat, milk and cheese from local farms were sold in nearby towns and cities. Beyond the Peak there were important industrial and manufacturing areas to the east around Chesterfield and Sheffield. Similarly, there was trade with the salt-producing areas of the Cheshire Plain and potteries in Staffordshire and to the east of the Pennines. Millstones and lead from the Peak went to Hull, from where they were shipped to other parts of Britain and in the case of lead, to the rest of the world.

The Cavendish Family at Chatsworth

The Cavendish family first became involved in Chatsworth in 1549, when William Cavendish and his wife Elizabeth ('Bess') of Hardwick purchased the old hall here, together with its deer park on the slopes above and farmland on both sides of the river. Over the generations, their descendants, soon Earls of Devonshire and later Dukes, have periodically rebuilt, enlarged and modified the House and its gardens, adding to their splendours according to the fashionable tastes of different generations.[3] The present landscape park to the north, south and west of the House was started in 1758–59 under the direction of Lancelot 'Capability' Brown and finished several years later. The medieval deer park, sited on the land running high above the House to the east, became redundant and later in the 19th century was largely subdivided into fields and plantations out of view from the House. Over the generations the Estate holdings were also gradually extended to their present bounds. This included an acquisition in the early 19th century, when large tracts of land were exchanged with the Duke of Rutland, which allowed the 6th Duke of Devonshire to extend the park a significant distance northwards.

Much of the designed landscape of the park we see today was created in the 18th century and modified in the 19th. The present gardens owe much to the work of Joseph Paxton and the 6th Duke in the 1820s–50s. The extensive farmland has had the Estate's stamp applied in more subtle ways. Some parts have developed in organic fashion over many generations. However, other areas of fields are pieces of ambitious planning, with what was there before swept away and replaced with the then current 'state of the art' field layouts and farm buildings. Other places were taken out of agricultural production at the 'home farm' or tenanted holdings and planted with trees as both long-term cash crops and decorative landscape features. These types of change are one of the characteristics of great estates; they could afford to make rapid radical alterations and improvements, whereas at the other end of the spectrum the typical hill farmer could not. The Chatsworth moorlands owe their survival not so much to their altitude and poor soils, but more critically to the family's interest in grouse shooting in the 19th century; elsewhere in the Peak similar land away from the estates of the Dukes of Devonshire and Rutland was often enclosed and improved.

In the first half of the 20th century, Chatsworth, like many great estates, fell upon relatively hard times and no radical changes to the landscape were made. However in 1950, when the late 11th Duke inherited, a reverse in its fortunes was instigated. He, and the now Dowager Duchess, spent decades building Chatsworth into one of the most attractive and successful of Country Estate tourist businesses. It is now visited by many thousands per year, who come to spend time at this most tastefully presented of 'great houses'. The 12th Duke and Duchess have now taken up the reins.

The Cavendish family also once owned much land elsewhere in the Peak District and North-East Derbyshire, as well as in other parts of England and Ireland; while some is still in their possession, a number of their estates were sold in the 20th century. These lands are all beyond the scope of this book, which exclusively describes the extensive current holdings in the vicinity of Chatsworth. To draw this distinction, the areas described are referred to throughout as the 'Core Estate'.

The Chatsworth landscape

This landscape of great scenic beauty lies in the heart of the Peak District. The House and park are in the Derwent Valley, with high wooded scarps to the east and desolate moors beyond, each with distinctive but very different types of appeal. Elsewhere in the valley there are extensive areas divided into fields, with villages, hamlets and farmsteads. These again have their own charm, with vernacular stone buildings, grassy fields, hedgerows, field walls, and woodlands.

No part of the Estate, or for that matter the Peak District has been left untouched by people over the last 10,000 years. While the geology of the area has determined the landforms and to an extent governs what grows here, it is people who have shaped everything that we see today from the soil upwards. Even the mix of plants and animals is determined by how we have managed and continue to manage the land. At a landscape scale nothing is how nature would have intended if left to its own devices. After the last Ice Age trees spread and carpeted much of the local landscape. They would still be here if it was not for people; many of the fine landscape vistas for which the Peak District is famous would not be visible. Even Chatsworth's heather moorlands are not 'natural' in the sense that these are entirely the product of people removing trees in prehistory and maintaining upland grazing here ever since.

The historic landscape in the Chatsworth Core Estate is not one integrated whole but has three distinct parts which will be frequently separated throughout the book, each with strongly contrasting geology, topography, history and

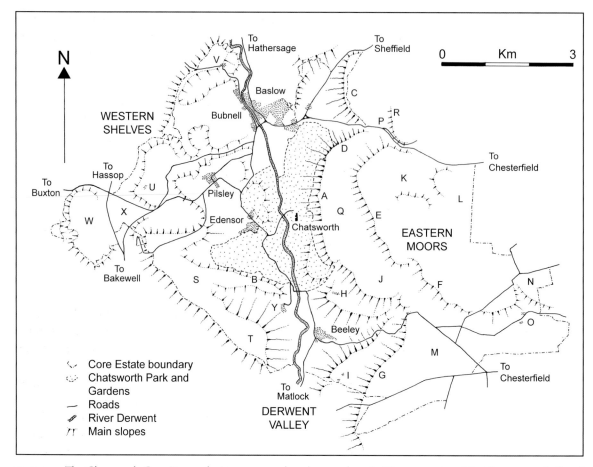

FIGURE 3. The Chatsworth Core Estate, showing topography, places and roads (Places mentioned in Chapter 1 – A: Stand Wood, B: New Piece Plantation, C: Gardom's Edge, D: Dobb Edge, E: Bunkers Hill, F: Harland Edge, G: Fallinge Edge, H: Beeley Hilltop, I: Fallinge, J: Beeley Warren, K: Gibbet Moor, L: Brampton East Moor, M: Beeley Moor, N: Longside Moor, O: Harewood Moor, P: Robin Hood, Q: The Old Park, R: Birchen Edge, S: Calton Pasture, T: Lees Moor, U: Birchill, V: Bramley, W: Cracknowl Pasture, X: Birchill Flatt, Y: Calton Lees).

surviving archaeology. The parkland with the House and gardens is at the heart – the enclosed farmland surrounding this, which is also focussed on the Derwent Valley but includes shelf-lands to the west – and the high moorlands lie to the east. Each has great time depth with a wide range of archaeological features, but before we come to these we need to understand something of the underlying geological backbone.

The natural background; constraints and resources

The River Derwent, which Chatsworth House overlooks, is one of the key features of the Peak District, providing a topographical 'artery' running north/ south between higher ground to east and west. The main scarp of the gritstone uplands to the east dominates the scene. The land beyond is high and the peaty soils have inhibited settlement for the last two millennia except for an occasional farmstead. In prehistory this land was inhabited more widely, at a time after the natural forest was first cleared, when soils were more fertile than they are today. These eastern moors flank the Derwent for much of its upper course. They run from above where its headwaters enter the broader Hope Valley at Bamford some 10 miles north of Chatsworth, to where the river starts to run out of the upland beyond Cromford a further 10 miles to the south. The start of the central limestone plateau of the Peak District, historically an important area for settlement, agriculture and lead mining, lies only about 3 miles west of Chatsworth. However, there is very little limestone country within the Core Estate, the exception being at Cracknowl Pasture. Between the Derwent and the plateau, there is a local dissected area of further shelves, higher ridges and steep scarps, where the rocks comprise beds of sandstone and shale.

The Derwent Valley

The River Derwent follows a deeply incised valley past Chatsworth at a little over 100m above sea level, with the land a short distance away to the east often rising steeply. Only at Baslow and Beeley are the valley-bottom lands wider due to brooks entering from the east. To the west, in places the valley side rises only gradually to low shelves, as around Bubnell, Pilsley and Edensor. These topographic considerations have had a strong influence on where the main villages are located, sited at places where good low-lying agricultural land is maximised. Parts of the flat valley-bottom land would have been liable to flooding, particularly prior to canalisation of the river by the Estate and before the building of reservoirs in the Upper Derwent Valley just after the turn of the 20th century.

The main rock type in the valley is easily eroded shale of the Middle Carboniferous era. Higher in the geological sequence, there are also interleaved thin beds of sandstone and siltstone, together with much thicker beds of coarse sandstone known as millstone grit. These erosion-resistant beds form the tops of the valley-side scarps.

Shale-based soils in the valley, derived from decomposition of this parent rock, are heavy and poorly drained clays. However, the bottom lands often have alluvium deposits containing many sandstone cobbles which are relatively infertile compared with those in the lowlands. The steeper upper parts of the valley's sides often have thin, poor soils and are strewn with boulders derived from erosion of the gritstone scarp above.

The Derwent Valley would naturally be thickly wooded. However, in the valley bottom much of this land has probably been largely clear of trees since prehistory. In contrast, many of the steep upper valley sides are covered in trees today, but this has not always been the case and the situation here is complex. Large woods such as Stand Wood above the House and New Piece Plantation

on the other side of the valley are largely 18th century replantings on ground that had a much reduced tree cover in the period immediately before. It is thought that the standing timber on poorer ground in the Peak District had been much reduced from the late medieval period onwards, used for large-scale lead smelting and other industrial processes; elsewhere extensive clearances on good agricultural land were already ancient, cleared for arable, grazing and fuel. As a result, by the end of the 16th century if not before, surviving and newly established woodlands in the Peak were often probably carefully managed coppice that provided a renewable resource for industry. However, given the lack of archaeological and documentary evidence, this does not appear to have been so in the case of Stand Wood within Chatsworth's late medieval deer park, presumably because this was primarily reserved for hunting. While late 16th century lead smelting took place briefly in the deer park, the timber removed may well have been from the shelf land above the main scarp. On the main valley side extensive woodland still existed in 1617 and this was only gradually depleted over the next 100 years.[4] In contrast, on parts of the lower scarp slope later incorporated within the mid 18th century landscape park, today there are still a significant number of splendid veteran oaks. Local tales of them being a remnant of Sherwood Forest are not true; the administrative boundaries of that medieval hunting forest never came this far west. Similarly, there is no positive support for the idea that they are a remnant of natural wildwood that has always

FIGURE 4. The Derwent Valley, with the southern end of the Park, New Piece Plantation and the Calton Lees valley in the background, and Beeley Hilltop in the foreground.

been there and certainly in historic times woodland has not extended unbroken from Nottinghamshire; pollen analysis shows that the extensive moors above Chatsworth have been clear of trees since prehistory.[5] While the oldest oaks have been here since late medieval times, some at least relate to the ground being taken out of normal agricultural production with the creation of the deer park. This is demonstrated by individual trees in the southern part of the landscape park that overlie medieval cultivation terraces.

The eastern moors

The main scarp above Chatsworth to the east rises to between about 200m and 290m above sea level. Parts of this steep edge have millstone grit cliffs at its crest, especially at Gardom's Edge and Dobb Edge, where these have been

FIGURE 5 (*right*). The Chatsworth moorlands, with Harland Edge at the skyline, from Beeley Warren.

FIGURE 6 (*below*). The western shelves, showing Handley Bottom with the Birchill shelf beyond.

enhanced by quarrying. Behind, to the east there is a broad shelf with an upper scarp beyond. The upper scarp, at Bunkers Hill and Harland Edge, rises up to a maximum of 370m above sea level and is often boulder-strewn.

This simple topographic picture is more complex further south. The beds that formed the scarp at the western edge of the main shelf to the north rise to Fallinge Edge, becoming in effect the equivalent of the upper scarp. Below, to the west, a lower shelf rises to prominence. This is first obvious in the southern part of the park where it is a narrow shelf half-way up the main valley side. As this shelf runs southwards it becomes wider at Beeley Hilltop, while at Fallinge its edge forms the equivalent of the main scarp further north.

Further topographic complexity is created by the erosion of the scarps by three streams. To the north Bar Brook and Heathy Lea Brook run down steep boulder-strewn valleys through the main scarp to either side of Gardom's Edge, with a confluence near Baslow in the Derwent Valley bottom. Further south, Beeley Brook runs down a similar valley between Beeley Warren and Fallinge Edge.

The high moors behind the upper scarp, at Gibbet Moor and Brampton East Moor, have upland streams in shallow valleys, with marshes at their heads and undulating land between. Further south, Beeley Moor is relatively flat, poorly drained and windswept. As one passes eastwards to the edge of the Core Estate, flat ridgetops at Longside and Harewood Moors are flanked by narrow but deep valleys that drop into the dissected landscape of the Coal Measure foothills.

The scarps of the eastern moors are formed by thick beds of millstone grit and sandstone, while softer interleaved shale beds outcrop at the shelves between. The main scarp above the House comprises Chatsworth Grit, while further south the Beeley Hilltop/Fallinge scarp is Ashover Grit. The upper scarp is Crawshaw Sandstone, which is the lowest hard bed in the Coal Measure sequence of Upper Carboniferous date. All three of these beds have been quarried in the past, producing such items as millstones, troughs and gateposts.

Outcropping on the main shelf is the lowest local coal bed, the Baslow Seam. In the past this has been worked at Robin Hood, in the old Chatsworth deer park and on Beeley Moor. Further east, above the Crawshaw Sandstone, there are several other coal seams, including one known as the Belperlawn or Soft Bed Seam which has been investigated on Gibbet Moor.

From the time of prehistoric farming in the last two to three millennia BC onwards, the soils over much of the high flatter ground on the eastern moors have deteriorated and they have become peaty. In hollows deep peat deposits have formed, but mostly the land is covered with shallow blankets of peaty soils. The buried now-inactive soils beneath vary according to whether the rock is sandstone or shale. Overlying the former rock type, the topsoil was originally a rich brown earth but now this is often heavily leached. The shales have heavy clays. The situation is further complicated by the frequent redeposited clay and gritstone-boulder deposits that concentrate on the scarp slopes but sometimes spread over shelf land below. In contrast to the moors, on improved enclosed land ploughing has mixed the peaty soils with whatever was below.

While the eastern gritstone uplands would naturally be covered in trees, with oak and birch dominant in most places, on the flatter land and perhaps elsewhere they had largely been removed by the end of prehistory. Rough grazing has predominated for the last two millennia, but in the Bronze and Iron Ages the parts with sandy soils were more intensively farmed, in places for upwards of two thousand years. Extensive archaeological remains survive because of subsequent non-destructive use.

Today's peaty soils on the eastern moors support a mixture of heather and coarse grasslands maintained by grazing and heather burning. Trees could recolonise if management were changed, despite the degraded soils, as well illustrated just north of the Estate on the shelf between Gardom's and Birchen Edges. Here, after an intensive moorland fire in 1959, many self-seeded birch saplings started to grow, the windblown seed coming from Chatsworth Estate land below Gardom's Edge; large areas quickly became covered in scrub.

The western shelves

The western area of the Core Estate is part of a distinctive triangular area of land between the rivers Derwent and Wye where the landscape is dominated by discontinuous gritstone shelves and ridges, with steep scarps facing roughly west, and small steep-sided valleys between. That at Calton Pasture and Lees Moor is by far the largest and highest. The long south-western crest of this dissected ridge is two miles long and is between 265m and 305m above sea level. Thus, it is comparable with the main shelf east of the Derwent, although here much of the moorland vegetation had been removed by the early 18th century at the latest. Further north the four main gritstone plateau-like shelves and ridges at Pilsley, Birchill, Bubnell and Bramley are lower, reaching about 195m–240m above sea level. Each supported a medieval settlement and its fields. To the far west of the Estate there is a topographically similar area at Cracknowl Pasture, but here the bedrock is limestone.

The limestones of Cracknowl Pasture are of the Monsal Dale Beds, belonging to the upper part of the Lower Carboniferous sequence. The limestone plateau contains many mineralised faults and these contain ores of lead that were extensively mined in the past, while more recently the accompanying minerals fluorspar, barytes and calcite have become economically important. Minor examples of such veins occur in this part of the Estate.

Further east the limestone rocks dip below those of the overlying Millstone Grit Series. The Birchill shelf and Bramley ridge are of Kinderscout Grit, while Calton Pasture and the Pilsley and Bubnell shelves are Ashover Grit. Around Birchill Flatt the dominant rock is shale, hence the low-lying wet character of this area.

As with the eastern moors, the soils are acidic sandy loams or clays according to the local bedrock. However, to the west of the Derwent in the most favourable areas, soils of moderate fertility have been farmed and maintained for several millennia, while the upper areas of Calton Pasture have had a post-medieval history of improvement; some parts of this higher land had probably not been cultivated previously since prehistory. While there are large woods on steep slopes in this part of the Estate, most are post-medieval plantations.

People in the Chatsworth landscape

The Chatsworth Estate has a wide range of archaeological features both in terms of their date and type. Some are thousands of years old, others much more recent. Some are abandoned settlements; others commonly relate to past agriculture, industry and transport.

When looking at the development of archaeological landscapes, the levels of destruction increase as one goes backwards in time by peeling off 'layers of the onion'. For earlier periods, in today's enclosed farmland, the lack of surviving features often does not imply that these areas were little used by people, but only that later farmers have swept away the surface evidence.

For some periods there are a significant number of features that have survived, as for example with the exceptional number of settlements, fields and ritual monuments from the Bronze and Iron Ages. Medieval earthworks are also common, and not surprisingly features created and used over the last few hundred years are in parts dominant. In contrast, virtually nothing survives of earlier prehistory, a time when people left little in the way of permanent marks on the land. Surprisingly, only a few scraps of pottery tell of the Roman period, despite a strong Peak District native population and a military and administrative Roman presence. There is also a similar lack of material from the early medieval period, but this is common for much of Britain.

Earthworks, field walls and buildings of all periods tell us not just of themselves but they also inform about how people lived and worked in the past, often in radically different ways to ourselves. People then were technologically simpler rather than being worse-off and weak reflections of modern society. They saw the world differently. While the archaeological features found obviously tell about their locality, they also are part of a bigger picture and, to a lesser or greater degree, tell of broader trends as well as local distinctiveness.

As the archaeology of Chatsworth Estate is the main subject of this book, little more needs to be said here on its character by way of introduction. However, a brief summary is given below of why this book came to fruition and how data was gathered, followed by an outline of how the text is ordered.

The archaeological survey

Because of the outstanding scenic, aesthetic, historical and ecological value of the Chatsworth landscape, conditional exemption from inheritance tax was granted by Government in 1993 in return for managing the Estate in integrated sympathetic ways leading to ongoing conservation of these important elements in the landscape.

In 1993 formally recognised historical and archaeological features of high conservation value in the Core Estate included 16 Scheduled Monuments and 127 Listed Buildings. There were also a number of other archaeological sites listed in Derbyshire County Council's Sites and Monuments Record and in National Park Authority archives. However, these were the product of ad hoc work in the past. There had been no systematic collection of data so coverage was variable and there was considerable variation in quality, both in terms of reliability and in the breadth and depth of what had been recorded.

The Trustees of the Chatsworth Settlement commissioned a series of surveys, funded by English Heritage, to obtain as complete a record as possible for the Core Estate.[6] This includes most or all of five modern civil parishes as well as parts of five others. Fieldwork was undertaken between 1996 and 2000. Assessments included a main archaeological survey,[7] complemented by work on buildings, field boundaries and woodlands.[8] Where possible, historic Estate maps and documents were used to put flesh on the archaeological bones, but a comprehensive study of the extensive Estate archives was beyond the scope of the project. The whole was summarised and interpreted in an archive report completed in 2004.[9] This work was complemented by another project which specifically assessed the designed landscape of Chatsworth's park and gardens.[10] Taken together, these set monuments in context with much greater confidence and understanding.

The results of the surveys stand in strong contrast with what was known previously. The main archaeological survey, where a total about 5000 hectares of land were assessed, identified 682 nationally or regionally important archaeological sites and a further 915 locally important features. Over 280 individual entries were made during the buildings survey,[11] while 1499 individual field boundaries were recorded and 73 woods and plantations were assessed. The Estate is wonderfully rich in important archaeological remains, with virtually every field and corner of park and moor having something interesting that tells of people in the past.

It is rare that landed estates have been studied in their entirety by archaeologists, although this process has started.[12] The Chatsworth survey helps break new ground by looking at everything within a large estate in detail, demonstrating some of the values of such a multi-period approach.

Chatsworth through time: changing landscapes and themes

Chapters 2 to 8 follow a chronological framework, starting with prehistory. However, as archaeological evidence becomes more plentiful for the last 500 years, the evidence is also divided thematically. Here we start with direct impacts made by the Cavendish Estate in creating a designed landscape, followed by agricultural and then industrial landscapes, the latter now masked in a landscape that at casual glance erroneously appears to have been a quintessential rural idyll for time immemorial. Last comes changing communication routes between places in the Core Estate and the wider world with the development of the modern road network in the 18th and 19th centuries. Chapter 9 celebrates the richness and character of what survives from the past in the present landscape. Suggested places for people to explore are given in Chapter 10 and finally a few thoughts on past, present and future are given in Chapter 11.

Throughout the book, often subdivision into themes is made for convenience of description and sometimes this inevitably sets false or over-simplistic distinctions. For example, prehistoric agricultural features and ritual monuments are described separately. While monuments such as stone circles and barrows are overtly ritual, other aspects of prehistoric peoples' lives, such as farming practice, undoubtedly were intimately interwoven with ritual practices. Conversely, in their frame of reference, these ritual acts would be seen as just as practical as planting crops or tending animals.

Given that the book describes one of the major estates in the country it seems appropriate to draw a distinction between the 'designed landscape' of the parkland and the enclosed farmland and moorland beyond. Villages, farms and fields are of course designed for people, but while aesthetic values apply, these are different from the often intellectualised perfection incorporated in the Estate's overtly polite landscape.

CHAPTER TWO

An Ancient Land:
Farms and Monuments in Prehistory

....

Prehistoric survivals

While evidence for people inhabiting the Peak in earlier prehistory, in the Mesolithic and before, is restricted to scatters of flint and chert in ploughsoils and buried under peat, there are exciting survivals from later prehistory, from the Neolithic to Iron Age, that tell of settlement, farming and ritual.[1] A nationally important concentration of archaeological remains from this period extends along the eastern gritstone moorlands from Bamford Moor in the north to Beeley Moor in the south; the southern third lies within Chatsworth Estate. These remains lie within a near-continuous band of moorland that exceptionally allows detailed study of how people lived and organised themselves in the landscape between 4000 and 2000 years ago.

The picture is somewhat different on the region's central limestone plateau, where a wide variety of scattered but sometimes imposing Neolithic and Bronze Age ceremonial and ritual structures date to as much as 6000 years ago. These include chambered tombs, long barrows, two large henges, and many round barrows. Some are visible from afar, sited on many of the high points in this landscape. After a break in the Bronze Age when large monuments were not erected, in the last millennium BC a series of hillforts were built, often sited close to the edge of the plateau, where they dominated contrasting landscapes that held different resources and opportunities. However, in the wider limestone landscape not much has survived of the places where people dwelt and farmed for the last four millennia BC; these would have left less imposing earthworks and much has been swept away by later people as they ploughed extensively. The exceptions are a number of sites, often in isolated areas cut off by limestone outcrops, where earthworks of small settlements and fragments of field systems remain; these are often of Romano-British date, but some are known or suspected to have earlier origins.[2]

The land surrounding the limestone plateau offers differing landscape histories. The Derwent and Hope Valleys, for example, have been a focal area for settlement over the last 2000 years and little left by earlier peoples survives. To the north and west, much of the Peak is high and bleak, and remains are restricted to a small number of isolated round barrows. In strong contrast the

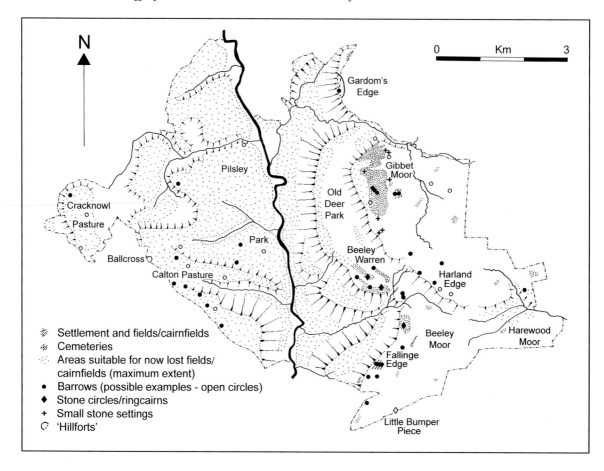

N

0   Km   3

Gardom's
Edge

Pilsley

Gibbet
Moor

Old
Deer
Park

Cracknowl
Pasture

Park

Beeley
Warren

Ballcross

Calton Pasture

Harland
Edge

Harewood
Moor

Beeley
Moor

Fallinge
Edge

Little Bumper
Piece

🕸 Settlement and fields/cairnfields
〰 Cemeteries
⁙ Areas suitable for now lost fields/
    cairnfields (maximum extent)
•   Barrows (possible examples - open circles)
◆   Stone circles/ringcairns
+   Small stone settings
⊙   'Hillforts'

FIGURE 7.
The Chatsworth
landscape in Later
Prehistory.

eastern gritstone moors were well suited for prehistoric farming communities. Here survival is exceptional because of the lack of later farming except for upland grazing over much of this land. Broad swathes of remains are available for study, although inspecting the evidence is often difficult as the surviving features are frequently small and low and the heather is high; heather burning allows disjointed glimpses of the true richness of the evidence. This includes house sites within a multitude of field boundary banks and stone-clearance features, together with small stone circles and settings and round barrows. Put together, these features tell of extensive use of this landscape from the Later Neolithic/Earlier Bronze Age to the Iron Age. The moorlands above Chatsworth lie at the heart of this 'prehistoric landscape'.

Although little survives from earlier prehistory around Chatsworth, from a time when people trod lightly on the land, large areas of the more-sheltered and/or better-drained parts of Gibbet Moor, Beeley Warren and Beeley Moor are covered with many unobtrusive but nationally important features that tell us much about how people lived two to four thousand years ago. Here the types of archaeological sites noted above are all well represented; there is also an

FIGURE 8. One of the Chatsworth Estate round barrows, high on Calton Pasture.

exceptional large Later Bronze Age enclosure above Gardom's Edge. In contrast, the enclosed farmland and parkland of the Estate have much more fragmentary visible evidence due to destruction of prehistoric surface features by later farming and other activities. These scattered survivals mainly comprise round barrows, but are complemented by a rare flat grave and a small 'hillfort'.

The ancient ways: hunting and gathering

Up until about 4000 BC Britain was inhabited by people who passed along paths from season to season, travelling between places where wild resources could be optimally harvested or hunted at particular times of the year.

The land now within Chatsworth Estate was undoubtedly inhabited by these Mesolithic people for several millennia from early post-glacial times, starting about 10,000 years ago, and perhaps before. These people have left only token traces of their presence. They would have moved about the region in an ordered seasonal round. Detailed knowledge of their 'home range' undoubtedly led to knowing which paths to follow to take advantage of a variety of natural resources as they became available. Their dwellings were often temporary or movable structures, although they also built more permanent dwellings as 'home bases', perhaps commonly used for over-wintering. No examples have as yet been found in the Peak, although one at Deepcar near Stocksbridge was excavated several decades ago.[3] Many of their tools, weapons and other accoutrements were made from materials such as wood, bone and skin that have not survived. The only common traces of these people's lives are small, lost or discarded stone tools that can be occasionally picked up when soil is disturbed.

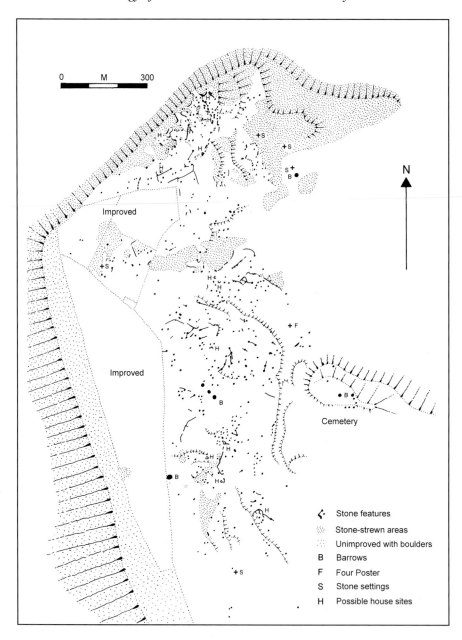

FIGURE 9. Prehistoric fields and cairnfields on Gibbet Moor.

Very few have been recorded on the Estate, as fields are not often ploughed and discovery on the moors has been dependent on rare accidental fires that have burnt off the peat and exposed patches of the soils beneath.

While these people led a technologically simple life, ethnographic parallels illustrate that gatherers usually have sophisticated social ties with their extended family and regional communities.

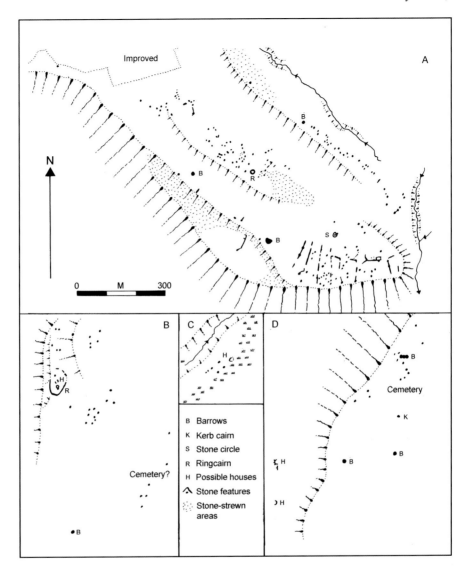

FIGURE 10. Prehistoric fields and cairnfields on the Chatsworth moorlands (A: Beeley Warren, B: Beeley Moor, C: Harewood Moor, D: Fallinge Edge).

Farming on the move?

With the advent of the Neolithic, from about 4000 BC, people in the Peak adopted farming ways, which included keeping herds and flocks of domesticated animals and the small-scale growing of cereals in tended 'garden plots'. However, their lifestyle in other ways may have been similar to their Mesolithic forebears in that they may have continued to move around the landscape seasonally.[4] It was perhaps not until the Later Neolithic or Earlier Bronze Age that people adopted a more sedentary way of life, establishing 'sustained' settlements and fields scattered across the landscape.[5] However, the extent to which farmers in the Neolithic were mobile or sedentary is a hotly contested issue amongst archaeologists.[6] Several decades ago it was unquestioningly assumed these people were sedentary, whereas more recently the pendulum has swung the other way. In the last decade more and more evidence has been found for permanent buildings, often large rectangular structures, particularly in Ireland and Scotland. The debate now is whether there were strong regional differences in the way people lived; there is no reason to think not. At the end of the day, the debate may well be over-simplistic and it is likely that elements of both lifestyles were common.[7] In the Peak District, the posthole layouts of two or probably three large rectangular buildings were excavated in the 1980s at Lismore Fields on the outskirts of Buxton.[8] Given the sheltered location of this site, it would not be surprising if this was a place where a local group over-wintered, whereas in summer many of the people took herds of cattle and flocks of sheep up onto the hills where there was extensive grazing. Some perhaps stayed to tend 'gardens' nearby containing small plots of cereal and root crops. However, the purpose of these large buildings is still unclear. Were they typical houses or were they special meeting places for extended-families or clan-groups? Perhaps people who stayed at the site dwelt in slighter structures that could be moved at will, leaving little archaeological trace.

In the Neolithic, small extended family groups would have come together occasionally in tribal gatherings, perhaps once or twice a year. People in this period built impressive communal monuments and in the Peak the limestone plateau is where these are found.[9] Disparate groups from around the region are most likely to have met in this central zone as this is where the richest pastures are, where there would have been a natural tendency for people coming from different directions to bump into each other more often. Often different groups would have been strangers or only met occasionally. Seasonal meetings presented opportunities to socialise, trade and meet prospective 'marriage' partners. It was also a time of potential tension, where groups could disagree, for example over tenure of land, or vent long standing disputes. Monuments were focal points where the flowing of traditional ritual practices provided an accepted way of minimising conflict. Barrows and chambered tombs reinforced land tenure by visually reminding people that the ancestors had long inhabited the place. Later, the large henges at Arbor Low south of Monyash and the Bull Ring at Dove Holes provided purpose-made and evocative stage-sets for gatherings.

In contrast to the limestone plateau, in areas like the Derwent Valley and eastern gritstone moors, some of the same Neolithic groups who visited the limestone pastures probably used the land beyond extensively at certain seasons but chose not to build monuments as this was not relevant here. This applies to the Chatsworth Core Estate where nothing of certain Neolithic date has been identified.

Settling down: the later-prehistoric farmed landscape

Later in prehistory the character of farming in the Peak gradually changed, with families each adopting more sustained relationships with particular places.

Areas surrounding farmsteads were given over to bounded fields and small family monuments were placed nearby. Beyond the fields there were extensive open pastures and farmers almost certainly claimed tenure to these by placing monuments containing the bones of their family ancestors overlooking this grazing land. Many of the monuments date from the period 2500–1500 BC, in the Later Neolithic and Earlier Bronze Age. Later their construction ceased, presumably as the pattern of land use developed by specific family groups had become so established that it was no longer contested. It may be that all these changes go hand in hand with developing ideas of ownership rather than tenure, and with a more sedentary lifestyle. However, it should not be assumed that these people had become farmers who would be easily recognisable as the forebears of Chatsworth farm tenants of a hundred years ago; the ways they lived and thought may well have had radical differences.

This picture is largely derived from the eastern moors, where the high quality of survival allows the character of settlement and farming to be studied in depth. A lot can be interpreted from what can be seen, while recent extensive excavations at Gardom's Edge have both confirmed much and raised new issues.[10] With the exception of a few monuments, to the uninitiated much of this surface evidence comprises little more than low piles of stone. It is when the positions of these are carefully plotted that a picture starts to emerge. While evidence for the fields and field clearance is readily identified, that for the settlement is more subtle. Buildings were generally made of impermanent materials that once abandoned soon rotted leaving little trace. Thus, often all that is visible without excavation are slight circular platforms terraced into sloping land; where the land is flat there is nothing to see. Hedges and probably fences originally defined many of the yards, garden plots and fields that surrounded the farmsteads. These again have gone, but often can be intermittently traced by slight lynchets and banks along their lines or by linear piles of field clearance stone placed against them. There are also many small circular heaps that were placed at close intervals within fields as the stony ground was prepared for use. When this land was cultivated the soil was probably turned by hand rather than by plough, thus the piles were not a hindrance.

People probably started adopting a more bounded way of life in the Later Neolithic and/or Earlier Bronze Age. While at this time they first established 'sustained' agricultural areas, many fields at these locales were used into the Iron Age and it is often difficult to date specific features exactly. Extensive areas of the gritstone eastern moors had these 'sustained' areas, with scattered 'farmsteads', each surrounded by fields. The land here was attractive. It was naturally lightly wooded, with oak and birch predominant, probably with open glades. The scarp tops, with gritstone and sandstone bedrock, once had a light sandy soil cover, which while stony was easy to cultivate. In the last 2–3000 years these soils have deteriorated and peat growth has rendered them waterlogged. The prehistoric farmers almost certainly practised mixed farming, using their fields for growing small quantities of cereals and other crops, and probably as hay meadows and also for cattle, sheep and pigs. Beyond the fields there were extensive open pastures on the higher and less attractive parts of any given farm; these undoubtedly were also extensively used for grazing. The overall farming emphasis was probably on the stock, both as the subsistence base and as a form of portable wealth. However, the acid soils have destroyed any bones, so this remains impossible to demonstrate.

We move now to describing the archaeological remains on the Chatsworth Estate; more general interpretations will be returned to at the end of the chapter.

Farming the Chatsworth uplands

The circular buildings of the prehistoric farmsteads were made with wooden posts, wattle and daub walls, and turf or thatch roofs. They are found, singly or in small groups scattered amongst the fields. As no stone footings were usually used, more undoubtedly remain unlocated. Amongst the eleven probable and possible unexcavated examples identified on the Chatsworth moorlands, there are two below Fallinge Edge.[11] These are the only known examples on the eastern moors that are located below a scarp rather than on the dip slope behind. The only part-excavated example is on Beeley Moor, but the only find there was a small patch of burnt earth.[12]

Up to 24 prehistoric agricultural areas are recognised from the clearance heaps and occasional earthen banks and lynchets.[13] There are particularly extensive areas of fields and agricultural cairnfields on Gibbet Moor and Beeley Warren.[14] On Gardom's Edge a small part of a similarly large area falls

FIGURE 11. This clearance cairn on Gibbet Moor became clearly visible several years ago when bracken was removed.

within the Estate but also extends well to the east.[15] These were core areas for prehistoric agricultural activity, with houses amongst the fields. In the case of Beeley Warren, the remains are found in three discrete areas. While this is in part governed by geology and topography, with the remains following the distribution of light well-drained prehistoric soils, each area has its own monuments and this may suggest that discrete family units farmed them. Similar observations can be made for Gardom's Edge and other locations on the eastern moors.[16]

These large examples of prehistoric agricultural areas today still have relatively well-defined field boundaries. The fields are variable in character, and distinctive types can be noted. The southern part of Beeley Warren has good examples of thin fields with co-axial boundaries,[17] which lie adjacent to an area of rectangular and irregular fields to the east.[18] The fields within the main Gibbet Moor area are less clearly defined but there are examples of the same two types of fields.[19] At the northern end of this group of fields, and on Gardom's Edge, there are also what can be termed 'plot edges', where clearance material has been placed along the irregular edges of particularly stony ground rather than field boundaries proper. Another indicator of the planned character of some agricultural areas is the placing of cairns in non-random arrangements. For example, again at Beeley Warren, several cairns are placed near the centres of fields, on the lines of visible linear boundaries, or midway between them.

There are somewhat smaller cairnfields, at Beeley Moor and possibly at other places such as Fallinge Edge where there is uncertainty over their interpretation and date.[20] The cairnfield on Beeley Moor may not have been occupied over such an extended period as the larger examples. It faces north, and is unusual in that there is an oval enclosure containing a house and a small ritual monument, while the surrounding agricultural areas have no present-day boundary definition. The enclosure measures about 90 × 55m and is defined in part by a low and narrow rubble bank, while elsewhere there is only a lynchet. One sector to the north-west now has no definition. What we do not know is whether the enclosure functioned as a small field, a stock enclosure, or a garden-plot/yard. The bank is not a tumbled wall but comprises agricultural clearance stone, probably piled against a hedge or fence. Such settlement or stock enclosures, while common elsewhere in Britain in prehistoric contexts, are rare in the Peak District.

In addition to the main agricultural sites, scattered across the moors there are a few agricultural cairnfields which are very small.[21] One such example is at Harewood Moor. There are also others where it is impossible to be certain whether small groups of cairns are agricultural or funerary.[22] Most of these small cairnfields occur on less favourable land and it may well be that some at least are the sites of short-lived attempts at cultivation of Neolithic to Iron Age date, often on land at a relatively high altitude.

The Chatsworth enclosed farmland and parkland

The extensive remains on the gritstone moors and their interpretation raises questions as to the character and extent of prehistoric cultivation in what is now Chatsworth Estate enclosed farmland and parkland. Did similar prehistoric activity once take place where the evidence has now been swept away?

Part of the large Gibbet Moor cairnfield extended into now-enclosed fields, where it has been swept away, except in one particularly stony field.[23] The main gritstone shelf below, in the old deer park area above Stand Wood, has been fully improved and while parts were presumably farmed in prehistory, the extent to which this happened is unclear. Large parts were probably excessively stony near the scarp edge itself or had unsuitably heavy soils; only isolated possible clearance cairns survive.[24]

West of the Derwent the relatively high gritstone outlier of Calton Pasture is ideally suited for prehistoric agriculture and the survival of at least six barrows spaced along its top supports this view.[25] As we will see below, such monuments often cluster around areas of prehistoric fields. There are also barrows on lower shelves suitable for agriculture at Cracknowl Pasture, near Pilsley and within Chatsworth Park.[26]

The discovery of three barrows on relatively sheltered valley-side shelves within Chatsworth Park, all surrounded by medieval ridge and furrow where ploughing may have removed the normally slighter evidence for prehistoric houses and fields, suggests that people used such areas more extensively than the rare surviving evidence elsewhere in the Derwent Valley has superficially suggested previously. The survival of the barrows within the 18th century landscape park, together with the exceptional preservation of medieval ridge and furrow here stands in contrast with other areas of the Derwent Valley, and once-similar evidence beyond the park presumably has suffered the ravages of later 19th to 20th century ploughing. Using the eastern moors evidence as a model, it may be there were scattered prehistoric farmsteads surrounded by fields in favourable sites within the Derwent Valley and open grazing above. Steeper slopes and marshy areas may well have been heavily wooded in all areas.

Whether the valley-bottom land of the Derwent was extensively used in prehistory is unclear, for while these areas are sheltered, they largely have heavy soils and/or were liable to flooding. In the summer they may have been mosquito-ridden. There were certainly people around, as demonstrated by the recent accidental discovery of a Bronze Age flat grave near the river at Beeley, one of only a handful of such sites known in the region.[27] They may well be relatively common but are rarely identified because the region is dominated by pasture rather than arable and thus not brought to the surface by ploughing.

Living with the spirits of the land: monuments for ritual and ceremony

While large Neolithic ritual monuments are found only on the limestone plateau in the Peak, the gritstone moorlands have a number of small stone circles and similarly designed sites, while unchambered round barrows are found across the region. Most of these were built in the Earlier Bronze Age, although some may be a little earlier. The local stone circles are mostly of a northern English type and have architectural traits that distinguish them from those in other parts of Britain.[28] The barrows on the Estate are part of one of the densest concentrations of such mounds in Britain; several hundred are documented in the Peak District.[29]

Barrows

The most common prehistoric ritual monuments surviving across the Core Estate are the ubiquitous round barrows; there are at least 33 examples.[30] Amongst these is the exceptionally well-preserved Gardom's Edge barrow, surmounted by three post-medieval commemorative cairns known as the 'Three Men of Gardom's', and a group of prominent if damaged barrows on

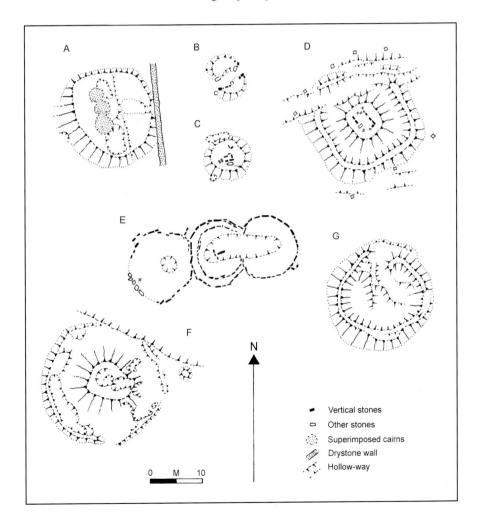

FIGURE 12. Prehistoric barrows on the eastern moors (A: Gardom's Edge, B: Harland Edge, C/E: Fallinge Edge, D: Hob Hurst's House, F/G: Beeley Warren).

Vertical stones
Other stones
Superimposed cairns
Drystone wall
Hollow-way

0   M   10

Calton Pasture. New and important discoveries include the two barrows and a possible third within Chatsworth Park, which together with an example nearby at Pilsley surmounted by a medieval cross base, confirm that such features were present in the Derwent Valley. Presumably elsewhere along the valley they have been destroyed, while in the Estate unusual circumstances have led to their survival.

Round barrows were built in the Peak District to bury the dead both during prehistory and later in the Anglo-Saxon period.[31] The majority date to the earlier period. Anglian mounds tend to be small and of earthen construction and there is no evidence for any of these being built away from the region's limestone plateau.

Most if not all the prehistoric barrows in the Core Estate were created by local farming families to bury selected representatives of their family as statements of their relationship to the world around them and to that of spirits and ancestors. Thus, by burying 'ancestors' in a prominent mound within or overlooking the land of the living, traditional claims to land tenure were legitimised.

The majority of the barrows in the Core Estate have simple circular mounds built of stone and earth. However there are notable exceptions. Perhaps the most atypical is the impressive Hob Hurst's House on Harland Edge, which is square with an outer bank and ditch.[32] The central mound, which is steep-sided and retained by a drystone wall, is just under 1.0m high. The ditch is equally steep and cut into the natural soil and rock to a depth of about 0.5m, while the low outer bank has an overall diameter of 21.0m. At the centre of the barrow are the remains of a small rectangular stone setting, built of vertically-set slabs. This setting, which measures 3.5 × 2.0m internally, is unusual as Bronze Age cists in the region are usually much smaller, only Neolithic chambered cairns having chambers of comparable floor area.[33] However, the setting does not fit comfortably within this tradition either, and it may be that, unusually, it was never covered by a capstone.[34] In other parts of Britain, particularly in East Yorkshire, square barrows were built in the Iron Age. However, there is no artefactual evidence in the Peak District from the only two square barrows, at Hob Hurst's House and another further east at Rod Knoll, to support an Iron Age interpretation.[35]

Another barrow that may have an outer ditch is located south-east of Beeley Warren. However, this may be better interpreted as the result of robbing for stone and this is clearly the explanation for another nearby barrow.[36]

A further very unusual site lies on Harland Edge and has an internal boat-shaped setting.[37] The mound measures only 8.5 × 6.0m across and is bisected by a stone setting, with entrances defined by portal stones set radially at the mound edge. The monument also had an outer kerb, traces of which survive and suggest it mostly comprised low stones, except near the entrance portals where it rises. The central setting is unique and appears to have affinities with both stone circles/ringcairns and chambered sites but it clearly does not fit comfortably within either tradition.

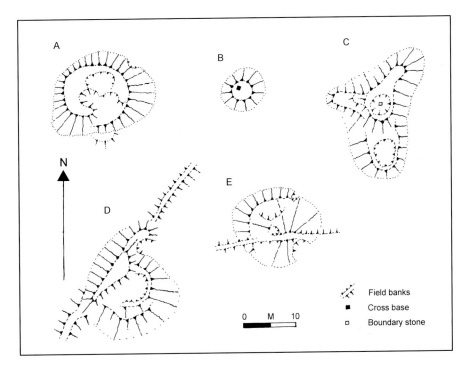

FIGURE 13. Prehistoric barrows west of the Derwent (A: Chatsworth Park, B: Pilsley, C: Cracknowl Pasture, D/E: Calton Pasture).

Field banks

Cross base

Boundary stone

0   M   10

Above Fallinge Edge there is a fully excavated triple cairn.[38] This comprises three stone-built barrows with kerbs, the central one possibly starting life as a ringcairn, all abutted together. A similar variation on the theme occurs further north, where three probable robbed barrows on Gibbet Moor are placed relatively close together in a north-west/south-east line.[39] Another robbed barrow nearby has damaged cists exposed.[40]

The north-western barrow on Cracknowl Pasture has an unusual ground plan in that it appears to have three lobes to the north-east, south and west.[41] These may be prehistoric additions to an original small circular mound, or they could result from partial destruction of a large circular mound which has had three parts removed by ploughing, leaving the lobes between, perhaps once surmounted by field boundaries. Some of the barrows on Calton Pasture have old boundary banks crossing them.

While simple architectural exteriors are the norm at round barrows, the evidence for variations in burial and ritual practice found within them is more varied. While external appearance could be copied by anyone who passed by, what was placed within the mound was only seen by those present at particular accompanying ceremonies. Several of the barrows on the Core Estate have well-recorded excavations and the examples given below show something of the variation found.

The central setting at Hob Hurst's House was excavated by the well-known local antiquarian Thomas Bateman in June 1853.[42] He appears to have found traces of fire throughout the interior, together with a layer of charcoal, thickest to the east. In the south-east corner was a heap of cremated human bones together with charcoal and two lumps of burnt lead ore. The bones were separated from the rest of the interior by an arc of small burnt stones.

Bateman's excavations on Calton Pasture on the 2nd of May 1850 were less successful; four barrows were dug in one day![43] All had been previously disturbed. Three had displaced human bones, some 'burnt'. Two mounds had 'burnt' galena that may have been introduced during lead smelting, most probably in the medieval period. At one of two cists, there were the disturbed remains of a cremation and sherds of a Food Vessel. This may be the grave dug by Rooke in the late 18th century, when an 'urn' was found full of 'ashes' between two flat stones.[44]

While the excavations by Bateman are particularly useful in that they provided basic information on a large number of barrows, 20th century investigations of a much smaller number have often been far more thorough and revealed greater detail on burial practices. Excavations were undertaken at a round barrow on Harland Edge in 1960–62.[45] In the central area several Earlier Bronze Age funerary/ritual deposits were found beneath the mound. Amongst the highlights was a 2.0m deep rock-cut pit with burnt bone fragments and charcoal within a sand and rubble fill.[46] The pit may have contained an inhumation but because of the soil acidity no trace of any such deposit was

FIGURE 14. On Calton Pasture the larger barrows stand out as obvious skyline features from lower land.

found. There was also a shallow pit with a boulder placed above it. The upper fill had scattered burnt bone, charcoal and an unburnt flint knife.[47] The lower fill had a human cremation, two flint knives and two inverted Food Vessels. Elsewhere an inverted Collared Urn, containing a human cremation, had been placed on the old ground surface but had been crushed by the cairn above.[48]

The triple cairn above Fallinge Edge was fully excavated in 1967.[49] This again has evidence for multiple burials, placed over time. The easternmost cairn was built first and at its disturbed centre there were scattered remains of a cremation and a Cordoned Urn. A further cremation and urn sherds were found in the rubble of the cairn but a crude cist abutting the outer side of the kerb appeared to be empty. A worker on the Estate had previously removed a Collared Urn from somewhere in the mound in 1963. One side of the cairn incorporated a small later lead-smelting hearth. The interior of the central cairn may have been open for a time as a ringcairn-like structure, before it was filled with horizontally-laid slabs and a stone cist built. A cremation and sherds of a Cordoned Urn were recovered from the cist, found in a modern paper bag! At the centre of the western cairn was a crude cist with a disturbed cremation and yet another Cordoned Urn. Nearby, there were two cremations, each with a Collared Urn, one in a pit in the subsoil, the other inserted into the cairn. Outside the western cairn's kerb a Biconical or Cordoned Urn containing charcoal had been inverted in a small pit. At the northern junction between this and the central cairn a small rectangular platform had been built, under which was a cremation accompanied by a broken pot of simple Food Vessel type.

Small cairns and funerary cairnfields

In contrast to the large and sometimes highly visible barrows, there are a number of small cairns scattered across the moorlands that may be funerary in character but which go barely noticed and often can only be clearly seen after the heather has been burnt. They are found both singly and grouped together in small cairnfields. While many of the prehistoric cairnfields are agricultural in character, this is not always the case. Two small examples stand out as funerary and there are also four others where it is impossible to be certain whether small groups of cairns are agricultural or funerary.[50]

The two certain funerary cairnfields are in exposed locations and have a high number of structures with formal characteristics. That on Gibbet Moor is located on an isolated high knoll to the east of the main fields/cairnfield on this moor.[51] It comprises two small barrows and six to nine smaller structures.[52] Four of the latter have crude kerbs of gritstone blocks surrounding earthen interiors with virtually no height. These are amongst the best examples of 'kerb cairns' in the region, a monument form rare here but more common in northern and western Britain.

The other good funerary cairnfield is near the crest of Fallinge Edge.[53] It comprises the triple barrow noted above and up to thirteen smaller funerary

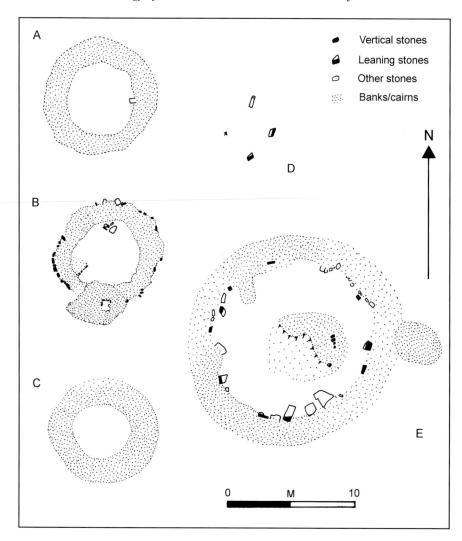

FIGURE 15. Stone circles and ringcairns on the eastern moors (A: Beeley Warren, B: Beeley Moor, C: Little Bumper Piece, D: Gibbet Moor Four Poster, E: Park Gate).

structures. One or possibly two of these are rectangular and the certain one was excavated in 1967.[54] This small structure was defined at its edges by a crude kerb of vertically-set slabs, and had horizontally-placed stones in the interior. Under the centre was a shallow pit containing a large amount of charcoal, a few fragments of cremated bone and a segmented faience bead.[55] Three of the other small structures are circular 'kerb-cairns' with stone kerbs and earthen interiors. Another may be surrounded by an outer bank. There are also two small barrows and a kerb cairn nearby to the south.[56]

There are also a number of other small cairns without obvious formal characteristics, which are found in relative isolation. Between 10 and 14 examples are at exposed locations that are unlikely to have been utilised for cultivation.[57] In 12 to 22 other cases, it is difficult to determine if they are agricultural in character, at the site of small short-lived cultivation plots, or are again small funerary cairns.[58]

Settings in stone

A variety of monuments, mostly small and unimpressive with vertically-set stones and rubble banks, exist on the Chatsworth moorlands. Such monuments were built by local farming communities, presumably to hold ceremonies that were concerned with the seasonal round and with rites of passage associated with birth, puberty, 'marriage' and death.

The Park Gate stone circle on Beeley Warren is the largest of the group and is similar to several others elsewhere on the eastern moors. This has a somewhat wrecked circle of 11 to 15 surviving low standing stones in a 12.5 × 12.0m ring, set on the inner edge of a circular bank.[59]

A related architectural form to the stone circle, the ringcairn, has the bank but not the ring of standing stones (although without archaeological excavation it is impossible to be sure such stones have not been removed). There is an excavated example on Beeley Moor.[60] This has a rubble ring with an external diameter of 9.0 × 8.0m. The excavator suggested the site was a house, on the basis that no burials were found. It has subsequently been realised, after work elsewhere, that ringcairns do not necessarily need to contain burials, as these were primarily ritual monuments where local communities carried out a variety of ceremonies. In contrast, excavations on Gardom's Edge have shown that house sites have large numbers of artefacts in and around them and this is not the case on Beeley Moor.[61] Here, a south-western break in the otherwise continuous

FIGURE 16. The Park Gate stone circle on Beeley Warren, where only its larger stones protrude from the long grass.

bank was not a true entrance but was the result of secondary robbing to build a small cairn over and against the outer edge of the bank. A possible crude cist at the cairn centre had no surviving contents but perhaps originally contained a votive deposit such as a food offering that has fully decayed. This said, the cairn may have been an agricultural clearance feature.

On Beeley Warren there is a circular rubble bank, which measures 11.5m externally, with one possible fallen standing-stone at its inner edge.[62] The possibility that it is an embanked stone circle or a robbed clearance cairn cannot be discounted. Another ring in Little Bumper Piece also has a circular rubble bank, which measures 8.0 × 9.0m externally, but it may alternatively be a barrow which has had its centre removed by wall builders.[63]

What other monuments on the Chatsworth moors lack in size they make up for in interest. They are a highly localised and idiosyncratic group, which commonly borrow from far-flung traditions as far away as Scotland rather than using the usual architectural forms of the Peak District. Complementing these are the unusual barrows at Hob Hurst's House and on Harland Edge which have already been commented on. All these atypical monuments allow a glimpse of long-range contact and the local distinctiveness of each farming community on the gritstone moors.[64]

One of these unusual monuments stands on Gibbet Moor and is of a type known as a Four Poster. This example has three small vertically-set stones which barely peep above the vegetation.[65] These slabs are each aligned south-west/north-east, so as to define three corners of a square as opposed to a circle, with sides of only about 2.0m long. It is probable that a fourth stone has been removed, probably in antiquity since there is no visible robber pit. This is the only Four Poster in the Peak District and their main concentration is in Central Scotland, although smaller numbers are found throughout the rest of northern and western Britain.

Even smaller settings are identified with varying degrees of confidence. There are two examples each with two stones, both again on Gibbet Moor. One comprises two small upright gritstone slabs in a north-west/south-east line adjacent to a possible mutilated barrow.[66] The stones lie 3m apart and stand 0.6 and 0.5m high. Their long sides are not quite on the same alignment as each other, but visually roughly form a line with a single standing stone nearby. The other two-stone setting lies on higher ground to the south, sited on the crest of a large natural knoll, possibly aligned on a nearby gritstone outcrop.[67] It comprises a small standing stone that stands 0.9m high and, 0.7m away, a second smaller stone that is less-certainly erected. Nearby to the south there are three probable and possible small cairns that may be funerary in character.

There are also single standing stones on Gibbet Moor. One is probably prehistoric and stands 1.2m high, while there is another comparable example in now-enclosed ground to the west, which is just slightly shorter.[68] Two smaller stones are less certainly interpreted.[69]

While the distribution and character of all these particularly small and simple settings suggest they were erected for ritual purposes by the local farming communities, their exact purpose is unknown.

Display and defence in later-prehistory

In the last millennium BC, in contrast to much of the Bronze Age when monuments were generally small, people again started building large communal monuments at a scale often exceeding anything built in the Neolithic. The later sites are very different in character and are often referred to as 'hillforts'.[70] What most have in common is that their boundaries are defined by banks and ditches, in some cases best described as ramparts. However, while they show an underlying concern with protection and defence, these sites may well have been built to display the power and importance of the community rather than there having been a real direct defensive need to build such massive earthworks.

Three or four large 'hillforts' exist in the Peak close to the interface between the limestone plateau and the Derwent Valley, at Mam Tor near Castleton, Burr Tor above Great Hucklow, Fin Cop west of Ashford and possibly at Cranes Fort near Youlgreave.[71] These, and several smaller local sites, have a variety of designs and may have been built for a range of purposes at somewhat different dates, all possibly in the late second and/or first millennium BC. Some of the slighter earthworks may be little more than stock enclosures. Elsewhere sites may have been occupied permanently by many people, while others may have been symbolic focal points that were only visited intermittently by the whole community. Mam Tor has a large number of platforms for buildings terraced into the slopes within its interior. Excavations here produced pottery, some of which is comparable to that of Later Bronze Age/Earlier Iron Age date from the unenclosed houses recently excavated on Gardom's Edge.[72] The ramparts remain undated.

East of the Derwent, a large enclosure at Gardom's Edge is unparalleled on the main gritstone moors, and while similar in size to the four large 'hillforts' listed above, it is very different in character. Two undated and atypical enclosures with rocky interiors perhaps provide parallels, the well known 'Carl Wark' near Fox House, and one on Harthill Moor.[73] However, these are much smaller.

Gardom's Edge

This strange enclosure is the largest prehistoric site on the Core Estate.[74] Three excavation trenches were dug along its perimeter in the late 1990s and, until radiocarbon dating results were obtained recently, it was tentatively interpreted as Neolithic in date.[75] However, the dates show it was built in the Later Bronze Age which has resulted in the eating of a few academic hats.

The two ends of the enclosure bank, adjacent to the cliffs of Gardom's Edge, lie on Chatsworth Estate land. However, the majority of this impressive monument is on the moorland behind the Edge, owned by the Peak District

National Park Authority. It comprises a massive bank, built of many thousands of surface-gathered boulders and smaller stones, is 610m long and between 6m and 9m wide, with at least three entrances. The bank encloses the highest parts of the Gardom's Edge crest and the interior covers about 6 hectares. Where excavated, a kerb of large boulders was found at the bank's outer edge and the whole appears to have never been much more than about 1m high. Both ends terminate at large boulders at the cliff top. The exact placing of this bank with regard to changes in slope behind the Edge suggests it is not well placed to be defensive; slight changes in position could easily have been made if this had been the intention. The excavations showed that part of its bank at least was built in two phases and these were preceded by a line of well-spaced timber posts along its line. The first bank, with outer kerb, was later widened to double the width when large fires were lit immediately inside and stones placed or thrown into this. No parallels for this strange act are known.

The size and character of the Gardom's Edge enclosure suggest it was a focal place for a large community. The architecture and the fire-lighting activity revealed by excavation would be seen by many as more at home in the Neolithic. Yet in the Peak they were doing things in similarly-strange ways 2000 years later. Archaeologists have long recognised that people in the Neolithic commonly did things for now somewhat-alien 'ritual' reasons, but the Later Bronze Age has commonly been interpreted from a more functional perspective. However, researchers are now no longer surprised by the idea that people throughout prehistory imbued their everyday lives and communal activity with overtly ritualised statements. While monuments are rare, with the exception of 'hillforts' and similar enclosures that have both 'functional' and 'ritual' aspects to their design,[76] there are many late prehistoric examples of acts, in the form of disposal of prestige artefacts in rivers and marshes, and structured deposition in pits, which illustrate something of the ritualised lives that people continued to live.

This said, why this strange enclosure above Gardom's Edge was built is still not known. Its boulder-strewn interior suggests sustained large-scale settlement is not a primary function. A simple communal stock enclosure seems equally unlikely as the architecture is wrong, for the bank is wide but low and does not extend along the scarp edge. What then are we left with? The land in the immediate vicinity could never have supported a population large enough, living here year-round, to build this massive feature. People must have come from miles around to construct it, perhaps over a number of years or even decades, and they presumably continued to use it for intermittent gatherings once finished. Test pits dug through much of its interior showed that nothing widespread in the way of buried artefacts was left behind to give us clues. We can speculate about seasonal gatherings, probably including feasts and ceremonies, and the exchange of surplus goods and imported raw materials. The coming together en masse also allowed the Later Bronze Age peoples of the Peak to discuss past and future subsistence strategies, to meet prospective 'marriage' partners and to strengthen 'tribal' identity. The building of a bank defined an enclosed internal space where non-everyday activities could take place, which included not only formal meetings with strangers but perhaps also other ritual activities. Thus, perhaps the everyday world was defended from a potentially ambiguous or threatening special place by being enclosed within a massive stone bank.

What is clear is that sometime later, probably in the Earlier Iron Age, people either stopped using the site, or at least no longer respected it in the sense that agricultural clearance cairns were placed on the bank and in one of the entrances, and small patches of usable land in the interior were cultivated.

Ballcross

This small 'hillfort' on Estate farmland at Ballcross at the edge of Calton Pasture has no public access.[77] Small excavations many years ago produced pottery that appears to be relatively early in date.[78] Thus, it may have been built at roughly the same time as the Gardom's Edge enclosure. The main visible features are an embankment, with footings of a later stone wall on top, and an external ditch, all surrounding a relatively small interior. It may be better described as a defended farmstead rather than a communal focal point. Whether the

FIGURE 17. The Ballcross 'hillfort'.

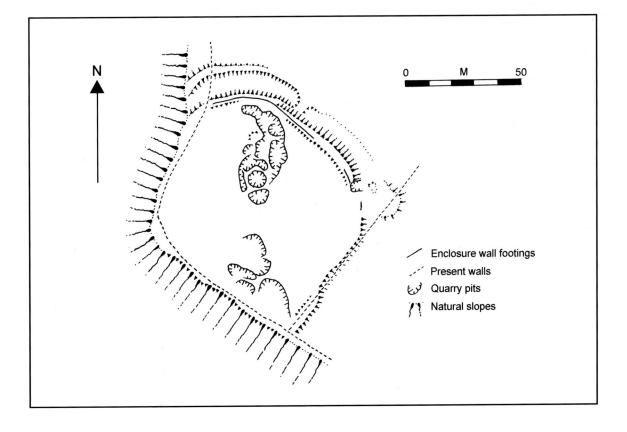

earthworks were primarily designed for defence, as a statement of prestige, or both, is a matter for debate. The site was later remodelled, perhaps in medieval times, possibly as a stock fold.

Living in the land: later prehistoric communities

Drawing together the strands of evidence discussed above, something of the way people organised themselves in the landscape and the character of local society can be explored.[79]

Much of the prehistoric story to be told for the Peak is consistent with that for the rest of Britain. However, in some important ways it diverges in later prehistory from that found in general textbooks. These are often based on areas like Wessex where much antiquarian and archaeological effort has long been expended. In the Peak the chieftains identified in Wessex from rich goldwork in Bronze Age barrows are invisible in the archaeological record. More importantly, an examination of the character and distribution of local barrows strongly suggests these were built by ordinary farming families. This illustrates that while similar ways of living may have extended over wide areas, we should never lose sight of regional and local identities. People have often done things somewhat differently from place to place.

On the eastern gritstone moors all stone circles, ringcairns and stone settings are found within or very close to settlements and their fields. However, the barrows can be divided into two groups according to their relationships with the prehistoric agricultural foci. While some are sited close by, others are set well away. In some cases a clear pattern is obvious in that barrows sit in splendid isolation high on the moors. Where the evidence for prehistoric fields has been destroyed, as over much of the Chatsworth enclosed farmland, such patternings are impossible to reconstruct, thus the discussion below concentrates on the moorland sites.

A further element in the prehistoric landscape is the two or more funerary cairnfields set apart from the agricultural remains. They lie within 'funerary zones' in the landscape, where there is also a thin scatter of small cairns, sometimes associated with larger barrows, which are usually on higher, less-favourable land than nearby 'field-areas'. Although these zones contain no obvious agricultural features, this does not imply that they were set aside exclusively for ritual activity. There is no reason to believe that this land was not also used for grazing or other everyday activities.

If every small farming group had its own monuments close to hand, as seems to be the case, then traditional interpretations of burial in round barrows as an indication of status cannot apply. Rather, all farming families expressed their place in the world and the prestige and aspirations of the family. In the case of those barrows placed away from the farmsteads, a careful examination of their siting also tells the same story. These barrows are normally placed off the exact line of watersheds, with extensive views only in specific directions. Thus,

FIGURE 18. The relationship between prehistoric settlements with their surrounding fields and monuments in the wider Chatsworth landscape (1–6: see text).

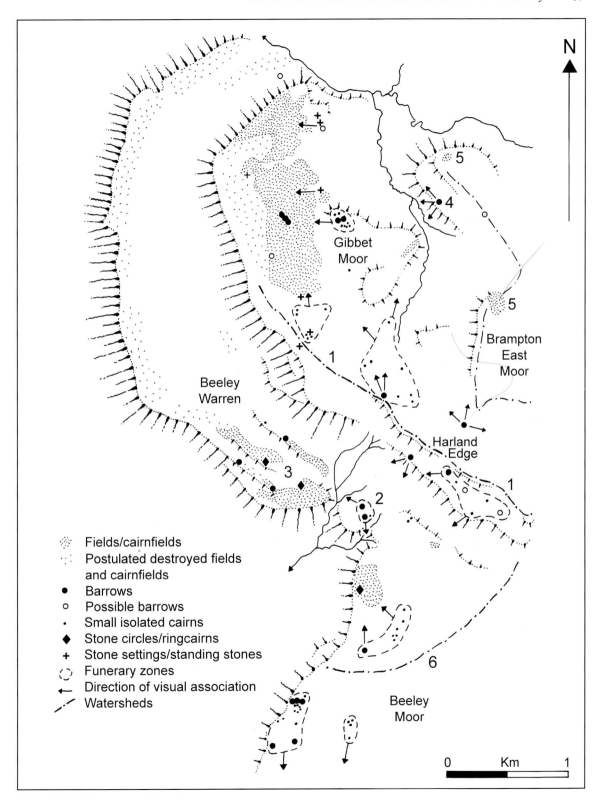

N

5

4

Gibbet
Moor

5

Brampton
East
Moor

1

Beeley
Warren

Harland
Edge

1

3

2

Fields/cairnfields
Postulated destroyed fields
and cairnfields
● Barrows
○ Possible barrows
· Small isolated cairns
◆ Stone circles/ringcairns
+ Stone settings/standing stones
⟲ Funerary zones
← Direction of visual association
·–·/ Watersheds

6

Beeley
Moor

0   Km   1

they 'lay claim' to grazing areas that were probably used by specific farming groups.

Much of the farming from the Bronze Age onwards was probably what can be best described as 'sustained' in that particular areas became locales where farming effort and time was committed through the creation and maintenance of fields. The recurring siting characteristics for monuments also reflect this patterned use of the land. However, a minority of features may relate to earlier and more fluid land use in the Neolithic. Of particular note are the small clusters of agricultural cairns, many of which are sited in high and out-of-the-way locations. These give the impression of short-lived cultivation plots, tried for a season or two and then left, either because the land proved unfavourable, or because the people involved chose to go elsewhere in subsequent years. A recently excavated small cairn high on Sir Williams Hill above Eyam has provided support for the idea they are early. Here an enlargement of a clearance cairn covered pits with late Neolithic/early Bronze Age Beaker pottery and other artefacts.[80] Two radiocarbon dates from these pits show they were dug somewhere between 2150 and 1900 BC; the initial clearance cairn is earlier still.

In some instances, areas of favourable agricultural land, of the type normally occupied by prehistoric cairnfields and fields, are blank. This suggests that local farming communities had long-term patterns of land use that prescribed some areas as out of bounds for sustained agriculture, perhaps because they lay at boundaries between groups, or because they were used in other ways.

FIGURE 19. The Ballcross 'hillfort' from Moatless Plantation.

Taking an example, the area centred on Harland Edge provides visible relationships between 'field-areas' and monuments. The Edge forms a watershed (Figure 18:1), with monuments placed to either side, mostly with views directed to fields at Gibbet Moor to the north and Beeley Warren/Beeley Moor to the south-east. A boundary between the two southern areas is suggested by the uncultivated shelf with two barrows (2). At a more local scale, the number and placing of monuments on Beeley Warren (3) suggests that each of the three discrete 'field-areas' may have had a separate social identity. Brampton East Moor is more ambiguous in that a large barrow but no adjacent cairnfield (4) strongly suggests a boundary along the shelf, while two small areas of cultivation on the ridge superficially contradict this (5). Such cairnfields may well be early in date and did not develop further once local communities had established traditional grazing boundaries. Further south, the high but flat and windswept part of Beeley Moor (6) is the equivalent 'watershed' to Harland Edge, with monuments placed to either side, with views directed to fields at Beeley Moor to the north or Fallinge Edge to the south.

While farmsteads in later prehistory were usually unenclosed, people started to again build communal monuments that expressed their identity, as at the massive enclosure on Gardom's Edge which seems to have been a seasonal gathering place. On the crest of the Ballcross ridge there was a small 'defended' enclosure; perhaps built for people of higher status. However, no flesh can yet be put on these bones as such sites are so rare and not well enough understood.

CHAPTER THREE

The Elusive Romans

Lost evidence

This chapter is short; around Chatsworth evidence for the Roman presence and that of the native population at this time is elusive. This should not be taken to imply there was nobody living here.

On the eastern gritstone moors many of the prehistoric settlements described in the last chapter probably continued to be occupied through the first half of the Iron Age, but there is little evidence of a significant farming presence by the late Iron Age and Roman period in the extensive areas that reverted to moorland. Why people abandoned many of their farmsteads and fields here is far from clear. After hanging on once the climate had become colder and wetter from the earlier 1st millennium BC, in a landscape where soils had a tendency to deteriorate if not carefully managed, families may one by one have given up and moved to lower ground. In some cases they remained for several centuries; it is difficult to abandon the family home. Later still, there were new potential livelihoods to be made elsewhere in the Peak, with the arrival of Roman soldiers and administrators. In these changing times opportunities no doubt arose for servicing their various needs and mining the newly desirable lead. These perhaps provided fresh impetus to move away from the eastern uplands. A minority probably stayed, farming those small most-advantaged parts of the upland where farms still exist today.

In contrast, in the case of settlements in the Derwent Valley around Chatsworth, which currently are very poorly understood, farming may well have continued unabated in Romano-British times. The introduction of iron ploughs perhaps allowed heavy soils here to be made more productive and capable of supporting a larger population.

No certain evidence of habitation in the Roman period has been identified on the Core Estate, except for a scatter of Romano-British pottery sherds picked up in ploughed fields on the favourable shelf-land west of Bubnell and two further examples found in topsoil during excavation of a prehistoric funerary site at Beeley.[1] No doubt much of the surface evidence has been removed by later agricultural activity.

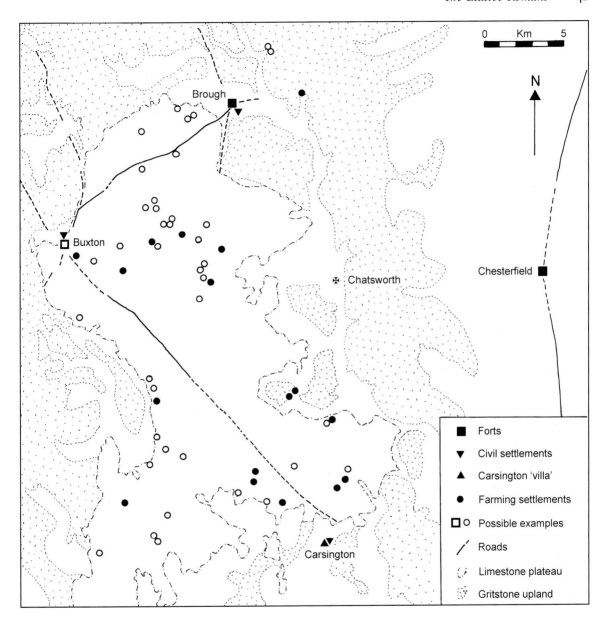

FIGURE 20. The White
Peak, Derwent Valley and
North-East Derbyshire in
the Roman Period.

The Roman administration

The Romans first arrived in force in the Peak District itself in the late 70s or
80s AD and quickly established forts linked by military roads.[2] The nearest
forts to Chatsworth are both a little less than 10 miles away. To the north-west
is Brough, originally called Navio, in the heart of the Hope Valley. To the east
Chesterfield had been established in the first push northwards in about 55 AD.
There may well have been another fort a little further away to the west at Buxton

but this has never been located. Here there was a civil settlement called Aquae Armemetiae, which grew up around the mineral spring.

In the first half of the 2nd century AD the forts were abandoned as military efforts were concentrated further north. However, Navio was reoccupied in 154–58 AD and continued in use until the mid 4th century. Sited in the heart of one of the main centres of civil population it doubtless had an administrative as well as military role in this northern part of the Peak.

One of the reasons the Roman administration was interested in the Peak District was its mineral resources, primarily the lead found on the limestone plateau.[3] This valuable metal was used for plumbing and in pewter, two of the necessities for 'civilised' living. Lead ores are also the world's main source of silver, which occurs in small quantities within the unrefined base metal. Such potential sources of new wealth for the Roman government may well have been one of the factors behind the Roman occupation of Britain. However, Peak District ores extracted in later times were mostly silver-poor and the Roman administration perhaps soon lost some of its interest in this strategic resource.[4] A lost documented 'place' called Lutudarum is thought to have been the administrative 'centre' for the lead production. Lead ingots which originated from smelting associated with the Peak mines have been found both in the region and beyond; some have this name inscribed in abbreviated form.[5] These concentrate in the southern part of the orefield. There has been much speculation as to where Lutudarum was located; amongst the favourites are Carsington or a short distance further east, somewhere around Wirksworth. At Carsington, excavations prior to the creation of Carsington Water reservoir found two Roman sites. One had a small 'villa-type' building within a ditched enclosure. The other was badly damaged but clearly had been more than a typical farmstead.[6] Wirksworth was one of the main focal points for lead mining in medieval and later times and there were rich mines nearby, although good Roman evidence has so far proved elusive. Another possibility is that Lutudarum was not a specific place, but derives from the name of the company that administered the lead production.

Farming away from the forts: business as usual?

While some local people no doubt moved to be near the forts and other Roman centres, to take advantage of the opportunities presented, most native families would have continued to live at farmsteads scattered throughout the countryside. Although people took advantage of some of the products introduced by the Romans, such as better quality pottery, or adopted the tradition of living in rectangular as opposed to circular dwellings, in other ways it seems likely that farming life continued much as before. This said, the region might have been wealthier because of the presence of the mines, administration and troops, supporting a larger population in the hinterland.

On the limestone plateau, and at a few places elsewhere, there is surviving upstanding archaeological evidence for buildings and fields dating to this period.[7] At those sites with a few rather than one building, the size of the community is unclear, for without excavation it is not known which are dwellings and which are outbuildings. Similarly, it is not known which were in use at any one time, and which replaced others. Superficially, in most cases scattered farmsteads and small hamlets seem to be the norm. However, while no larger 'villages' have been identified, the Romano-British settlement archaeology is found at sites that were marginal to arable production in medieval times, which was presumably also the case earlier. In an upland limestone landscape where surface water is at a premium, only being found at the base of deep gorges and along a limited number of spring-lines elsewhere, there has presumably long been a strong tendency for settlements to stay in the same favourable places rather than migrating through time. Today's villages are optimally sited and while most existed in medieval times a significantly earlier origin should not be ruled out.

CHAPTER FOUR

Medieval Communities:
Villages, Farms and Fields

Beginnings: Anglo-Saxon kingdoms

Knowledge about people on the Chatsworth Estate during the early-medieval period is as much of a blank as in the Roman period. While small farming communities were probably present, nothing is now known of them.

The influence of new Anglo-Saxon ways on local people had a strong impact in the Peak by the 7th century at latest.[1] The region was the land of the Pecsaete or 'People of the Peak'. In the second half of this century, members of the Peak's Anglian elite group, within the sphere of influence of the Mercian heartlands around the Trent Valley, were commonly interred in burial mounds.[2] By the end of the 8th century the Peak had been fully subsumed within the kingdom of Mercia, although this upland area was always something of a backwater. It was near the border with Northumbria to the north, which may have also had some influence in this buffer zone.

Anglo-Saxon carved crosses are found both in several Peak churchyards and out in the countryside. Some, as at important population centres at Bakewell, Eyam and Hope, are tall monuments with complex carvings that include figurative elements. Others are smaller and exclusively have intricate abstract knotwork designs. The latter are found in a wide variety of places, ranging from medieval church sites to high moorland locations miles from the nearest settlements. While those crosses with just knotwork are generally agreed to be 10th century in date and to be in an Anglo-Scandinavian style, experts do not agree about the date of the larger crosses. The traditional view is that they date to the late 8th and early 9th centuries and are part of a Mercian sculptural tradition, but it has more recently been suggested that they date to shortly after 920 AD.[3] At this date King Edward of Wessex, as part of his attempt to unify England, came to Bakewell and here was accepted as overlord by Danish, English and Scottish leaders. The crosses may have symbolised the new order, erected as statements of power and influence.

A fine shaft of a small pre-Conquest cross, of the Anglo-Scandinavian type with abstract knotwork designs, was discovered about 1927 buried in a field close to Gladwin's Mark near the southern edge of the Chatsworth Core Estate, on what had until recent centuries been high and bleak moorland.[4] After being moved several times, it was finally re-erected in Bakewell churchyard outside the south porch. Exactly where this cross was originally sited and what its purpose was is not clear.

Lords and communities: manors and townships

The origins of medieval manors in the Peak lie well before the 1066 Norman Conquest and are poorly recorded, but this system of land governance is thought to have started in the 8th or 9th centuries and been consolidated in the 10th and 11th.[5] These local administrative and land-holding units were granted by kings to important lords and their followers, to provide a means of support in return for fealty.[6] Sometimes a manor focussed on a single settlement, but often they had several and each was within its own local 'township'.[7] In some cases

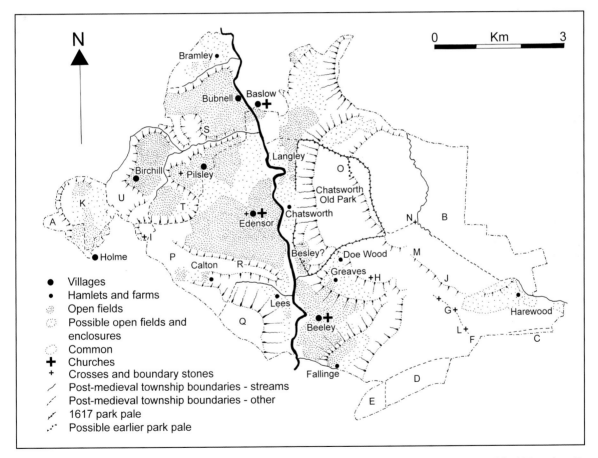

FIGURE 21. The Chatsworth landscape in the Medieval period (Places mentioned in Chapter 4 – A: Ashford Township, B: Walton Township, C: Ashover Township, D: Darley Township, E: Little Rowsley Township, F: Approximate site of the Gladwins Mark cross – now gone, G: Harland Sick cross base, H: Beeley Warren cross base, I: Ballcross, J: Harland Edge, K: Cracknowl Pasture, L: The 'Shirl Fork Post' stone, M: Hob Hurst's House, N: Umberley Well stone, O: Earthwork above Park Gate Farm, P: Calton Pasture, Q: Lees Moor, R: New Piece Plantation, S: Bubnell Cliff, T: Handley Bottom, U: Birchill Flatt).

the settlements themselves may well have origins well before the development of the manors, while at others the medieval villages reflect radical re-organisations of local farming populations by their lords at this time.

The manorial system goes hand-in-hand with the rise of medieval feudalism, where local people subsisted by farming the land in return for providing labour services and/or paying rents. Often this included working land, known as the 'demesne', set aside for the lord's own use. Communities were governed by manorial courts that regulated a complex series of traditional rights and constraints.

It is only in the 11th century that a picture of the medieval land organisation around Chatsworth can start to be reconstructed. As with much of the rest of the Peak, the first documentary reference to local settlements is in Domesday Book, compiled in 1086.[8] This records Chatsworth, Langley, Edensor, Beeley, Baslow and Bubnell, all in the Derwent Valley, and further west Pilsley and Birchill.[9]

Chatsworth and Langley had been privately owned prior to the Conquest as 'berewicks' of Edensor, but had reverted to the Crown by 1086.[10] They had taxable arable land, meadow, woodland pasture and scrubland, with five villagers and two smallholders paying tax. Edensor itself comprised two privately-held manors prior to the Conquest, which later had both been granted to Henry de Ferrers. In 1086 it had taxable arable land and meadow, with the taxpayers comprising ten villagers and seven smallholders. Pilsley also had been granted to Henry de Ferrers but was 'waste' in 1086. Previously it had taxable arable land, meadow and scrubland. Beeley, once also privately owned had reverted to the Crown by 1086, had taxable arable land and meadow, with three villagers and five smallholders paying tax. In the cases of Baslow, Bubnell and Birchill these settlements were 'berewicks' in the royal manor of Ashford and no breakdown of what was taxable at each is given.

Comparison of these statistics with entries for the rest of the Peak District,[11] shows that Edensor was one of the larger villages in the area, with more ploughland and a higher taxable population than most, probably only matched in the near vicinity by the royal manorial centres at Bakewell and Ashford.[12] Only in the southern fringes of the Peak, between Tissington and Wirksworth, was settlement more generally on a similar scale. Amounts of meadow, wood pasture and scrub around Chatsworth do not stand out as particularly high or low.

Church and state: expressions of power

Throughout the medieval period there was dynamic tension between secular lords and the church, both vying for power and influence. This extended from kings and archbishops down to local lords of manors, priests and monks. At the same time there was also alliance, for example, lords built churches and granted land to monasteries, while in return their souls were protected. The Peak District was something of a backwater. While a few motte and bailey timber castles were built in the Norman period, the only one built in stone and continuing in use over the longer-term was Peveril Castle at Castleton. Similarly, the Peak has its share of stone-built parish churches but lay a long distance from the cathedrals where the church hierarchy was centred. There were no grand abbeys, but several of those in surrounding regions held property here and monastic farms known as granges were common.[13]

There were two medieval churches within today's Core Estate. That at Beeley still retains much of its medieval fabric, but with parts in a heavily-restored state, including a Norman south doorway, a squat west tower and an aisle-less 13th century chancel.[14] In contrast, the church at Edensor was replaced by a more imposing building in the late 19th century. Nothing is to be seen today of monastic farm buildings at Chatsworth and Harewood.

There are also four medieval cross bases in the Core Estate, each a dressed plain block of gritstone with a square socket hole at the top for the cross shaft. That at Edensor lies within the churchyard and may always have been there.[15]

FIGURE 22.
Beeley Church.

The Pilsley cross base is placed on a prehistoric barrow adjacent to a long-established routeway within what was a medieval open field west of the village; the site seems to be original and erection of the cross as a way marker is one obvious explanation.[16] The cross base is said to have once been removed to a local farmstead for use as a trough, but was returned soon afterwards following a run of bad luck. Two of the medieval cross bases lie on moorland. That above the head of Harland Sick is in an isolated location on flat land at the heart of Beeley Moor.[17] In contrast, that on Beeley Warren is at a prominent site overlooking the Derwent Valley.[18] Both are adjacent to hollow-way routes and may be both way markers and boundary stones. Another cross base existed in the 19th century on what had once been a common next to a major hollow-way at Ballcross, but this is now lost.[19]

We know that there was a manorial hall at Chatsworth in the late medieval period but nothing remains. Its size is not known, but it would be surprising if it were on such a grand scale as that erected over the hill at Haddon, long occupied by the Vernon family.[20] Most halls were less ambitious affairs and some were normally occupied by stewards rather than the lord, particularly when an estate included several manors and these were spread widely, often over several counties.

Across much of England in the medieval period there were extensive areas of land set aside for hunting game.[21] These 'forests' were sometimes vast. The Crown owned the Forest of the Peak which covered much of the north-west part of the district. Others were privately held, as at Duffield Frith south of Wirksworth and Malbanc Frith and Macclesfield Forest in the Cheshire and Staffordshire parts of the Peak.[22] Private deer parks were also created in the medieval period, often smaller and enclosed by a pale.[23] While these were common in some regions, little is known of those in the Peak District, although a few certainly existed, as at places like Haddon and Harthill. Another example was at Chatsworth itself (see below).

Living together or apart: villages and farmsteads

Today long-established villages are found throughout much of the central and eastern parts of the Peak District. Here, at some point in the thousand years before Norman times, these nucleated settlements became the norm for the first time, whereas prior to this many people are thought to have lived in scattered farms and hamlets. While some villages at prime locations may be considerably older, present evidence suggests that local nucleation, when several scattered farmsteads spread across the townships were probably brought together, commonly took place from the early 10th century.[24] This was coincident with the rise to dominance of the manorial system and the development of the open field system of agriculture.[25] While at some favoured sites it is likely this happened well before the Norman Conquest, on less advantageous land some villages were not created until as late as the 12th century. These late sites include examples of one of the region's classic types of village, carefully and regularly planned around single straight streets lined with buildings in regular parcels, with open fields behind. Even when settlements are named in Domesday, it should not be assumed that entries always refer to nucleated villages. While the named administrative units existed, there is a possibility that the villages themselves could result from later manorial re-organisation.

In other areas of the Peak, particularly to the west and north, but including the eastern gritstone upland, nucleated villages were never created or were rare superimpositions. Here the landscape was dominated by scattered hamlets and farmsteads throughout the medieval period. The dissected and often higher land was more suited to this way of farming. Thus, the Peak District is not only one of contrasting topographies but also traditional ways of living.[26]

Today Chatsworth's Core Estate includes several villages, notably Edensor, Pilsley, Bubnell, Beeley and a small part of Baslow, together with hamlets, including Calton Lees and Birchill. All have medieval origins and their present layouts reflect this, with the notable exceptions of Edensor and Birchill which are significantly smaller than they once were.[27] Birchill is reduced to a single farmstead and associated dwellings, while the footprint of Edensor was halved in size and the appearance of the remaining part radically altered by the Estate in the 19th century. There are also several farmsteads and hamlets on the Estate that are known to have existed in medieval times, including some still occupied today, reflecting an older dispersed type of settlement pattern of great antiquity. At Chatsworth itself, there is now a grand stately home, which replaced a smaller hall in the 16th century.

Although all the settlements noted above have medieval or earlier origins, with the notable exception of churches at Baslow and Beeley, the present buildings mainly date from the 17th century onwards. However, it may well be that sub-surface medieval archaeology commonly survives beneath later structures and in adjacent gardens and closes.

In any planned village, when first laid out, each tenant was allocated a small strip of land, called a toft, upon which buildings were placed. It has often been the case that while buildings have migrated around these plots over the centuries as new replaced old, the ownership boundaries have been retained. Thus, the overall medieval plan can sometimes still be seen; this is the case with some of the main Core Estate villages. In contrast, identifying distinctive medieval plans for irregularly laid out villages, small hamlets and dispersed farmsteads is usually not possible, although documentation can demonstrate occupation at this time.

Edensor

The eastern half of Edensor was removed during radical reorganisation in the late 1810s to early 1840s. It seems likely that this once large village had a relatively complex medieval plan. Something of this is seen on an early 17th century map, when most buildings followed a long somewhat-sinuous village street running from Chatsworth old bridge in the direction of Bakewell.[28] The church lay near the top of the village, adjacent to a crossroads with a road from Baslow to Calton, again flanked by houses. Some houses near the crossroads appear to lie within medieval toft boundaries while others closer to the river on the north side of the road to Chatsworth Bridge may have been removed when an adjacent warren was created.[29]

Beeley

At Beeley the medieval/post-medieval village plan is also complex and somewhat irregular, with post-medieval farmsteads, houses and cottages flanking several streets. No unambiguous toft boundaries exist and it may be that the village never had a planned origin but developed in 'organic' fashion. There is a main north/south through-route a short distance to the east of the church.[30] Two routes coming in from the east are probably also ancient and align roughly with the church, which now lies to one side of a short lane running away from the main street westwards towards the river. In the late 18th century there was a small green, between the main street and the churchyard, which would have been a village focal point.[31] The old Beeley Hall lies on the more southerly of the approaching east/west routes. Further east several properties may have origins as squatter dwellings built at the sides of a long livestock 'funnel' following Beeley Brook upwards to the commons. A second focal point today for roads coming from the east is the Devonshire Arms, but it may be that the road following Beeley Brook was originally primarily used by traffic bypassing the village itself.[32]

Pilsley

In contrast with Beeley, at Pilsley the medieval layout appears to comprise a single planned east/west street, now with post-medieval farmsteads and cottages to either side. Those to the north are built in modified medieval tofts, while those to the south, which are all cottages, probably do not. This suggests that the original planned settlement had dwellings on only one side of the street, whereas those on the other side developed later in a more piecemeal fashion. However, even at Pilsley the situation may have been more complex, for in 1785, the date of the earliest map of the village, there was a green set apart from the main street.[33]

Bubnell

At Bubnell the farmsteads are all sited along one side of the street, with the River Derwent close by on the other. The large gaps between present farmsteads and other houses suggest there has been some shrinkage of the settlement. Compared with today, two additional dwellings existed in the 1840s. There are also surviving low earthworks of possible medieval buildings and boundaries

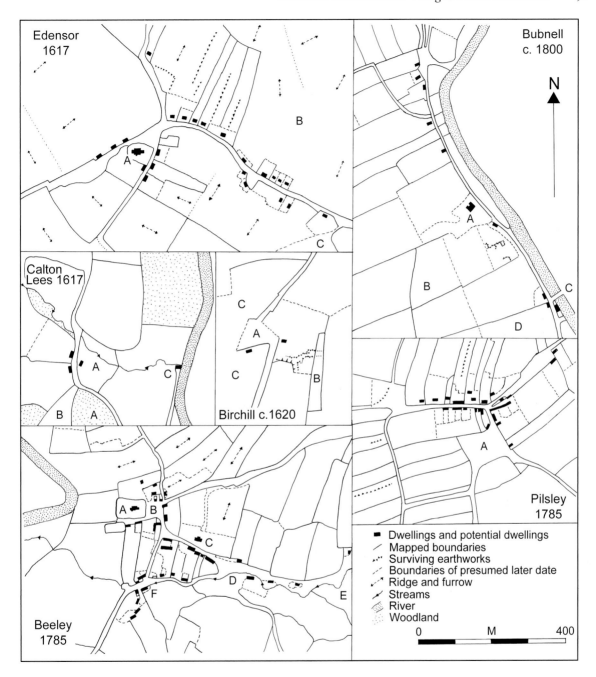

FIGURE 23. Schematic layouts of villages based on the earliest post-medieval plans available, with dwellings and assumed dwellings shown (Edensor – A: church, B: warren, C: sheepwalk) (Bubnell – A: hall, B: The Warren, C: Baslow Bridge, D: Baslow Township) (Calton Lees – A: 'freeholds', B: sheepwalk, C: possible mill) (Birchill – A: 'Waste', B: freehold, C: 'Town Rowes Groundes') (Pilsley – A: green) (Beeley – A: church, B: green, C: hall, D: livestock funnel and squatter dwellings, E: common, F: Devonshire Arms).

south-east of Bubnell Hall, where fieldname evidence suggests there was later a small warren.[34]

Birchill

The first detailed map of Birchill, a settlement which has existed since before the Norman Conquest, is that by Senior drawn in the early 17th century; this shows two buildings, both dwellings.[35] These were a short distance to the south-west and south-east of today's buildings and were at the edge of an irregular 'green-like' area marked on the map as '*Waste*'. There is the possibility that at least one other dwelling also existed at this time, not depicted by Senior as it was on freehold land nearby.[36] Nearby there are still earthworks of a sinuous lane, with probable medieval origins. In 1778, the date of the next available map of the township, this route was shown as a footpath to Pilsley.[37] By this time the settlement had been reduced to a single farmstead, with buildings occupying the same site as today.

Calton Lees

Today Calton Lees has five stone-built dwellings sited to either side of a short street, but there are no clear signs of tofts or of medieval open field strips behind. In 1617 only three dwellings existed; by the river there may have been a mill.[38] There has been a settlement at Lees since at least 1205, when first documented, but it may never have been large.[39]

Farmsteads and lost settlements

There are several lost medieval settlements within the Core Estate.[40] Chatsworth hamlet was probably at approximately the same site as the later grand mansion or a little to the south-west, while the exact site of Langley is unknown but lay somewhere within the northern part of Chatsworth Township. Senior's early 17th century survey shows a small field named 'Langley' immediately east of the 1760s kitchen gardens, although the medieval buildings were not necessarily at this exact site.[41]

When Chatsworth and Langley were depopulated is unclear; only Chatsworth Mill and the grand house and outbuildings started in the 1550s by William Cavendish and his wife 'Bess of Hardwick' existed to the east of the river by the time Senior drew his survey in 1617. Documentation shows that Langley was certainly still in existence in 1431.[42] The records of lay subsidies to the Crown for 1448–49 list Chatsworth as 'devastated and laid waste'.[43] However, a manorial hall already existed at this time, as there is a 1441 reference to this building. By this date it is possible that the hall was the only dwelling that stood and it has been suggested that the deer park was also first created around this time.[44]

It should be remembered that names used in Domesday Book denoted

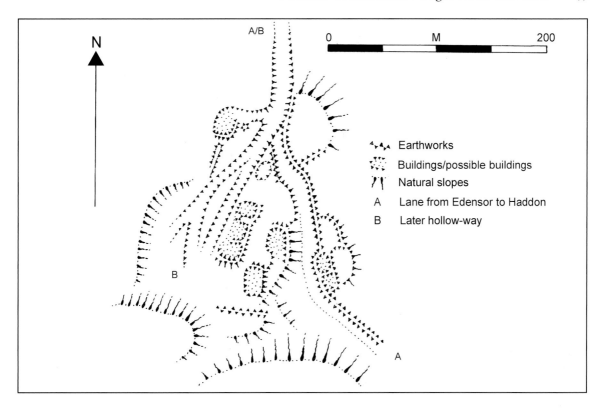

N

A/B

0   M   200

Earthworks
Buildings/possible buildings
Natural slopes
A   Lane from Edensor to Haddon
B   Later hollow-way

B

A

FIGURE 24. The earth-
works of a deserted
settlement high on
Calton Pasture, probably
of medieval date and
possibly that named
Calton in medieval
documents.

administrative or manorial units, therefore other un-mentioned farmsteads
and hamlets may well have been present. Some are known to have existed
on the Estate somewhat later in the medieval period. A place called Besley,
somewhere in Chatsworth Township, was established by the late 13th century
and continued to be mentioned until at least 1355.[45] On higher land, medieval
settlements included Fallinge and Greaves (now called Beeley Hilltop), both
documented from the 13th century.[46] Doe Wood Farm, which has now gone,
was documented from the early 14th century.[47]

West of the Derwent, again on relatively high land, Bramley was also first
documented in the 13th century.[48] Also in Bubnell Township there was once
a settlement called Butterals. This now lost place was first recorded in 1316
and was presumably a single farmstead or small hamlet.[49] The meaning of the
place-name is thought to be 'butere halh' – water meadows with good pasture,
suggesting a low-lying and flood-prone location. There were probably two
settlements south of Edensor, one called Calton, the other Lees; the former
was first recorded in the late 12th century, the latter in the early 13th century.[50]
While Lees is clearly today's Calton Lees, Calton is either now deserted or less
probably was an alternative name for Lees.[51] Earthworks of a deserted farmstead
or hamlet have been identified on Calton Pasture and it is possible this is the
site of medieval Calton.[52] The earthworks define an irregular arrangement of
three to five building platforms to either side of a lane, with yards or garden

plots. Presumably the buildings were a mixture of dwellings and outbuildings and they were not necessarily all in use at any one time.

Harewood Grange at the eastern edge of the Core Estate belonged to the Premonstratensian abbey of Beauchief on the south-western outskirts of Sheffield. The land in the demesne of Harewood was given to the abbey in the late 12th century.[53] While Harewood Grange now lies within Beeley Parish, when owned by the abbey it was a separate township and land charters outline its boundaries, which included wastes and commons on Harland Edge to the north-east.[54] It also had grazing rights on the wastes and commons of Beeley.[55] Before the property was given to Beauchief Abbey it is likely there was a farmstead or hamlet at Harewood, which appears to have lain within Beeley Township before being granted to the abbey.[56] Thus, it may have existed in 1086 but was not mentioned in Domesday because it paid taxes as part of Beeley.

A grange also existed at Chatsworth, mentioned only once in a document of 1355.[57] Which monastic house held this is unknown and it is unclear if it stood within Chatsworth hamlet or was elsewhere in the township.

Ploughing for crops and rearing animals: open fields and hedged closes

Large parts of the parkland and enclosed farmland of the Core Estate once contained open fields associated with its medieval villages and hamlets.[58] The archaeological earthwork evidence comprises swathes of strip lynchets and broad ridge and furrow.[59] These are sometimes obvious features in the landscape, as on both sides of the river within Chatsworth Park, in fields around Pilsley and Beeley, and on Cracknowl Pasture. Later field boundaries sometimes also 'fossilise' parcels of medieval strips, although this is no longer a strongly defined pattern anywhere within the Core Estate, in contrast to surviving field-wall layouts in some other parts of the Peak.[60]

The open fields of the Peak District villages were extensively used for arable and pasture from at least the 10th until the 14th century. However, with population decline in the 14th to 15th centuries, exacerbated by climatic fluctuations, the Black Death and later political unrest,[61] some villages declined. The feudal ways of organising communities and their land started to break down and livestock farming gradually became more the norm. Some settlements were abandoned as people migrated to other places with more to offer. From this time onwards, if not before, open cultivation strips started to be enclosed, but with the boundaries frequently retaining the distinctive sinuous pattern of the earlier strips in 'fossilised' form, often with between two to ten strips being made into single fields. In some instances the process of enclosure was not complete until the 18th or early 19th century, with small surviving areas of strips in the centuries immediately prior to this still farmed traditionally, each strip being allocated to different farmers from year to year. When these areas were normally used for pasture, several people had rights to graze previously agreed numbers of animals.

FIGURE 25. The surviving evidence for medieval cultivation strips within Edensor Parish (A: 'The Arable Feeld', B: Warren, C: old Chatsworth bridge; D: now lost river bend; E: possibly part of the open fields of Pilsley in the medieval period).

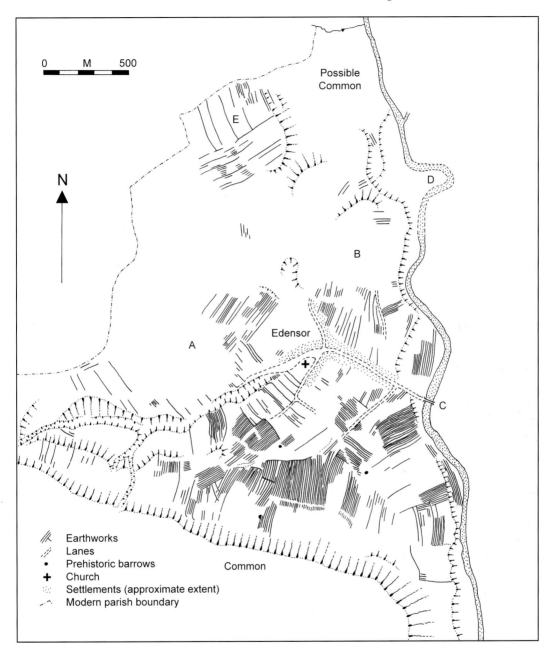

Edensor

The most extensive survivals in the Core Estate of vestiges of strip cultivation within open fields are found around Edensor. Swathes of surviving earthwork remains within Chatsworth Park,[62] while other good but more fragmentary evidence lies within enclosed farmland.[63] Senior's survey of 1617 shows that the open fields beyond the warren were fragmented by this date, but that some parts were still divided into strips and one parcel was known as '*The Arable Feeld*'.[64] However, this record was made at a time when large areas of what was previously open field, presumably once in the lord's demesne land, had been subsumed within a large rabbit-rearing warren belonging to Chatsworth House.[65] The extensive distribution and complexity of the surviving earthworks suggest there were originally probably several open fields around Edensor village, although the exact number is not known. Given the size of the village and the surviving remains, by analogy with other places, there were perhaps three or four. The area of earthworks on relatively high ground within the park south-west of the village is particularly interesting in that the distribution of strips, with small parcels overlying others with different orientation, shows this was in effect an outfield where cultivation only took place intermittently.

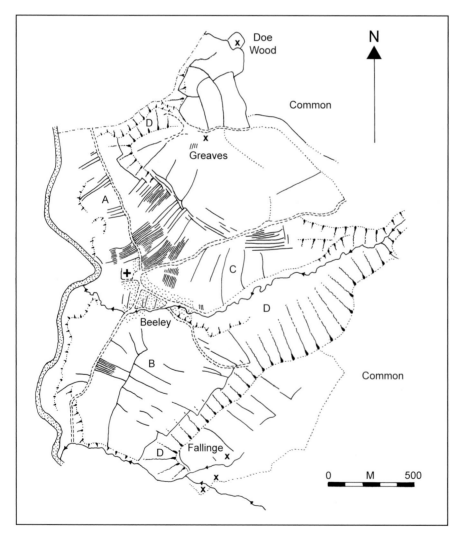

FIGURE 26. The surviving evidence for medieval cultivation strips within Beeley Parish (A: North Field, B: Nether Field, C: Upper Field, D: lowlying Common) (For a key see Figure 25).

Beeley

The enclosed Derwent Valley parts of Beeley Township have extensive archaeological evidence for open fields. While 'fossilisation' is still apparent in today's field layout, much of the evidence comprises strip lynchets and ridge and furrow.[66] The village has three documented open fields, named South, Nether and Upper Fields.[67] The first two lay to either side of the village along the lower slopes of the Derwent Valley, while Upper Field lay on the south-facing slopes of Beeley Brook. Above this field, strip lynchets extend northwards onto the gritstone shelf.[68] Some of these earthworks, together with 'fossilised' boundaries that are clear on a late 18th century map, may well suggest cultivation strips as far as Beeley Hilltop, or to give its older name, Greaves.[69] It is unclear whether the open field here was farmed from Beeley, or used exclusively by the residents of the hamlet.

FIGURE 27. The surviving evidence for medieval cultivation strips within Pilsley Parish and at Cracknowl Pasture (A: Possible continuation into Edensor Parish, B: The site of the Handley Bottom field) (For a key see Figure 25).

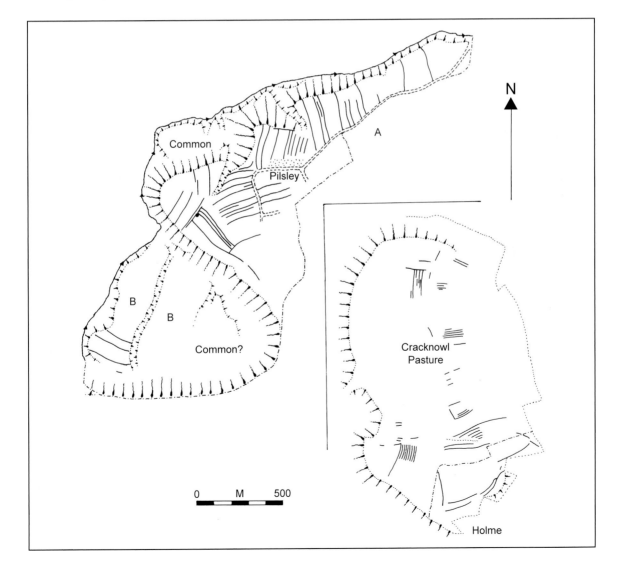

Pilsley

Archaeological evidence for medieval open fields is also good at Pilsley. Immediately to the south-west of the village, and in more degraded form to the north-east, there are field boundaries 'fossilising' strips that are still obvious in the present field layout; historic maps show an even clearer pattern. This is complemented by important examples of strip lynchets and ridge and furrow

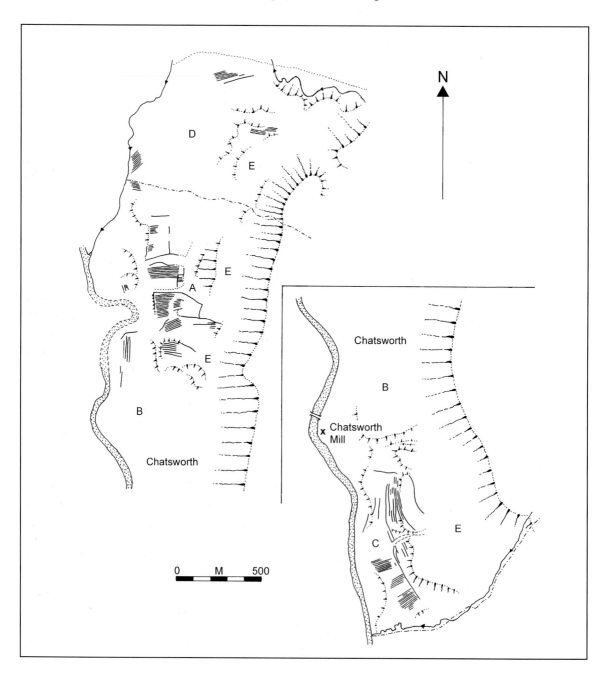

in the same areas.[70] The eastern field may have once extended into what is now part of Edensor Parish. At the south-western end of the township, at Handley Bottom, a low-lying and largely poorly drained area, there is now little evidence for cultivation strips at a third open field. However, estate maps of 1785 and 1805 clearly indicate the western half of this area was not part of Pilsley's common but divided into strips.[71]

Bubnell and Baslow

Archaeological evidence for medieval open fields is slight for Bubnell, while the small parts of Baslow within the Core Estate have scattered survivals of ridge and furrow and other documented evidence for open fields.

Birchill

Today there is little surviving evidence that Birchill ever had medieval open fields. However, an early 17th century survey shows much of the surrounding land as a large unenclosed pasture named *'Birchill Ffield'*; an adjacent pasture was called *'The Ould Ffield'*.[72]

The smaller settlements

As we have seen above, small medieval settlements, either individual farmsteads or small hamlets, existed in less favourable areas of the Core Estate. While there is archaeological evidence that most of these places had small open fields, what is less clear is whether they also had significant areas of enclosed farmland in the medieval period. While some of these settlements may have been nothing more than isolated farmsteads, elsewhere in the Peak rare survivals suggest strip cultivation took place at such places despite the lack of any obvious communal basis for this practice. This is well exemplified at Lawrence Field near Fox House, where a single longhouse and a smaller outbuilding are associated with a large oval enclosure divided into a series of cleared strips.[73] Similar practices are well attested in other parts of Britain, as for example on Bodmin Moor in Cornwall, where small hamlets had shared strips.[74]

FIGURE 28. The surviving evidence for medieval cultivation strips within Chatsworth Parish and the Baslow part of the Park (A: The fields of Langley, and possibly Chatsworth to the south, B: Evidence destroyed by later gardens – presumed site of fields of Chatsworth, C: Block of fields possibly farmed from Besley, D: open field cultivation within Baslow township; E: former open commons) (For a key see Figure 25).

On the eastern side of the Derwent within Chatsworth Park there are strip lynchets and broad ridge and furrow.[75] These are found in two areas that are much smaller in extent than those over the river associated with the large village at Edensor. The small size of the cultivation areas here is consistent with what is known of medieval Chatsworth and the lost Chatsworth Grange, Langley and Besley, which are all believed to have been inhabited by only a few people. It may well be that what we see today are the small 'open fields' of some or all of these places. It is unclear whether the strips were cultivated communally or alternatively worked by individual farmers.

Further south on this side of the river, the case for Greaves (Beeley Hilltop),

having its own cultivation strips has been noted above, whereas at Doe Wood Farm a short distance away there is no evidence for them. The fields around Fallinge are now widely improved. However, a map of 1785 shows a series of boundaries around the farmstead that may well follow 'fossilised' strips within what once was a small open field; these have now mostly been removed or straightened. [76]

Near Baslow the land below Gardom's Edge may perhaps once have been within an area which had ancient closes, farmed from an isolated farmstead or separate hamlet. A settlement called Woodhouse is documented somewhere in Baslow parish, but the location of this is unknown. [77]

On the west side of the Derwent, Bramley has few surviving signs of medieval cultivation strips except for fragmentary earthworks in Bramley Dale south-west of the settlement. [78] However, the predominantly rectangular fields here may be the result of post-medieval re-organisation.

The Cracknowl Pasture limestone ridge has extensive if somewhat fragmented evidence for medieval cultivation strips. This consists entirely of earthworks, as no 'fossilisation' took place and the present layout of large rectangular-type fields had been established by the early 17th century at the latest. [79] These medieval strips in part at least were presumably within the open fields of the now-shrunken settlement of Holme, which today lies within Bakewell civil

FIGURE 29. Ridge and furrow is often difficult to see until a light cover of snow transforms the landscape, as here in the north-eastern part of Chatsworth Park, perhaps once associated with the lost settlement of Langley.

parish. At various times from the 17th century onwards Cracknowl Pasture has been seen for various administrative purposes as part of Ashford, Great Longstone and Hassop.

Suitable land for open field cultivation at Calton Lees was somewhat limited. However, a small area of broad ridge and furrow on valley-bottom land indicates its former presence.[80] High on Calton Pasture, in an area that was probably wastes and commons in the late medieval period, there are two small areas with surviving strip lynchets.[81] These may be associated with the medieval farmstead or hamlet of Calton rather than Calton Lees. It is unclear if the full extent of strips survives, or whether, as is perhaps more likely, they were once part of a more extensive layout that was largely swept away when short-lived rectangular fields were created in post-medieval times.

The land enclosed around Harewood Grange in the medieval period is clearly defined to the west by surviving boundary earthworks that are roughly coincident with the present enclosures, which are still surrounded by moorland on three sides.[82] The ground within the medieval bank and ditch is of variable quality and in the medieval period it may well have been divided between enclosed fields, possibly with some strip cultivation, and larger 'unimproved' areas used for private grazing.

Wastes and commons: a rich communal resource

In the medieval period and sometimes continuing until the late 18th or early 19th centuries, the unenclosed land beyond open fields and closes was an important resource. In the Peak District, these often-high 'wastes and commons', today still in some cases moorland, were used by the occupants of the townships for grazing and for raw materials such as stone for building, peat and scrub for fuel,[83] and bracken or heather for thatching and animal bedding. They also provided wild foods such as bilberries and fungi. Mineral rights and wild game were usually reserved for the lord of the manor, although the former were sometimes leased to others. People had free right of access across wastes and commons, thus a complex network of routeways developed.

More sheltered parts of the commons, often on steeper slopes unsuitable for agriculture, would have been wood pasture, although the extent of coverage is now difficult to gauge. Such woodlands would be relatively open in character, managed for the grazing capacity of this land, as well as for timber and other arboreal products. While the timber usually belonged to the lord of the manor, other aspects were a communal resource. The trees were a vital source of fruits and nuts, as well as leafy fodder such as elm, oak, lime and holly for livestock. Beneath the trees grew berries and herbal plants. The veteran oak pollards in the park at Chatsworth are the last visible vestiges of wood pasture. Today lime occurs rarely at Chatsworth except for decorative examples planted in the landscape park, but there is a fine specimen of a veteran large-leafed lime near Moor Farm at Beeley. Along the river valley alder carr and willow beds were probably actively managed. Alder makes good charcoal and willow has many uses due to its pliability, for example in basketry, fencing and buildings.

Details of how the grazing of the wastes and commons was organised locally is not clear. Each family within a township would have traditional grazing rights for an agreed number of animals. In cases where commons are conjoined it is probable that grazing was shared by different communities, rather than each area of open ground being strictly for the use of people from any one township.

The Eastern Moors

East of the Derwent, the manors of Baslow, Beeley and Walton had extensive wastes and commons, large parts of which were later retained as private moorland by the Cavendish Estate after Parliamentary Enclosure Awards in the first half of the 19th century. However, 19th century encroachments did create enclosed fields at former common, particularly east of Beeley around Moor Farm, Hell Bank Plantation and Fallinge.[84]

The delineation of townships boundaries, now reflected by those for modern civil parishes, has been constant since at least the late 18th century. However, there are two ancient boundary stones that do not conform. These both lie on what was relatively flat moorland common between the upper reaches of Harland Sick and Millstone Sick.[85] Both are inscribed with crosses and may well be medieval in date, associated with Harewood Grange to the north-east which was subsumed within Beeley parish in early post-medieval times. They lie to either side of a medieval cross base and all three may have lain on a common boundary.[86] The south-eastern cross-marked stone was probably sited at the junction of boundaries between Beeley, Harewood, Darley and Ashover. It, or the medieval cross, may well be the 'Shirl Fork Post' referred to in land charters dating from the late 12th century onwards.[87] The other boundary stone presumably lies on the boundary between Harewood and Beeley, and this may have continued round to the prehistoric barrow at Hob Hurst's House and then on to Umberley Well, where there is another cross-marked stone, first recorded in 1614, placed on the present boundary junction between Baslow, Beeley and Brampton (previously Walton) Townships.[88] Alternatively, this medieval boundary may have run to another surviving medieval cross base on Beeley Warren, perhaps also erected by the monks at Harewood.[89]

The present boundary of Chatsworth Township follows the deer park pale mapped in the early 17th century.[90] However, it seems likely that there had been boundary re-definition with the creation of the park in the medieval period, perhaps in the mid 15th century. The earlier medieval boundaries of Chatsworth and the lost Langley, Besley and Chatsworth Grange are now obscure. Much of the high land within the deer park above Stand Wood was in effect bounded 'wastes and commons' taken-in for hunting. Interestingly, there is a surviving earthwork within the final deer park boundary, half way up the steep slope in

FIGURE 30. Medieval cross bases on Chatsworth moorland at Beeley Warren (left) and Harland Sick (right), and the 'Shirl Fork Post' in a field south of Harewood Moor (centre).

the wood above Park Gate Farm, which is either an earlier line of the pale for a somewhat smaller original park, or an earlier boundary between enclosures and common.[91]

Medieval Commons west of the Derwent

The identification of the extent of medieval wastes and commons in the townships west of the Derwent is often difficult because the land is now fully enclosed and there were no Parliamentary Enclosure Awards.[92]

Extensive open grazing areas that were associated with Edensor and Calton Lees are shown on Senior's 1617 survey; these included all of Calton Pasture as well as Lees Moor and areas of what is now parkland south of Edensor. Large parts of this private grazing area were presumably wastes and commons in the medieval period. The main exception is the area between New Piece Plantation and Edensor that today has extensive evidence for medieval open field cultivation. As noted above there is also evidence for strip lynchets of potential medieval date in small areas high on Calton Pasture, which illustrates that medieval land use may have been more complex than is easily reconstructable today. Perhaps parts of the commons here were originally shared between Edensor, Calton and Calton Lees. Later, after Calton was abandoned, Lees Moor was used by Calton Lees and Edensor had the rest.

Further north, areas of common can be postulated but these were often enclosed before the first surviving detailed estate maps. For example, to the north-west of Bramley there is a high hillside with a planned post-medieval field system of small but ruler-straight rectangular fields. Here it may well be an area of common was enclosed en masse as part of a private agreement between farmers and the Duke of Rutland's Haddon Estate. Other potential candidates for commons include parts of Bramley Dale, the dissected area west of Bubnell Cliff farmstead, the extensive steep slopes to the north and west of Pilsley, parts of Handley Bottom, the steep slopes to the west of Birchill and the low poorly-drained Birchill Flatt to the south.

Working the land: the medieval landscape

By the time of the Norman Conquest in the 11th century the land around Chatsworth, as with large parts of England, was a very different place to what it was in later prehistory. By 1066 the physical 'skeleton' of today's historic landscape was in place, including villages, farmsteads and fields, although people lived in radically different ways and had different social values to those of more-recent times. Most land was farmed in tenure, held by the lord for the Crown and worked by the community on their behalf. The emphasis was on feudal traditions, with boon work[93] and customary payments provided by the farming community to manorial lords and the church, in return for secular protection and spiritual well being. It was only in the later medieval period that this system broke down, when more and more services and obligations were gradually commuted to money payments.

In the idealised community, as embodied in lowland villages of Midland England, village crofts and tofts were surrounded by large communal open fields, with commons beyond. The whole formed a township, which in turn was part of a manor. In practice, particularly in an upland area such as the Peak, the situation is likely to have been more complex. The majority of medieval England was not dominated by villages. While these were common in a band from Northumberland via the central Midlands to Hampshire, in contrast in East Anglia, south-east England and all western counties the landscape was dominated by hamlets and scattered farmsteads.[94] In places like the Peak, near the boundary between these zones, the types of settlement have more localised distributions. Villages were common on the limestone plateau and to a lesser extent in the Derwent Valley, while elsewhere settlement was more dispersed.[95]

Putting together the strands of evidence discussed earlier in the chapter for the land around Chatsworth, a picture emerges of a busy and well-organised landscape in the medieval period from the Norman Conquest onwards, but where earlier development is shrouded in obscurity. Relatively large villages at Edensor, Beeley and Baslow are located at particularly favourable locations, have complex layouts, and had extensive open fields surrounding them; these may well have long been foci for settlement and farming. Pilsley, Bubnell and perhaps Birchill were somewhat smaller villages with open fields. These may have originated as planned settlements that were imposed on the landscape by feudal lords. In less favourable parts of the landscape on both sides of the River Derwent, but most common to the east where only relatively small areas of suitable arable land existed, there were a number of scattered hamlets and farmsteads. These settlements were arguably not farmed on a communal basis, although feudal obligations to a manorial lord would still have existed. Cultivation in small 'open fields' with strips was practised.

As with large central parts of the Peak District, the medieval landscape in what was later to become the Chatsworth Core Estate may have been one where, in strong contrast to today, there was hardly a wall in sight. Building in stone in the Peak was for the large part a post-medieval tradition, other than for the notable exception of churches and halls. In contrast with today, the village dwellings would have been made from timber, clay and thatch. The fields beyond comprised large open areas, with earthworks at their edges dividing them from the open commons on higher ground. There may possibly have been later-medieval walls defining closes at this interface, which are the potential exception to the rule, but the evidence for these is, if extremely tentatively, negative.[96]

While the open fields were used extensively for arable, livestock farming was also important and animals were grazed both in the open fields and on the land beyond. Here there were extensive commons on the higher ground and probably small areas of meadow alongside the river. There were probably what can be termed 'infield' and 'outfield' arrangements in many townships, the infield around the village used regularly for arable, the outfield sited on less favourable land and only used occasionally in this way. The arrangement of ridge and furrow high in the Park south of Edensor provides such an example.

The extensive high commons, which from today's perspective are near-useless moorland ground, while not suitable for intensive agriculture in the medieval period, were an important communal resource. To the east of the river, because of the upland topography, the commons were particularly extensive and probably shared by several local communities. To the west, the commons were smaller, sited on the locally higher areas and steep slopes. In more sheltered areas, some parts of the commons were no doubt used as wood pasture.

As we shall see in Chapter 8, many of the long-used field lanes, and the hollow-ways across moorland commons had origins in the medieval period. These provided access between village, open fields, quarries, mines and common, and led beyond to market towns and administrative centres. Similarly, Chapter 7 details medieval 'proto-industry' on the high commons near Chatsworth, including the important activities of millstone making and lead smelting.

While cultivation strips around the main villages were initially laid out in open fields, it may well be that parts of these had started to be enclosed in the later-medieval period. Those areas held directly by the lord of the manor, known as the demesne, were easier to enclose in that only one person had traditional rights and in some manors perhaps this took place wholesale in the 14th to 16th centuries. Many of these closes, and probably others created in areas that were never part of the open fields, may well have been predominantly used for pasture. Interestingly, in Edensor in the early 17th century, traditional arrangements survived for some land parcels, where different people were allowed to graze a pre-arranged number of animals within the same close.

In later medieval times, some of the less favourable settlement sites were abandoned, or in the case of Chatsworth, a hall with a private high-status deer park and warren were developed. These will be explored in the next chapter.

CHAPTER FIVE

The Cavendish Era:
The Designed Landscape

The Splendours of Chatsworth

The House, gardens and park at Chatsworth are world famous for their beauty and grandeur, fulfilling our vision of an archetypal Ducal country seat. This reputation is well deserved, for few stately homes can boast the involvement in the 18th and 19th centuries of a 'dream team' of architects and designers that includes such illustrious names as William Kent, Lancelot 'Capability' Brown, James Paine, Jeffry Wyatville and Joseph Paxton.

The Cavendish Estate

The Cavendish family acquired Chatsworth in 1549 and much has been written about the subsequent history of this noble family, their grand house and its pleasure grounds.[1] This will not be repeated in detail here. Instead, the emphasis is placed on providing a summary of the designed landscape they created and archaeological survivals from different phases.

The Estate at its height included much Peak District land beyond the present Core and the Earls and then Dukes of Devonshire were 'lords of manors' over even greater swathes of the local landscape. Important examples include Ashford, Sheldon, Blackwell, Buxton, Hartington and Wetton. The landscape histories of these manors lie beyond the scope of this book, although it should be remembered that the income they provided helped shape the designed landscape around Chatsworth.

Today's Core Estate was only gradually acquired. Two sets of estate maps that cover all Estate holdings at specific points in time provide key dates. Senior's surveys show that by 1616–17 the Estate around Chatsworth comprised: the whole of Chatsworth Township; much of Edensor, Calton Lees and Birchill Townships with the exception of small areas of freehold land; roughly half of Cracknowl Pasture; and small parts of Pilsley Township.[2]

Unwin's 1831 map shows that extensive additions to the Estate farmland had been made.[3] The northern part of Chatsworth Park and farmland nearby, all within Baslow Township, had been acquired by the 6th Duke of Devonshire in an exchange of land with the Duke of Rutland in 1823–25. The Manners family

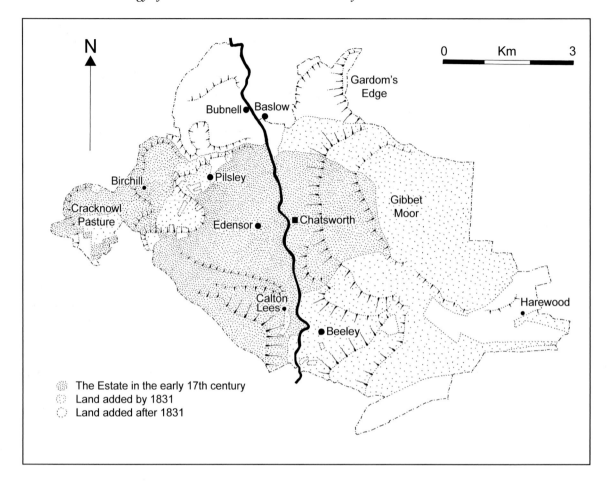

FIGURE 31. The growth of the Chatsworth Core Estate in the early 17th century (as depicted by Senior), 1831 (following Unwin) and today (note: small freehold parcels have been omitted).

(latterly the Dukes of Rutland) had held Baslow Manor since 1565, at which date they inherited it from the Vernons who had long been Lords of Baslow.[4] By 1831 the Cavendish family also held much of Pilsley and Beeley Townships. The 3rd Duke of Devonshire acquired the lordship of the Manor of Beeley in 1747 and thereafter gradually acquired property here.[5] Elsewhere, smaller acquisitions also took place.[6]

Significant additions to the Estate after 1831 include Harewood Grange, which had been part of the Sutton Estate from 1535 to 1832, when it was sold to Richard Arkwright. It was still part of the Arkwright Estate in the late 1840s, but was sold to the 6th Duke of Devonshire shortly afterwards. Bubnell Township was exchanged with the Duke of Rutland in 1870, and parts of Baslow parish at and below Gardom's Edge were acquired at the Rutland sale of their Longshaw Estate and associated lands in 1928.

That none of the Chatsworth Estate moorlands east of the House are shown on Senior's 1617 survey presumably indicates that these uplands east of the deer park were not part of the Estate at this time. In contrast, Unwin's map of 1831 shows that much of this moorland was seen as belonging to the Estate.[7]

The history of the moorlands prior to the early 19th century cannot be easily reconstructed in any detail. These were manorial wastes and commons prior to the Enclosure Awards and thus in a sense were not in private ownership. This changed with awards for Baslow in 1826, Brampton in 1831 and Beeley in 1832.[8] Thereafter the moors were effectively privatised, and passed to Chatsworth Estate.

The 6th Duke of Devonshire only gained rights to Gibbet Moor in Baslow Township, as part of the major land exchange with the Duke of Rutland in the 1820s. Interestingly, as early as 1719 the Cavendish Estate had driven the Umberley Brook leat across the southern part of this moor to provide water for the formal gardens, presumably with the agreement of the Haddon Estate.

The House and its gardens

Chatsworth House is arguably the premier seat in the Peak District, although other important houses include nearby Haddon Hall, long held by the Dukes of Rutland and one of the main rivals for influence in the region. Hassop Hall, at a similar distance, was the home of the Eyre family, Earls of Newburgh in the first half of the 19th century.[9]

The present Chatsworth House was started in the 1550s by Sir William Cavendish and 'Bess of Hardwick', replacing an earlier manor house, and it has

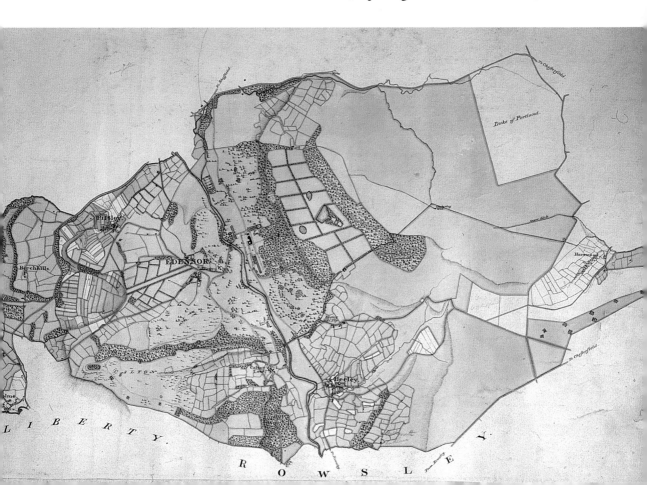

had formal gardens from an early date. Both have been significantly remodelled over the subsequent centuries.[10] The mansion as seen today is faced on all sides in Classical style, dating from major remodelling started by William Talman in 1687 or shortly before, and finished by Thomas Archer in 1708. From 1820 Jeffrey Wyatville extended the House northwards to provide a large service wing and apartments. The grand stables were built in the 1760s; before that date the main outbuildings were closer to the House.

In 1617 Senior depicted a garden that was very different to that of today. The House entrance front was to the west, while east of the House there was only a relatively small rectangular formal garden and an adjacent enclosure with central pond called 'Old Orchard'. To the south, between the formal garden and the road running upslope from old Chatsworth Bridge there was an irregularly-shaped walled area called 'The Newe Parke'. To the north-west of the House, in an area that today is open parkland, there was a more extensive formal area accessed by a series of walks, with large ponds and tree plantings, one of which was 'Roe Park'. A garden building at the centre of one of the ponds later became known as Queen Mary's Bower.

One of the most significant discoveries of the archaeological survey undertaken in the 1990s was the earthworks surrounding Queen Mary's Bower.[11] These low grassy banks and hollows reflect both the design of parts of the formal orchards and ponds laid out as part of the pleasure gardens in the 16th century and subsequent modifications. The main area with earthworks escaped the de-formalisation of gardens and parkland landscaping of the mid 18th century and part of these were retained as a wooded garden known as the 'Rookery' that continued in use until 1822. Only the Bower, which was remodelled, was retained. The surviving earthworks stand out in strong contrast to the mid 18th century parkland within which they sit, giving a glimpse of more formal fashions of layout that once surrounded the House, rather than the more 'naturalistic' settings that replaced them.

By the time Kip and Knyff's drawing of the House and gardens was made in 1699, the formal gardens had been much enlarged, taking in the earlier 'Newe Parke' to the south and extending across a large area to the north and east. The gardens now comprised a formal series of square and rectangular compartments, containing parterres, fountains, a bowling green with bowling house, and ornamental 'wilderness' plantings. The ponds shown by Senior to the north-west remained, but several of these had been remodelled to form an impressive canal.

After Kip and Knyff were at Chatsworth, a second equally large canal pond, running through gardens south of the House was constructed in 1702–03 when the gardens were extended further to the south. To allow this to happen the 1710–11 coach road running up from Chatsworth Bridge was diverted. A small late 17th century cascade coming down the hill was enlarged in 1703–08. At the top is Thomas Archer's impressive Cascade House, erected between 1703 and 1712.

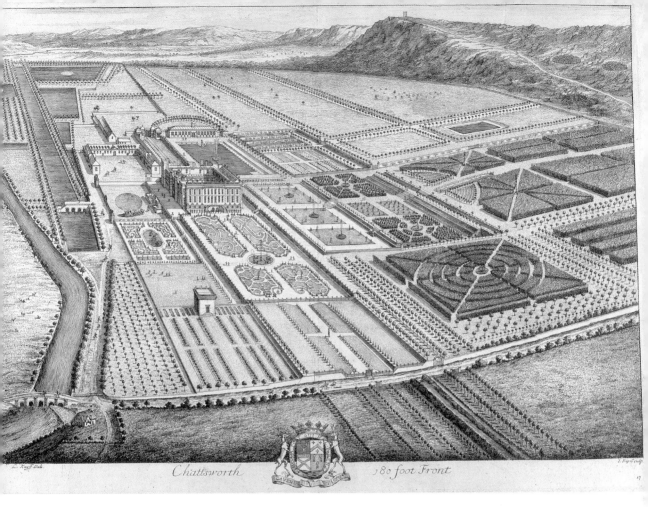

Chattsworth   180 foot Front

Despite radical later changes, some early garden features remain today, notably the South Canal, the Triton and Sea Horses fountain closer to the House, the Cascade and Cascade House. The Bowling House and First Duke's Greenhouse remain but have both been moved and rebuilt, and Queen Mary's Bower has been restructured. Another feature worthy of note is the icehouse at the southern end of the Canal Pond.[12] This functional structure was probably built in 1728 and is complemented by two other later icehouses in Chatsworth Park.

By the time the landscape park was started in 1758–59, radical changes to the gardens were well underway. A broad lawn close to the House's eastern front had replaced formal gardens, perhaps instigated by the garden designer and architect William Kent.

In 1773, when the first plan was made that shows Chatsworth after the park was completed, all the formal parterres and geometric wilderness areas in the gardens had already been replaced by open lawns and sinuous walks through informal woodland plantings on the slopes above.[13] The formal garden to the west and north of the House had been removed and landscaped as part of the park, with the exception of the small area at the 'Rookery'. The kitchen gardens were also moved in the mid 18th century, placed at the then northern edge of

FIGURE 34. Chatsworth in about 1743, as painted by Thomas Smith.

FIGURE 35. The rock-works and informal plantings at the heart of the Gardens at Chatsworth were added by Paxton in the 1840s.

the park. There was now an uninterrupted view of the House from the west, allowing its setting in the new park to be viewed to best advantage. Hand in hand with this was the moving of the House's entrance front to the north, while the grand stables were set back and made an imposing landscape statement in their own right.

Radical alterations to the gardens were again made in the first half of the 19th century, and much of what exists today, and the general character and atmosphere of the place, reflects the vision of the 6th Duke who worked hand in hand with Joseph Paxton, the chief gardener between 1826 and 1858. The starkness of the 18th century layout was mitigated by the creation of an extravagant variety of ornamental gardens and features, including the Broad and Rough Walks, the Emperor Fountain, the Great Conservatory, serpentine paths linking impressive rockworks, a grotto, streams and ponds, a rose garden, a large arboretum and Wyatville's high formal terrace to the west of the House. The gardens were separated from Stand Wood by a high wall. Beyond this, the woods had a variety of wilderness walks and drives, passing the 'Ruined Aqueduct' designed to be seen from the gardens far below, and going to a series of ornamental lakes and ponds built as header reservoirs for the garden waterworks. Some of these had been created as early as the late 17th century, but it was only in the 19th century that it became fashionable for these to be seen rather than hidden away. More convenient kitchen gardens were added behind the stables.

Many of the 19th century garden features continue in use today. However, the most imposing building in the gardens, Paxton's great conservatory, built in 1836–40, had to be demolished in 1920. This massive glasshouse was the precursor and inspiration for the Crystal Palace in London. Its site is now occupied by a hedge maze created by the late 11th Duke and the Dowager Duchess, but the impressive formal earthworks that surrounded the conservatory still survive.[14] The underground boiler house complex has recently been opened to the public, while the flue and chimney that removed fumes also remain, if in somewhat ruinous condition.[15]

Twentieth century additions to the gardens have been more modest, but include those made by the late 11th Duke and Dowager Duchess, such as the pleached limes flanking the south lawn, the serpentine hedges beside the Rough Walk, and a new greenhouse.

Beyond the gardens: landscapes for the elite

Turning back nearly 400 years, in the areas beyond the House and gardens, in 1617 Senior again shows a very different landscape to that of today. The slopes east of the House were wooded and there was open land on the high shelf above, both within a deer park. Similarly, open areas west of the Derwent included a rabbit warren as well as large sheepwalks. These were in full view of the house and no doubt a source of pride, and this can be paralleled, for example, by the warrens at both Quarrendon and Wing in Buckinghamshire.[16] Deer and rabbits

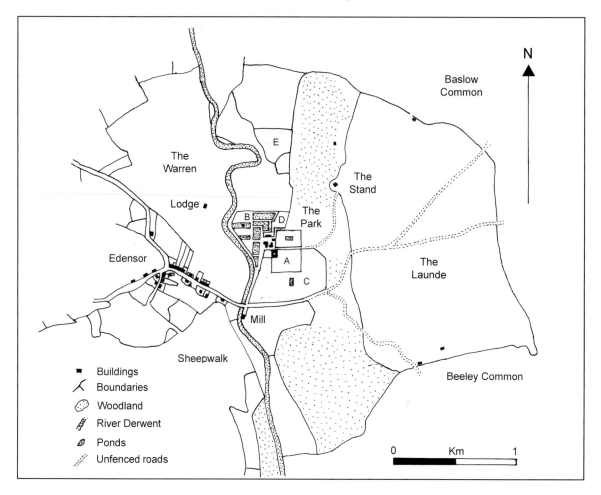

were prestige foods and deer parks were used for leisure, for both hunting and banquets away from the formality of the House.[17] Conversely, the various ornamental ponds in the gardens designed to be enjoyed for their aesthetics were stocked with fish for the table. Orchards provided fruit.

Radical change came to Chatsworth from 1758 into the 1760s, with the building of Lancelot 'Capability' Brown's landscape park in line with then fashionable aesthetic values, which idealised 'nature'. The deer park and warren were old fashioned and not what a cultured family wanted to show to their guests. The warren, which by then was divided into fields, together with other fields on both sides of the Derwent, was swept away for the new landscape park. The old deer park became redundant and its upper parts out of view of the House were eventually subdivided into agricultural fields in the late 18th century.[18] An important part of Brown's design was new tree plantings in Stand Wood to enhance this area as a scenic backdrop to the park, matched on the other side of the river by the creation of New Piece Plantation.

Recently it has been realised that the landscape park was preceded by an

FIGURE 36. The landscape around Chatsworth in the early 17th century based on the maps made by William Senior in 1617 (A: The House and gardens, B: formal orchards and ponds, C: The 'New Park', D: The 'Roe Park', E: 'Langley').

earlier and less ambitious scheme to decorate the landscape visible from the House, which was probably instigated by William Kent in the 1730s.[19] For, not only had the gardens been simplified, but several strategically-placed tree-clumps had been added in the agricultural landscape beyond.

The park was significantly enlarged in the 1820s, involving removal of further swathes of hedged fields on both sides of the river. To the north of the House the most ambitious changes were made possible after the 6th Duke acquired extensive lands in Baslow Township from the Duke of Rutland in exchange for property elsewhere. Around Edensor, imparkment took place at the time this village was being partially removed.

The old deer park

There has been a deer park at Chatsworth since before the mid 16th century when the Cavendish family acquired the property. At the top of the main scarp slope here, visible for miles and with fine views both down to the House and across the broad shelf to the east, a hunting or prospect tower known as The Stand was constructed in the 1570s and survives today. In the early 17th century Senior recorded small enclosures called 'Newe Parke' and 'Roe Parke' near the House, presumably used for penning deer, both to facilitate their management and so they could be viewed from the House. Beyond, within the main park pale, Senior shows heavily wooded areas on the scarp slope above the House and a large unenclosed area, extending across the main gritstone shelf above and probably originally taken in from moorland, which was called 'The Launds'. The pale has long also been the boundary between Chatsworth Township and the manors of Beeley and Baslow. Most parts of the boundary to this, as shown on Senior's map, can still be traced on the ground today as a drystone wall. However, the nature and condition of the stonework suggests that for much of its length there have been significant rebuilds over the centuries.[20] Styles of build differ. For example there are superior coursed-walls with well-made later coping stones around Beeley Lodge, that are made to be seen by visitors entering the park and are consistent with 18th and 19th century rebuilding. Further east the wall is sinuous, winding its way up the boulder-strewn and steep slope of the main scarp. The wall here was built with containing deer in mind, as indicated not only by its height but by the fact that the side facing inwards is neat, with stones laid closely together, whilst on the Beeley side the through stones protrude to varying depths creating a rougher face.

In the 18th century landscape park to the north and south of the House, in areas that had formerly been within the old deer park, there are many exceptional veteran oaks. To the south these ancient trees are particularly common and in a few cases they overlie medieval cultivation terraces. Many of the oaks show signs of having been pollarded in the distant past, indicating use as wood pasture. Others, long ago, have been purposefully stripped of branches indicating they were used to produce browse for the deer.[21]

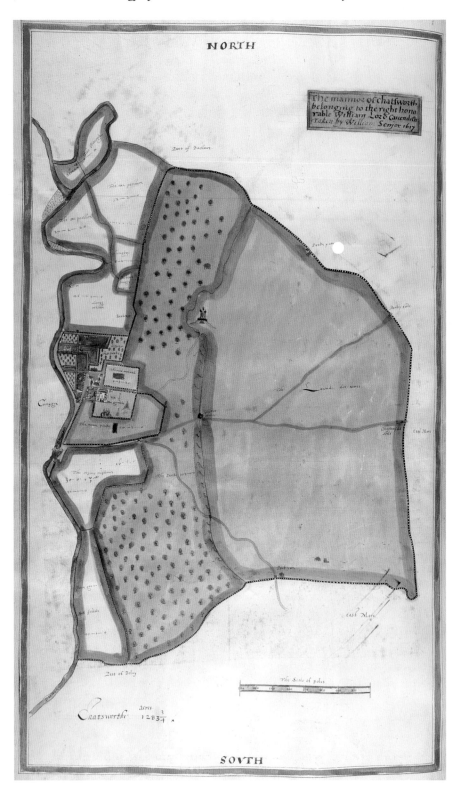

FIGURE 37. William Senior's 1617 map of Chatsworth.

FIGURE 38. William Senior's 1617 map of Edensor and Calton Lees.

A place for rabbits: the warren

One aspect of late medieval and early post-medieval farming on estates was the rearing of rabbits in warrens both to provide food for the table and for fur.[22] In 1617 Senior shows a large warren, named the 'Cunigre', adjacent to the river north-east of Edensor in what mostly was made part of the landscape park. This was an unenclosed area, bounded only at its edges, on land that had previously been medieval open field. Near the centre was the warrener's lodge.[23] An undated early 18th century painting, possibly by Leonard Knyff, shows the same situation.[24]

When this warren came into existence is unclear, but they were commonly created in the late medieval period with the population declines at this time leading to new uses being found for areas that were formerly cultivated. Eight oval mounds, which may well be pillow mounds, can still be seen today.[25] The 18th century Estate annual summary accounts, which survive intermittently from 1729 to the 1770s, make reference to the consumption and sale of rabbits from the warren.[26] For example in 1729–30, the earliest surviving entry, the warren produced a total of 415 rabbits, of which 319 were sold, 56 went to 'His Grace' and 40 went to Staveley. In 1756–5 a total of 335 couples were noted, but there was also an entry for ploughing and sowing 67 acres of the warren. In the 1757–58 account part of the warren was again ploughed and there is a note 'The Warren was destroyed 1758, sold all the rabbits'. The practice of rabbit rearing was clearly being phased out as plans for creating the grand landscape park were advancing.

While the warren survived until just before the landscape park was started in earnest, archaeological earthwork evidence indicates that some or more probably all of the warren had been enclosed into rectangular fields sometime earlier in the 18th century.[27] Rabbits were not the only animals kept in the warren, for the Estate accounts from 1729 onwards record the grazing of livestock here; the internal field boundaries were either added to facilitate stock management or to grow fodder for the rabbits.[28]

Reserved for stock: the grazing joysts

The 18th century summary accounts show that up until the end of the 1750s four large areas were regularly rented out under traditional agreements, as both winter pasture and hay production or rented grazing in summer.[29] A typical example, from the 1756–57 account, gives rents of £184 for 'Calton summer and winter joysts' and £73 for 'Chatsworth Park joyst', while 'Warren joyst' for £21 and 'Cracknewls joyst' for £17 were presumably smaller areas.[30] These grazing areas were at: the large open sheepwalk, formerly commons, on Calton Pasture; in the old deer park east of the House; in the warren west of the river; and at Cracknowl Pasture much further west. While the Park Joyst was presumably predominantly or wholly open grazing within the park pale, the others may well have been divided into fields in or before the first half of the 18th century.[31]

A rare survival of a Joyst Book, for 1745, indicates that while Cracknowl Joyst was grazed by cattle, sheep and horses, Warren Joyst had only cattle and horse grazing. The others were more specialised, with Chatsworth Park Joyst and Calton Summer Joyst exclusively for cattle, while the Calton Winter Joyst was for sheep.[32]

The agreements continued after the creation of the landscape park from 1758–59. For example, in 1764–65 reference to the warren was replaced by 'New Park Joyst', which was rented for £77.[33] This provides an important reminder that although 18th century landscape parks are usually appreciated today from an aesthetic viewpoint, they are still important grazing areas from an economic perspective and indeed needed this to maintain their character.

Liquid engineering: providing water for fountains and cascades

One of the most spectacular sets of features at Chatsworth, but not seen by the casual visitor to the House, is the lakes and ponds mostly shrouded in woodland high on the gritstone scarp above. From the late 17th century onwards these provided water for the cascade, fountains, canal and other waterworks in the gardens, taking water via ambitious leats from a wide catchment area on the moors above.[34] While the earliest ponds were just functional structures, they became ornamental features in their own right in the 19th century, together with others added then and designed to be seen from a circuitous carriage drive built for touring the grounds.

In the eastern parts of Stand Wood there are four artificial header lakes, one now disused. Old Pond and Swiss Lake were probably created in the 1690s (at the latest) and 1710–17 respectively. A fifth, Morton Pond on the slope below, is now within the upper part of the later gardens and was probably dug in 1700.[35] Old Pond, once fed by a small stream, is the smallest of the four on the high shelf and is now dry.[36] Swiss Lake is located nearby and was a much more ambitious undertaking with a large earthen retaining dam.[37] It was originally called the 'Great Pond' and only took on its present name in the 19th century when Swiss Cottage was built alongside. Initially this pond was fed by the Harland Sick Leat coming from the south-east.[38] However, water was soon supplemented by the Umberley Brook Leat dug in 1719.[39] This broad drain follows the contour on the upper moors from near Umberley Well and was piped down the upper scarp slope to the reservoir. These early leats came from commons in Beeley and Baslow Townships; nothing is known of the agreements made that allowed the 2nd Duke of Devonshire to take off the water.

Ring Pond and Emperor Lake were added in the 19th century, placed close together near to the scarp top.[40] Ring Pond was created in 1830–32.[41] The water came from Harland Sick Leat and fed the stream to the late 1830s 'Aqueduct' folly in Stand Wood as well as earlier garden features below. The larger Emperor Lake was started in 1845 and enlarged in 1849, designed to provide the head of water for the Emperor Fountain in the Canal Pond to the south of the House, created in anticipation of a visit by the Tsar of Russia.[42] This lake was fed by the broad Emperor Stream leat, first known as the 'Great Canal Aqueduct' and dug in 1847–48, which is over 2 miles long and takes water from the moors to the north-east.[43]

'Open Pond' is sited in an adjacent field to the other four.[44] This was probably created sometime between 1824 and 1831 and is not obviously fed by one of the major leats.[45] Another pond of similar size and probably created in the 1760s is located on Calton Pasture.[46] Both these ponds are decorative features and may have been built with wildfowling as well as livestock in mind.

Eighteenth and nineteenth century transformations: the landscape park

The landscape park at Chatsworth is considered one of the grandest and most beautiful in Britain. While it was designed for the 4th Duke by Lancelot 'Capability' Brown, it was created under the supervision of Brown's assistant Michael Millican between 1758–559 and the mid 1760s. This 18th century park was significantly enlarged to the north and north-west in the 1820s by the 6th Duke.

In the Peak, only at Lyme on the western flanks of the region is there a park on similar scale to Chatsworth. Closer by, at Haddon, the hall and its old deer park was neglected by the Dukes of Rutland in the later 18th and 19th centuries, and no major landscaping took place, as their main country seat was at Belvoir Castle near Grantham. Hassop Hall stands in a very private early 19th century park, its high wall cutting it off from the outside world as had become fashionable by that date. There is only a small area with scattered parkland trees below the house, while most parts within the wall have plantations surrounding workaday fields.

The park at Chatsworth fills the valley to either side of the Derwent. The House stands proud at its eastern edge, silhouetted by Stand Wood behind and mirrored in the river below. The wide expanses of rolling grassland on the lower valley sides, with scattered parkland trees, small stands and decorative plantations, are framed by long and steep wooded slopes to east and west. The Elizabethan hunting tower, The Stand, at the top of Stand Wood overlooking all, is visible on the skyline. On the slopes below, parts of the old deer park were incorporated in the 18th century landscape park and these are easily identified today by the scattering of stately veteran oaks. In the 18th and 19th centuries views were further enhanced to make them 'boundary-free' from strategic points with the building of intermittent ha-has, both within the park and in nearby farmland at Dunsa and Pilsley. Similarly, the parkland landscape was adorned with gates, lodges, bridges, drives and public roads; these are returned to in Chapter 8. Other buildings include the grand mid 18th century stable block and the now-ruined mill, together with the much earlier Queen Mary's Bower. To the western edge of the park is the model village of Edensor given its eclectic architect-designed appearance in the 1830s–40s. Green drives of 19th century

FIGURE 39. One of the fine veteran oaks in the north-eastern part of the 18th century landscape park, which once stood in the old deer park created in the later medieval period.

date lead to Calton Pasture, which from the 1760s has been in effect an outer park, and to the ornamentalised reservoirs in Stand Wood noted above. Other functional features in the park include a high-walled kitchen garden built in the 1760s at what was then its northern end. There are also an early 20th century game larder and two icehouses. The northern one, with a highly distinctive ice pond,[47] was built in the mid 18th century, while that now overlain by the later game larder had existed since 1734.[48] There was also once a venison house and three deer barns.[49] Of these only one deer barn survives, in the south-eastern part of the park.

The landscape park is exceptionally rich in archaeological features which reflect what was swept away when it was created.[50] Much of the land imparked

in the mid 18th century was previously enclosed fields, whose hedges were grubbed up, except for some of the trees which were kept to create the desired effect of an idyllic scatter of trees punctuating the swathe of grass.[51] Some old trees, particularly oaks, still stand today and their hedgerow origins are demonstrated by the low field banks upon which they grow. A few beeches planted for Brown also survive. The park was far more open in feel than the one we see today, its character having been changed somewhat by 19th century tree plantings.[52] These included limes, elms, beech, oak, sycamore, sweet chestnut and cedars.

The creation of the park involved significant labour and expense, with the wholesale removal of many field boundaries, the seeding with grass and minor landscaping to remove or infill unsightly features such as small quarries. However, the oft-repeated story of massive earth movements is not true; the pre-park archaeological earthworks show clearly that this did not happen in most areas. The only significant 'blank' is to the north of the House where the formal gardens were mostly removed, with canal and ponds filled. Other significant earthmoving was confined to the river, which was dammed and widened below the House to make it lake-like.

In the mid 18th century, landscape parks were the latest fashion. Formal geometric layouts and avenues were outmoded, and the great landowners of Britain vied with each other to turn vast tracts of land around their houses into landscapes of grass and scattered trees. These parks expressed the ideals of their owners who desired to surround themselves by 'nature', albeit a tamed and decorative pastoral idyll suitable for polite society that had little to do with how the landscape would naturally look. The character of such parks set them apart from the surrounding landscape and thus they were symbols of social segregation. While polite society was welcome and indeed Chatsworth has always been a 'public' place to be shown off, the agricultural peasantry, quarrymen and miners who subsisted in the surrounding parts of the Peak District would have felt excluded.

Several early 19th century changes were made to the park. Diversion to roads and drives took place in the 1820s and the woods and garden around Queen Mary's Bower were removed, with this now ancient garden feature retained and 'restored' under the auspices of Wyatville.[53] More radically, imparkment of fields and closes around Edensor took place to the south, east and north of the village. This went hand-in-hand with the removal of half of the village itself. On the other side of the river even larger extensions to the parkland were made, taking in all the remaining valley land in Chatsworth Township and then continuing northwards to farmland in Baslow Township which was acquired from the Duke of Rutland in 1823. Here, the northern end of the new park was hidden from the outside world by dense tree plantings, with lodges flanking the Golden Gates controlling access along a new drive to the House.[54]

Later changes were more subtle, except for the remodelling of Edensor in the later 1830s to early 1840s, which will be returned to below. Many trees

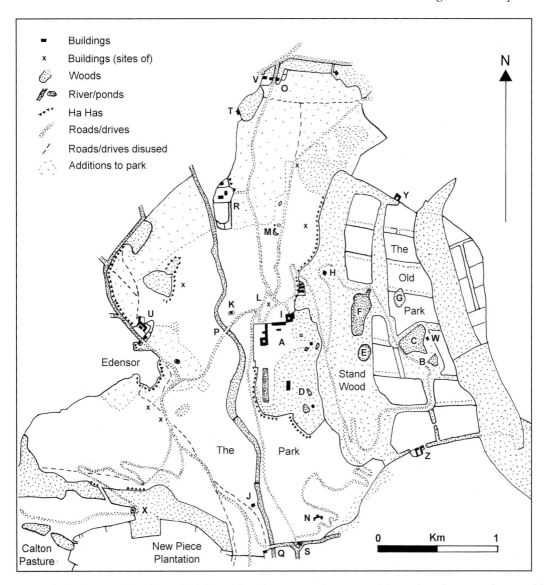

FIGURE 40. The landscape park and site of old deer park as they were in about 1900, showing the 18th century design and later changes and additions (A: House and gardens, B: Old Pond, C: Swiss Lake, D: Morton Pond, E: Ring Pond, F: Emperor Lake, G: Open Pond, H: The Stand, I: The Stables, J: The Mill, K: Queen Mary's Bower, L: Game Larder, M: Ice Pond, N: Deer barn, O: The Golden Gates, P: Three Arch Bridge, Q: One Arch Bridge, R: 18th century kitchen gardens and 19th century Barbrook House and White Lodge, S: Beeley Gate Lodge, T: Barbrook Lodge, U: The New Inn/Estate Office, V: Park Lodge, W: Swiss Cottage, X: Russian Cottage, Y: Parkgate Farm, Z: Park Farm).

were planted in the park in the 19th century, often under Paxton's auspices, creating the interplay between open and more wooded areas that the present visitor is familiar with. While the feel has remained the same, tree planting has continued to today as old trees pass maturity and are replaced with others, often in different places and this has slowly changed the park in subtle ways.

More recent additions are sculptures, an avenue and two circles of trees, and horse jumps for horse trials, all of which jar with what Brown, Wyatville and Paxton intended.

Eye-catchers in stone: architect-designed buildings

There is no distinct Chatsworth Estate style in the construction of the 18th and 19th century buildings found today within the park. Rather, successive Dukes took advantage of architectural designs from well-respected architects such as James Paine and Jeffry Wyatville. One of the greatest influences on the buildings of Chatsworth Estate was the close partnership between the 6th Duke of Devonshire and Joseph Paxton from 1826 until the Duke's death in 1858.

Paine, employed by the 4th Duke, made a major contribution to the architectural parkland landscape in the late 1750s and 1760s with the architecturally stunning designs for the grand stable block to the north of the House, the new mill at the southern end of the park, and the two bridges over the Derwent. They are mostly characterised by their clean lines, the exception being the Stables that are more ornately decorated.

While Wyatville did much at the House during his employment by the 6th Duke in the 1810s–20s, he also built the western terrace which separated the House and garden above from the park in imposing fashion. In the park he remodelled Queen Mary's Bower and four lodges were later built to his designs in the late 1830s and early 1840s. The two at Edensor flanking the main road are

FIGURE 41. Queen Mary's Bower, a 16th century garden feature that once stood within a larger pond, was 'restored' in the 1820s.

cottage-like in appearance, and two more formal examples in a style mirroring his work at the House flank the Golden Gates at the north end of the park.[55]

Paxton, head gardener, forester, agent, steward, friend and confidant of the 6th Duke, had received little formal education, but gained his knowledge through observation, experimentation and experience, supported by his employer and patron. The Duke provided the opportunity and resources while Paxton brought his skills and flair. The unique relationship between the two men has left a strong visual legacy at Chatsworth at the gardens, parkland, Edensor and to a lesser extent elsewhere.

One of the first areas to be reworked by Paxton was the Nursery at the 18th century kitchen gardens north of the House, where he also enlarged and redesigned a former cottage to create Barbrook House as his dwelling. Later he constructed White Lodge nearby and its associated gates in 1855.[56] The lodge was an ornate building for what could be termed the tradesman's entrance to Chatsworth, but it reflects the importance the 6th Duke attached not only to Paxton but also to the place where many of the plants for his gardens were grown.

The lodges and main entrances to any estate set the scene for visitors for what was to come, signalling that a special and exclusive landscape is about to be entered. Chatsworth was no exception. Each lodge here has its own character. Only one 18th century lodge survives, a plain building, now with an infilled central arch. It has long been just a dwelling, hidden behind the Estate Office at Edensor. Another, on the old drive north of the House, was removed in the early 19th century. There is also a small lodge next to One Arch Bridge of which little is known except that it pre-dates 1839. The lodges designed by Wyatville, at Edensor and the Golden Gates, were only brought to fruition in Paxton's time. Castle Lodge at the entrance to Edensor was built by Paxton in 1842, while the 1861 lodge at Beeley Gate was to a design by Stokes, Paxton's son-in-law.[57] Barbrook Lodge, probably of 1849, stands against a service lane from Baslow Nether End and is plain and functional, built in a cottage style.[58]

There are also architect-designed buildings at the fringes of the park. The stylish New Inn at Edensor, now the Estate office, unusually is built in brick in a plain classical style. This was erected at the top end of the village after the Devonshire Arms and the Parsonage at the bottom end were knocked down in the late 1770s to remove them from sight of the House. The New Inn was designed by Joseph Pickford of Derby just before the imposition of the Brick Tax of 1784. This tax of 2s 6d per thousand bricks raised to fund the war with the American colonies may have discouraged the use of bricks in much of the future building work on the Chatsworth Estate in the first half of the 19th century.

At the northern edge of the park, hidden in its own wooded grounds, is Park Lodge. This was not a lodge in the usual sense, but a rather grand house built in 1840–42 for the 6th Duke's physician Mr Condell to an Italianate design by John Robertson, Paxton's main architectural associate at Chatsworth and a former architectural draughtsman to Loudon. Paxton himself took the ornate

Italianate style into the wider landscape when he designed and built two large properties in commanding positions that could be seen from the main roads through the Estate. These are Dunsa House north of Edensor and Pilsley House on the outskirts of Pilsley.[59]

Two unusual Estate cottages were built as eclectic architectural curios designed to be seen by visitors using carriage drives which wind out of the park onto higher ground. Swiss Cottage on the water's edge at Swiss Lake has highly decorated barge-boards and was built about 1839–42 to have an Alpine feel.[60] Russian Cottage, hidden at the edge of New Piece Plantation and overlooking Calton Lees, was designed in 1855 in the style of a Russian farmhouse from a model sent to the 6th Duke.[61]

Most other buildings in the Core Estate, in the villages of Pilsley and Beeley and out in the countryside, even when erected by the Estate for their own use, are more vernacular in style. These buildings will be returned to in the next chapter.

The transformation of a village: Edensor

Today Edensor is a model Estate village at the edge of the landscape park that contains an eclectic range of buildings mostly designed, built or altered in the later 1830s to early 1840s as a showcase of tasteful building styles and of the 6th Duke's paternalistic altruism towards his estate workers. Contrary to common misconception, while a little over half of the village was demolished from the late 1810s to early 1830s, it was not moved wholesale. While this was possibly the original intention, the primary aim seems more likely to have been to remove the eastern buildings in order to have an approach to the House for coaches that didn't pass through the village. However, after what remained of the village had been hidden behind a screen of trees, in the late 1830s to early 40s, some of the remaining houses in the western half of the original village were given radical facelifts, while others were replaced by new buildings.[62]

The majority of demolished buildings, and associated garden and yard boundaries, have left little or no surface trace, although in drought conditions some of these are visible as parch marks in the parkland grass. Park Cottage, of typical local 18th or early 19th century vernacular style, predates the remodelling and stands in the parkland, isolated from the present village alongside the line of the former street.[63] It is far from clear why this survived.

Edensor appears as a design book brought to 'life' with its various cottage styles. Paxton, later in collaboration with Robertson between 1841 and 1844, created most of the main buildings in the village. They set about rebuilding some dwellings and modified others that already stood, making each a unique part of the village in its design and style. Care was also taken in creating appropriate linking walls and curtilage boundaries. In some instances there are distinct recognisable styles used and the more elaborate of these feature at more important or prominently placed buildings. Italianate was the most favoured

FIGURE 42. The village of Edensor, before and after the radical changes made in the first half of the 19th century, drawn from estate maps dated 1785 and 1856 (A: site of the Devonshire Arms, B: site of the Old Parsonage, both removed shortly before 1785).

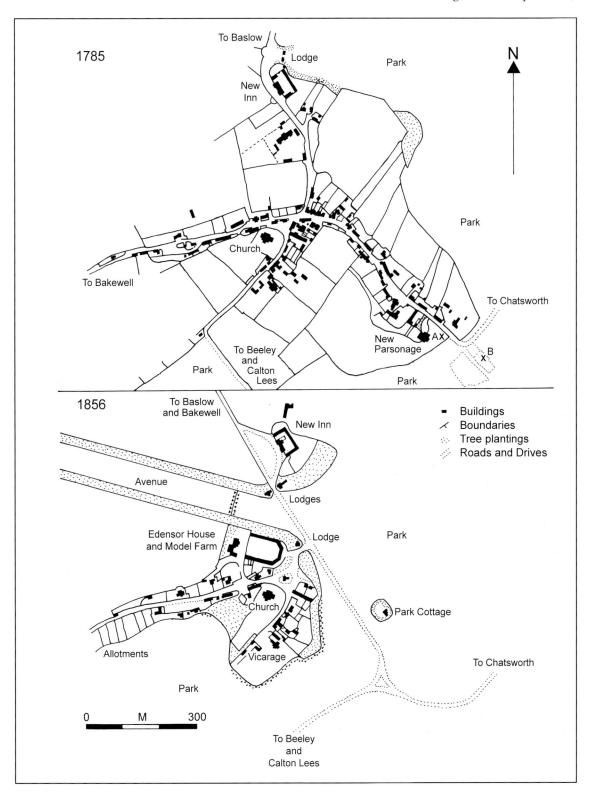

1785

To Baslow

Lodge

Park

N

New Inn

To Bakewell

Church

Park

Park

To Beeley and Calton Lees

Park

New Parsonage

A X

X B

To Chatsworth

Park

1856

To Baslow and Bakewell

New Inn

Buildings
Boundaries
Tree plantings
Roads and Drives

Avenue

Lodges

Edensor House and Model Farm

Lodge

Park

Church

Park Cottage

Allotments

Vicarage

To Chatsworth

0   M   300

Park

To Beeley and Calton Lees

style, with Norman and Tudor also being used. A few buildings have gothic details or decorative gable barge-boards suggesting Swiss influence. With less important properties there are few features in these characteristic styles although they are still good representatives of mid 19th century estate designs. It was rare for two properties of the same style to be placed next to each other. This ensured that each individual building stood in its own right accentuated by the natural topography of the small valley along which the village was strung out.

Another architect used at Edensor was Decimus Burton who built the model farmstead in 1836–37 in a severe classical style mirroring the 18th century mill in the park by James Paine. Edensor House was the original farmhouse and the outbuildings were laid out in a symmetrical 'U'-shaped plan.[64]

FIGURE 43. The architect designed cottages in the 1830s–40s model village of Edensor are overshadowed by the church built in 1867–70.

Later, another major building project in the village, financed by the 7th Duke, was the demolition of the medieval church and its replacement in 1867–70 with a much grander structure designed by Sir George Gilbert Scott. With its new spire, the church became a visually striking, and some would say over-bearing, centrepiece to the village. Its saving grace is that it provides a fine landmark from within the park. It may well be that the removal of the tree screen, which hid the village from passers-by, took place at around this time, opening up the village and its church to view.

Trees: aesthetics and income

Trees have been an important part of the landscape at Chatsworth for centuries. Woodlands have many practical uses but also planted trees have formed important parts of decorative landscape schemes, particularly from the 18th century onwards, where there have been strong aesthetic reasons for the positioning and character of treescapes.

In the Peak District the traditional management of areas of woodland for fuel, building materials, fodder and pasture has long been an integral part of manorial, estate and farm practice. Standards were grown to provide timber for construction as well as fuel, with oak bark used in tanning. Up until the late 18th century there was much coppicing in the Peak, some poles kiln-dried as 'white coal', others burnt to make charcoal, for use in the lead and iron smelting industries.[65] Coppiced woodland was regularly harvested as part of a cyclical rotation.[66] Farey, writing in 1813, refers to landowners in Derbyshire adopting a 24 to 25 year cycle in order to supply wood mature enough for pit props, ladders, soughs and gates in the lead and coal mines.[67]

In the 18th and 19th centuries new ways of managing woodlands were introduced from the continent and in particular from Germany. The aim of landowners was to produce high quality timber for specific purposes, which was achieved by managing the woods as plantations of standards rather than coppice. There was also at the same time a move towards linking wider landscapes with ornamental gardens. Woodlands in the designed landscape context were viewed as important structures that framed and enhanced views as well as providing a long-term cash crop and shelter for property and gardens. All of today's Chatsworth woodlands are of this type, although conifers have sometimes replaced deciduous trees. Species commonly planted on the Chatsworth Estate include sycamore, beech, oak, larch, Corsican pine, Scots pine and Norway spruce. Sweet and horse chestnut were also planted as specimen trees on edges of rides or close to plantation boundaries. While nearly all of the present plantation trees are of 19th and 20th century date, with some sites having been replanted more than once, there is a line of surviving veteran limes within New Piece Plantation that is probably 18th century in date and may be part of the original planting.

At Chatsworth there is limited evidence for earlier traditional woodland management. The many ancient oaks at the bottom of what was the old deer park have already been noted. There are also small fragments of possible former coppice still surviving on the Estate, for example within Doe Wood just beyond the south-eastern edge of the old deer park and Jumble Coppice at the northern end of the landscape park.

Planting by design: the parkland and the woodland backdrop

Within the park, in addition to the scattered decorative trees, there are small plantations and substantial plantings at its flanks that are designed to be seen. The 18th and 19th century designed landscape also continues well beyond the park, with strategically planted trees being one of key devices to visually extend the idealised 'natural' beauty of the place, both from the House and when travelling through the Estate.[68] Some plantations are carefully placed at highly-visible locations to strengthen the impression that the landscape is heavily wooded; in most instances this also served practical purposes, for these steep slopes were of little agricultural value and the Estate woodlands have always been a significant source of timber and are used for rearing game.

Unlike many great estates, the designed landscape at Chatsworth never placed great emphasis on grand avenues of trees through the park and beyond. Only two are known. One, visible on an undated painting, was planted sometime in the 17th century within the warren, running from the river for a short distance to the low ridgetop east of Edensor; this was possibly extended to the skyline a few years later. One end of another lost avenue can be seen on Kip and Knyff's 1699 drawing of the gardens, running southwards beyond these; the trees look immature and it had presumably been planted only a few years before. In both cases lines of trees defined the axes of the House and gardens and were designed to be viewed from the main rooms; they did not flank formal approach routes.

One somewhat later development, of which little now remains to be seen, is the planting of a series of decorative tree clumps, probably at the instigation of Kent in the 1730s.[69] There were four circular plantings to the south-west which were subsumed when New Piece Plantation was created at the time the landscape park was laid out from 1758–59. Three other possible oval examples lay in the warren on the low ridge above Edensor; there are boundary earthworks surviving for at least one of these.[70] Another oval earthwork lies within the later Paddocks Plantation west of Edensor at a high point on the ridge here, at a similar distance from the House to those in New Piece Plantation; by 1785 there was small wood at the same ridge-top location called Hackitts Plantation but its outline had been changed to square.

The most dramatic transformation to the treescape came in about 1760 when New Piece Plantation was created to flank the western edge of the landscape park as a visual backdrop, to match woodland to the east at Stand Wood which had been gradually replenished from the early-18th century onwards. West of

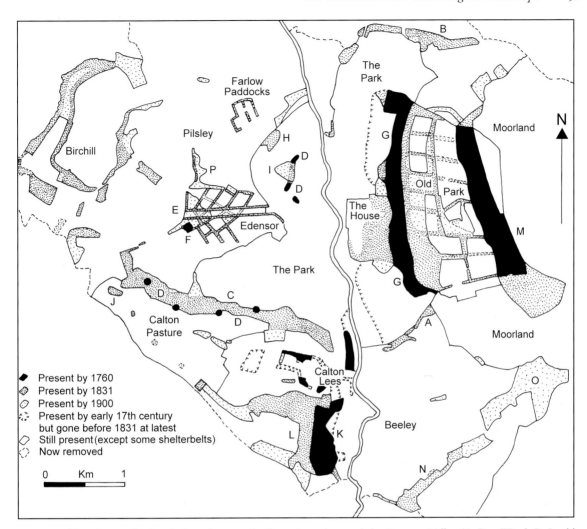

FIGURE 44. Historic woodland and plantations on the Estate in and around the Derwent Valley (A: Doe Wood, B: Jumble Coppice, C: New Piece Plantation, D: The Warren and Calton Pasture circular and oval plantations, E: Paddocks Plantation, F: Hackitts Plantation, G: Stand Wood, H: Buston Wood, I: Park Wood, J: Moatless Plantation, K: Lindup Wood, L: Lees Moor woods, M: Bunkers Hill Wood, N: Limetree Wood, O: Hell Bank Plantation, P: Broomhill Plantation).

the river, Buston Wood probably also dates to around 1760 but was not brought into the park until the early 19th century. Park Wood, which may well have origins as two of Kent's plantings, had been enlarged into a long linear feature known as 'The Shoulder of Mutton' in the late 18th or early 19th century and was modified again in the mid 19th. On Calton Pasture, Moatless Plantation and other smaller tree clumps were added around 1760 but only a few over-mature deciduous trees at one of these survive.[71] The rest have disappeared without trace, while Moatless Plantation has been replanted.

Turning now to land well beyond the landscape park, there are several large plantations, mostly confined to steeply sloping and agriculturally unproductive

land.[72] Woodland in the early 17th century was found not only in the deer park
and gardens, but also in and around the Calton Lees valley and nearby at the
larger Lindop Wood.[73] These were presumably primarily planted for practical
reasons rather than with any decorative intent, as were later woodlands at
nearby Lees Moor and elsewhere. Bunkers Hill Wood, high in the old deer park
on the upper scarp, was created in the 18th century. Expansion of the Estate's
plantations onto further steep-banks in the 19th century included Limetree
Wood and Hell Bank Plantation above Beeley.

Some of the larger plantations away from the landscape park have decorative
elements to their design. In the northern part of the Core Estate, Bramley
Plantation, which was created soon after the Estate acquired this land in 1870,
was visible as a skyline feature from outside the House and thus given a sinuous
lower boundary for decorative effect.[74] Similarly sinuous woodland edges were
created earlier at Broomhill Plantation north-west of Dunsa in the 1850s or 60s,

FIGURE 45. An unsigned
painting of Chatsworth,
now in Ombersley Court
in Warwickshire, possibly
painted by Leonard
Knyff shortly after 1710.
In the background is the
warren with its lodge and
avenue of trees aligned
on the House.

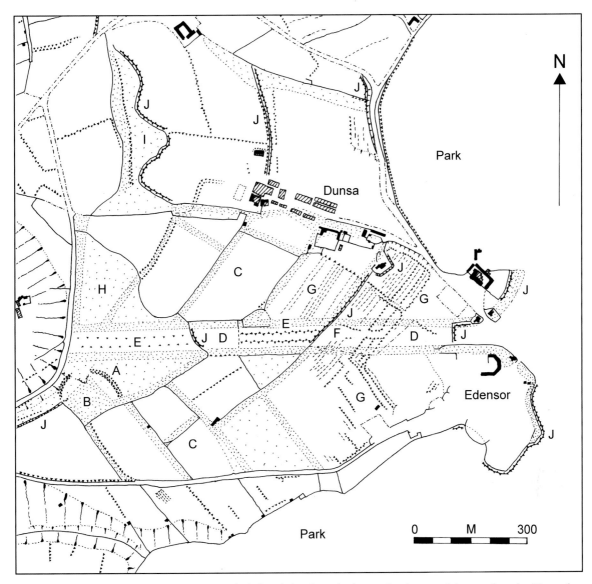

FIGURE 46. The Edensor avenue, ornamental shelter belts, later ha-has and other surviving earthworks (For a key see Figure 82). (A: Earthworks at postulated c. 1730s plantation, B: Later-18th century Hackitts Plantation, C: Later-18th century linear plantings, D: The 1820s avenue, E: banks flanking the unfinished drive – damaged to west, F: Unfinished road levelling, G: Medieval earthworks, H: Paddocks Plantation, I: Broomhill Plantation, J: 19th century ha-has).

and later along the northern edge of Lees Moor Wood south-west of Calton Lees in the 20th century.[75]

Estate maps show that trees were also used to create large-scale grid arrangements of ornamental shelterbelts. One of the most ambitious of these designed treescapes lay east of Edensor and was partly visible from the House and park. Here, shelterbelts arranged in a grid-like pattern at the edges of rectangular fields existed by 1785.[76] In the mid 1820s the layout was radically altered with the insertion of an avenue of close-planted trees aligned on the House from where it ran to the skyline. The intention was to build a drive down its centre, but this was never finished.[77] Sometime between 1855 and 1867 the large plantings at Paddocks and Broomhill Plantations were created along the ridgetop, subsuming parts of the shelterbelts. Thereafter, in the later 19th century most of the rest of the earlier planting scheme was gradually removed, although a few associated earthworks survive.[78]

A second example of shelterbelt planting once existed around Farlow Paddocks, east of Pilsley.[79] This was an ornamental arrangement similar to that near Dunsa but smaller. Again much of this planting existed by 1785.[80] Today only parts of the original design still retain trees.

A third similar planting on a grander scale was created on the main gritstone shelf east of Chatsworth House above Stand Wood in what had been the old deer park. When this was subdivided in the late 18th century, linear belts of trees surrounding rectangular fields were created.[81] However, the integrity of the design was lost in the mid to late 19th century and little now survives except at the southern end near Park Farm.[82]

Dukes and Commoners: The designed landscape in context

In the last 500 years the Peak District has in many ways changed in line with social and economic transformations that took place throughout much of Britain. It was far from London and was a social and agricultural upland backwater without many of the advantages of lowland England. However, two particular factors made it important. One major asset of the Peak was its mineral wealth. Lead was paramount, bringing significant wealth to its inhabitants, particularly in the 17th and 18th centuries. The other distinction is the creation of Chatsworth as a grand seat by one of the most powerful families in the country. Here the Cavendish family could escape the court, politics and the demands of fashionable society, leaving their London house for quieter country pleasures when circumstances allowed. At Chatsworth they 'held court', entertaining wealthy and influential visitors, in a place where they owned much land and were at the very apex of the social hierarchy.

When Senior surveyed the Cavendish Estate in the early 17th century, Chatsworth had been in their hands for nearly 70 years. A grand house had been built, surrounded by formal gardens, ponds, orchards, outbuildings and deer enclosures. To the east, on the steep slope and land beyond there was a large deer park with a tall hunting tower on the scarp top overlooking it all. On the opposite side of the river to the west, another prominent feature in the landscape was the large open expanse of the warren with a warrener's lodge at its centre.

The House and gardens were ambitiously added to and altered intermittently from the 17th century onwards, following architectural and garden design trends that were then fashionable. The House was given grand classical facades in the late 17th and early 18th centuries, and it was much extended just over 100 years later. Formal geometric gardens and wildernesses, with cascades and canals, covered an ever-increasing area until the early 18th century, but from then the layout started to be simplified, with open lawns replacing parterres. The gardens were transformed again in the first half of the 19th century under the 6th Duke and Paxton, creating many of the wide variety of features that are familiar to visitors today, including formal walks, lawns, and terraces near the House, while meandering paths above linked ponds, rockworks and arboretum. In the landscape beyond, the greatest transformation came in 1758–60s with the creation of Brown's spectacular landscape park for the 4th Duke.

Prior to the mid 18th century, beyond the House, gardens, deer park and warren, the landscape was one of enclosed farmland around villages and hamlets. In the early 17th century the farmland also still included small areas of unenclosed traditional cultivation strips. By this time much of the high open land above Edensor and Calton Lees, which had formerly been common, was an Estate sheepwalk. In contrast, east of the Derwent and beyond the deer park, there were vast upland commons not yet owned by the Estate; many of these remain moorland today.

The relicts of open fields, the warren and former commons west of the Derwent were extensively enclosed into fields over the 150 years leading up to the mid 18th century. Some of the sinuous field boundaries created at this time define small fields which reflect the shapes of cultivation strips. Many other fields are more rectangular in shape and ignored previous land use. In a few instances, as at Jack Flat near Yeld Wood, small irregular intakes had been taken in from commons.

Traditional field-lanes and hollow-ways across moorland commons, some of which had origins in the medieval period, continued in use in this period. In many instances they sustained more erosion as traffic increased due to rising populations together with much greater export of millstones, lead and coal. Imported products, often made of iron and ceramic, came from the embryonic industrial areas flanking the Peak District. The erosion from strings of packhorses, and in some cases wagons, created the obvious braided hollow-ways that are such a distinctive feature of the eastern moorlands today. At several junctions of routes there are fine guide stones, made more interesting by their non-standard spellings of place-names and three-fingered pointing hands.

Industrial activity on the Estate at this time developed from medieval origins. Much of what is visible of the important millstone quarrying at and below Gardom's Edge and Dobb Edge probably dates to the 16th to 18th centuries. Similarly, the lead mining on Cracknowl Pasture may date to this time, while coal is known to have been mined at the Baslow, Chatsworth Park and Beeley Collieries.

The creation of Chatsworth Park and Calton Pasture in the mid 18th century, with the sweeping away of much farmland, took place at a time when there was already a fully developed monetary economy after the final demise of feudal traditions and when moves towards large-scale industrialisation had begun. The need to idealise landscape came at a time when, beyond these oases for the privileged, the land was being parcelled by walls and dirtied by mines and factories, and people were starting to leave to live at close quarters in growing towns and cities.

In the second half of the 18th and early 19th centuries, the post-medieval farmed landscape of the Peak District was changed radically with the enclosure of many commons, and the privatisation of others. On the Chatsworth Estate the impact was not as great as in some areas; much of the better land was already enclosed. This said, the old deer park, which effectively became redundant after the landscape park was finished, was not finally divided into fields until the late 18th century. Similarly, some former moorlands, as above Beeley for example, were enclosed in the early 19th century. The extensive moorlands which have survived were not improved because it became fashionable to shoot grouse in the 19th century.

Many plantations were created across the Estate in the 18th and 19th centuries. Notable for their size and landscape impact are New Piece Plantation made at the same time as the landscape park, matched to the east by Stand Wood replanted a few years before and Bunkers Hill Wood above, also created in the 18th century. The Core Estate's fourth large wood, at Lindop, already existed in the early 17th century but was much enlarged in the 18th and 19th centuries. Another distinctive but now nearly-lost woodland feature of the Estate was the impressive late 18th century layouts of shelterbelts surrounding rectangular fields, as in the old deer park, and near Dunsa and Farlow Paddocks.

In the 18th and early 19th centuries traditional through-routes were gradually replaced by turnpike roads that allowed industrial products to be moved and commercial trade to take place, with relative ease. While most of these roads are still in use today, there are a few abandoned sections, as at the 1759 road in the park south of Baslow, leading down from the impressive but collapsing Millstone Bridge.

Of the 18th and 19th century industrial sites on the Estate some of the most impressive are the extensive stone quarries on Fallinge Edge, and those on the lower scarp at Burntwood and Limetree Wood. These retain many details that enlighten process and working conditions, including stone sheds and broken products such as millstones, pulpstones, stone troughs and gateposts. The coal mines on the gritstone upland continued to be worked into the 19th century, now at deeper levels underground, and there was an 18th century lead smelter at Harewood Cupola, the foundations of which still remain.

It is the 'everyday' landscape formed or modified over the 250 years since Brown was at work around the House which is inevitably most evident today; this is reflected in the length of the next three chapters and even then space only allows a summary of the wealth of historic features that are of interest.

CHAPTER SIX

The Cavendish Era:
The Farmed Landscape

An Estate of many parts

In the last few hundred years a strong dichotomy has existed between the House, with its gardens, old deer park, warren and later its landscape park, and the extensive farmland and moorlands beyond. The exclusivity of one is obvious, comprising landscapes overtly designed to show the wealth, aesthetic taste and superiority of the owners of Chatsworth; the other is more workaday. However, in important ways lines drawn between these different worlds have always been blurred. Farming and industry on the Estate provided the wealth for the creation and upkeep of the grand house and pleasure grounds. Conversely, the parkland was still farmed and many people were traditionally employed in the upkeep of this as well as the House and gardens. Beyond the park, the wealth of the Estate allowed long-term management, including the establishment of extensive woodlands and the making of wide-reaching agricultural improvements on the farmland implemented in line with fashionable practice. This contrasted with more normal landscapes of gradual 'organic' change or continuity elsewhere. Similarly, the survival of moorlands owes more to the elite pastime of grouse shooting in the 19th century than it does to the constraints of nature.

This chapter documents settlement and farming changes from the 16th century to today. The landscape is full to brimming with structures dating from this period, many still in use. In the majority of cases, as with dwellings, field boundaries or field barns, these at first glance seem insignificant because they are commonplace and familiar, but they are the heart of the historic landscape character we have inherited. Also, we must remember that what we take for granted today, thinking we understand it, was built under radically different social conditions and for different reasons than many think. We must avoid looking back through rose-tinted spectacles at the countryside that existed when our great-grandparents were young.

Living on a great estate: patterns of settlement

Two of the main villages, Beeley and Pilsley, are in many ways typical Peak District villages; they have thrived through the centuries and, like all others

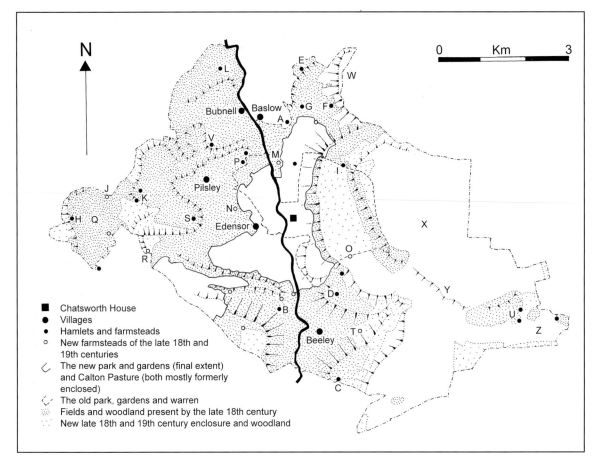

FIGURE 47. The Chatsworth landscape in post-medieval times (Places mentioned in Chapter 6 – A: Baslow Nether End, B: Calton Lees, C: Fallinge, D: Beeley Hilltop, E: Jack Flat Farm, F: Yew Tree Field Cottage, G: Baslow Far End, H: Cracknowl Cottage, I: Parkgate Farm, J: Station Farm, K: Birchill, L: Bramley, M: Home Farm, N: Dunsa, O: Park Farm, P: Farlow Paddocks, Q: Cracknowl Pasture, R: Ballcross Farm, S: Handley Bottom Farm, T: Moor Farm, U: Harewood Grange and Harewood Grange Farm, V: Bubnell Cliff Farm, W: Gardom's Edge, X: Gibbet Moor, Y: Harland Edge, Z: Harewood Moor).

nearby, had medieval origins. A third village, Edensor, was visually transformed in the 19th century into a model village, but in other important ways the inhabitants continued as before. The core of Baslow, the fourth village near Chatsworth, has always lain beyond the Estate, but came closer with the growth of Nether End to provide facilities for 19th century visitors to the House and grounds.

It is not just Edensor that has been visually transformed in post-medieval times. Stone-built dwellings and outbuildings gradually replaced timber-frames with wattle and daub from the 17th to 19th centuries, and thin sandstone slabs and later Welsh slates replaced thatch. More recently the pigsties, cowsheds, stables and barns, which nearly every cottage and farmstead had, have been replaced by the garage or converted into additional accommodation. People in local villages have also seen social transformations over the last few hundred years. Medieval feudal ways gradually went as emphasis swung towards ownership and profit, this change going hand in hand with improved farming practices and eventually industrialisation. Many people have long earned their living by being tenant farmers or labourers on the Estate, while others worked in traditional service trades. A significant number, far more than today, worked in the House and gardens, or maintained the Estate parkland, woodlands and moors. However, from the 18th century onwards, people started to move away from the Peak District to burgeoning industrial areas such as Chesterfield and Sheffield. In the 20th century with increasing mechanisation far fewer people were needed to work the land. Similarly, in recent decades, large numbers of house servants and gardeners could not be afforded. This depopulation has been offset by growth in the tourism industry and the viability of commuter-living in our post-industrial world.

The date, continuity and character of smaller settlements is varied.[1] Some have long been occupied, as with the hamlet of Calton Lees or farmsteads such as Fallinge and Beeley Hilltop. Others failed long ago, as with the farmsteads of Langley and Besley on the Chatsworth side of the river near the House. Most of today's buildings at the scattered farmsteads, as well as smaller houses and cottages, are 18th or 19th century in date. Some properties were probably not occupied for more than a few generations, as with Jack Flat Farm and Yew Tree Field Cottage east of Baslow.[2] Now abandoned, both were built in intake encroachments onto the commons, high on the rocky slopes above Baslow Far End. In contrast, the isolated small dwelling at Cracknowl House is 17th century in date and still occupied. Parkgate Farm may well be the site of The Horns Inn, used before the 19th century by packhorsemen and others as they crossed the moors.[3] Station Farm by Hassop roundabout is a 19th century creation, built in the 1860s as an inn adjacent to the entrance to Hassop Station when the Midland Railway extended its line from Rowsley to Buxton; it only became a farmstead in the 20th century.[4]

One very small but unique building lies high above and west of Bubnell, placed next to a narrow and now little-used lane that once was the 1759 East Moor to Wardlow Turnpike. This curious but carefully-built circular structure with corbelled roof is said to have been a lock-up.[5]

Villages and farmsteads: the vernacular buildings

Across the Chatsworth Estate there is a wide range of vernacular buildings, varying from humble field barns and small cottages to large farmhouses with suites of outbuildings.[6] Most are stone-built in typical Peak District post-medieval vernacular fashion with squared sandstone for the walls and dressed but often plain sandstone or gritstone surrounds to openings, beneath welsh- or stone-slate roofs. The latter came from local quarries, dug where the coarse sandstone was thinly bedded. Thatch was once common and former examples can be recognised from the roof pitch at re-roofed buildings. Only on Cracknowl Pasture is a different building stone used, limestone, which is the local bedrock here. While the buildings within and adjacent to the park are largely architect-designed, within the wider Estate beyond the vista of the House the farmsteads and cottages tend to be more functional in appearance with little or no adornment; there is no Estate building style. Often the only visual clue to ownership is the Estate livery of blue and white paintwork at doors and windows.

Farmhouses are often accompanied by outbuildings that commonly include loose boxes, stables, cattle byres, enclosed fodder barns, and implement and cart sheds. More rarely pigsties still survive. Large threshing barns are absent and open-sided hay barns were never common.

A minority of the vernacular buildings were built in the 17th century, often recognised by their small mullioned windows, dating to a time when the houses and outbuildings in the Peak commonly started being constructed in stone. However, the majority of today's stone buildings are of 18th and 19th century date.

Each of the main villages will now be briefly reviewed, followed by the outlying farmsteads and cottages.

Pilsley

The present dwellings are a mix of 18th and 19th century stone-built houses, with a cluster of 20th century homes built for estate workers and retirement accommodation at the southern entrance to the village. Former farmsteads are spaced along the street, mixed with houses and cottages which also had small barns, stables and cowhouses. A hundred years ago there were three farmsteads at the western end of the main street and at least one more at the eastern end.[7] In recent decades these have become redundant to modern farming needs, although the houses are still occupied and many of the outbuildings have been converted to other uses. The village post office/shop was formerly a bakery.[8]

Paxton's influence on the village extended in a limited way to Pilsley where he built in the Italianate style at Pilsley House.[9] He also designed Pilsley School in 1849, in this case built with coped gables, mullioned windows and hood moulds. Top House is also attributed to him.[10]

Beeley

The Estate owns many but not all of the village properties. Former farmsteads and cottages flank a north/south lane and other roads running eastwards, with a medieval church to the western side rather than at a focal point.

A detailed survey of the Estate properties in Beeley was undertaken in 1850 and this provides insight into what many of the cottages may have looked like before mid 19th century improvements.[11] What were probably the older buildings were often either low two-storey dwellings, or were single-storey with an upper level in the roof space. One, Pynot Cottage, today still has its 17th century mullioned windows.[12] Unlike today, in 1850 a significant proportion of the older properties were thatched.[13] Sandstone slates were also common, usually used on somewhat larger and slightly higher quality buildings. Today, thatched buildings are rare in the Peak District, although two still exist on Chatsworth Estate, at Thatched Cottage at Nether End, Baslow and Thatch Meadows in Pilsley parish.[14] These give some indication as to how many of the properties in Beeley, and also Edensor and Pilsley, would have formerly appeared.

A few houses described in 1850 as being in poor states of repair with roofs letting in water were either pulled down, or were rebuilt with heightened first floors and dormer windows, and re-roofed with Welsh slate or sandstone slabs. The village had numerous cow houses, stables, hay barns and pigsties that were used by the cottage occupants; three properties had cheese rooms. Most tenants kept pigs, one or two cows, and in some instances horses for carting or transport.

There was a public house, and this thrives today as the Devonshire Arms.[15] Last Cottage is also of interest as in 1850 this was a thatched shoemaker's premises with an outside staircase to the first floor.[16] The now-blocked doorway still retains the stone surrounds. It and adjacent buildings to the south were described as being 'altogether not worth much', not helped by the fact that the yard to the east was 'in a very filthy state being partly occupied with dung heaps and the drainage bad'! In the same group of buildings there was also a grocer's shop and a joiner's shop.

The 1850s survey also included five working farmsteads in the village core; there are none today. They included the Old Hall, where the farmhouse is one of the oldest surviving buildings in the village, dating from the early 17th century. There is a cruck-framed but stone-clad outbuilding behind that may be an even earlier survival. Norman House, on the opposite side of the street also dates from the 17th century, and is a substantial three-storey dwelling for what was a second relatively large farmstead. Both houses have windows with chamfered mullions, which are characteristic of Peak District halls built for the gentry, and farmhouses erected by yeoman farmers, at this date. At Norman House, one 19th century building is a fine six-bay open hay barn, with piers of stepped stone; these are rare in the Peak.

Another impressive building is the Duke's Barn, sited immediately to the north-west of the Old Hall. This large range, with a spandrel inscribed 1791, reflects Estate 'improvements' in agriculture at this period; it was reputedly built to house the 5th Duke's shire horses. By 1850, the eastern end was used by the Old Hall, but the rest was the outbuilding of a separate farm. Later the Barn was again used to house the Estate work-horses and wagons.[17]

As with Pilsley, the influence of Paxton is not immediately noticeable when compared with Edensor. The only obvious hand he played was at Beeley School built in 1841 and possibly at the adjacent School House.[18] The unusual architect-designed building near the Devonshire Arms, with three cottages in a Y-shaped plan, is attributed to G. H. Stokes, Paxton's son-in-law.[19]

FIGURE 48. There are many interesting details at the vernacular buildings across the estate. Here old pigsties at Beeley have well-dressed stones surrounding feeding chutes.

Baslow

The Estate owns only a few properties in Baslow Nether End, and one of the oldest surviving is the small 17th century Thatched Cottage.[20] In contrast, the much-altered Cavendish Hotel, previously known as the Peacock Hotel is reputed to be a former hunting lodge belonging to the Manners family.[21] It became the Cock Inn in 1700 and has remained a hostelry ever since. The present building appears to be of 19th century date, with modern additions, and traditionally catered for relatively wealthy visitors to Chatsworth.

Bubnell

A linear village which has medieval origins but is today probably much-shrunken, with now-spaced properties along a single street. The Estate owns two surviving farmsteads, both with complex suites of mostly 19th century buildings.

Calton Lees

This hamlet today has two sets of farmstead buildings and several cottages, mostly dating to the 18th and 19th centuries. Calton Lees House has a main front built in simple classical style, with the windows linked by continuous sill and lintel bands.[22] However, the rear wing has the remains of an earlier cruck frame; in the Peak District these commonly date from the late medieval period to the 17th century. In its final form, the relatively large size of the house and its architectural aspirations suggests that it was built as an Estate residence for a person of 'quality'. Calton Lees Farm has a plainer house.[23] In 1785 the outbuildings layout here was roughly rectangular but in the second half of the 19th century they were largely replaced by scattered buildings to the north of the main house. A rare three-bay hay barn with open front is somewhat earlier.

Farmsteads with medieval origins

Some medieval settlements are now reduced to single farmsteads, as at Birchill. Here, despite its long recorded history starting before the Norman Conquest, it retains no buildings that on external inspection at least date to before the 19th century. The present farmhouse, from its appearance, probably started life as three agricultural workers' cottages for the large modern dairy farm. Another older house standing nearby was probably once the farmhouse.[24]

The present buildings at the farmstead at Bramley in Bubnell Township again mostly date from the 19th century. The present house was built in 1802, while nearby there was an 'old house' recorded in 1847 which has now gone.[25] The archive evidence indicates that in the 19th century there was also a second occupied dwelling at Bramley, on the other side of the lane; perhaps a vestige of a once thriving hamlet. In 1847 this was noted as a 'house, cowhouse and garden' but was unoccupied by 1871 and has now gone. The vernacular outbuildings at the present farmstead include two long main ranges, set on terraces, built in the mid to late 19th century. Mostly the walls are plain, but the western end of the northern range is built of rusticated stonework and also may have been a former dwelling, presumably for a farm worker and family.

Fallinge is a small hamlet straddling the Beeley parish boundary high on the main gritstone shelf, with one surviving farmstead on Estate land, which has buildings of 17th to 19th century date.[26] This is laid out in a 'U' shape, with the farmhouse flanked by outbuilding ranges, with a small farm workers' cottage in the eastern of these.

The most imposing buildings of all the dispersed farmsteads are at Beeley Hilltop, once called 'The Greaves' after the resident family who owned the manor and built the fine hall here at this remote spot in the 17th century.[27] This rather gaunt but large high-status house has fine-quality ashlar dressings and quoins, and mullioned and chamfered windows with hood-moulds. It stood within small formal gardens, of which earthwork evidence still survives.[28] A farmstead courtyard stood close by to the east, but this has now been largely replaced by modern farm sheds. One survival against the lane has a wall with a line of unusual arched openings, now blocked. At some distance to the west there is a house with attached outbuildings forming two sides of what was a second farmyard, which is reached by an arched entrance.

Estate farmsteads of the 18th and 19th centuries

Classic large planned model farmsteads from the 18th and 19th centuries, when estates took a keen interest in then progressive agriculture, are not found at Chatsworth.[29] While these carefully designed farmsteads are a feature of landscapes in places like East Anglia, Northumbria and the Scottish Lowlands, they are not normally found in the Peak, as individual holdings were rarely large enough to warrant radical building programmes. Even at Chatsworth, the closest the Estate came are the less-grand planned farmsteads which were built in the 19th century at Home Farm (formerly Crimea Farm) sited in the Derwent Valley bottom south of Baslow, at Dunsa Farm beyond the north-western edge of the park, and at The Stud Farm at Pilsley. These were purpose-built by successive Dukes of Devonshire for Estate use and also as examples to visitors and tenants of how innovative and modern the Estate farming enterprises were at that time. All have well-built functional buildings in well-dressed gritstone. Any ornaments are discrete and normally confined to the roofs.

Home Farm, formerly Crimea Farm, has outbuildings in a planned 'U' shape set at a distance from the farmhouse. These are shown on a map of 1857, but not one drawn in 1848, and are constructed of finely-dressed stonework.[30] Even the yard walls are finely finished. Alterations, including larger yards with further finely made walls were made after 1867. The former farmhouse stands on the other side of Bar Brook, close to the site of Paxton's residence.[31] Its original name suggests that the house at least was built during or shortly after the time of the Crimean War of 1854–56. This farmstead may have originally been built as a dairy unit to supply milk and milk products to the Estate, as suggested by its location close to the main house in rich meadow pastures between Bar Brook and the River Derwent. The 9th Duke kept his herd of Shorthorns here in the early 20th century.[32]

The quietly understated but well-built farm buildings of Dunsa are set around a yard, built with functionality rather than ornateness in mind.[33] Dunsa evolved from two cottages present in the late 18th century, and there were two main phases of development. The first was in the early 1830s, when a 'U' shaped range of three cottages, with outbuildings and Estate kennels, was built. The second phase of building took place sometime between 1855 and 1879, when further farm buildings well to the west were constructed around a central yard; a southern range was added later. Only two ranges now survive and there are extensive modern buildings. Interesting original detail includes a fine pigeon loft in one gable end.

The Stud Farm at Pilsley was a planned suite of outbuildings for the 9th Duke's shire horses.[34] It was constructed in 1910 with a courtyard plan. Part of the former Stud is now occupied by the Chatsworth Farm Shop.

Several farmsteads on the Estate were also built or rebuilt for tenants, but space allows only brief notice of three of these. Parkgate Farm lies at the edge of the old deer park and the buildings here were wholly rebuilt sometime between 1867 and 1879. New plain and functional outbuildings were set around a courtyard with the farmhouse in the southern corner, possibly re-designed as a 'mirror' to Park Farm to the south of the old park, which also had some new buildings added at around the same time.[35] Park Farm was probably first developed as a small planned farmstead in around 1800 when this area was enclosed.[36] This good example of an Estate farmstead has a main courtyard with house, loose boxes, stables, an open-sided hay barn of two-storey height and other outbuildings, all with good quality stonework. Two further ranges of implement sheds enclosing a further yard area were added sometime between 1867 and 1879.

The next two farmsteads to be described are on land owned by the Dukes of Rutland until the 1820s. Yeldwood Farm lies on the western side of the 1803 Baslow to Sheffield turnpike road at Baslow Far End.[37] The farmhouse with attached cottage to the rear lies to the south of the double range of outbuildings and there are two further cottages to the south-west, all of which have been here since at least 1848. The roadside outbuilding range is thought to have been built as a coach house for overnight stabling, presumably associated with the hotels at Nether End.

Yeld Farm on the opposite side of the road was built against the 1803 turnpike sometime after this was constructed and the field pattern realigned.[38] This farmstead still retains many of its original buildings and also an interesting range of associated smaller stone structures such as troughs, a stone-flag dog kennel and pigsties. The first phase, with a house and two outbuilding ranges comprising cart shed and loose boxes with hay storage above, was built sometime prior to 1848, and loosely arranged around a yard. Another range, with a four-bay implement shed and further loose boxes, was added sometime between 1848 and 1879.[39] The house was also extended to the south-east during this time.

Grassland Mosaics: the enclosed agricultural landscape

Much of the enclosed landscape of the Core Estate that we see today is the product of farming practice over the last few hundred years. While local communities throughout much of this period have grown arable crops to meet their own needs, the mainstay of the farming economy has been livestock. Many field boundaries are still extant, but redundant layouts include notable examples in Chatsworth Park and on Calton Pasture. Both places have exceptional earthworks which, while low, are both extensive and of great interest for the rare picture they present of a complex agricultural landscape which was 'fossilised' in about 1760 and the 1820s. That within the park is much as left, while unfortunately at Calton Pasture ploughing and reseeding in recent decades has caused degradation.

The field boundaries of the Estate form an intricate pattern that changes in character from place to place.[40] These changes are vital to an understanding of the history of land use at each area. They also reflect evolving farming practice

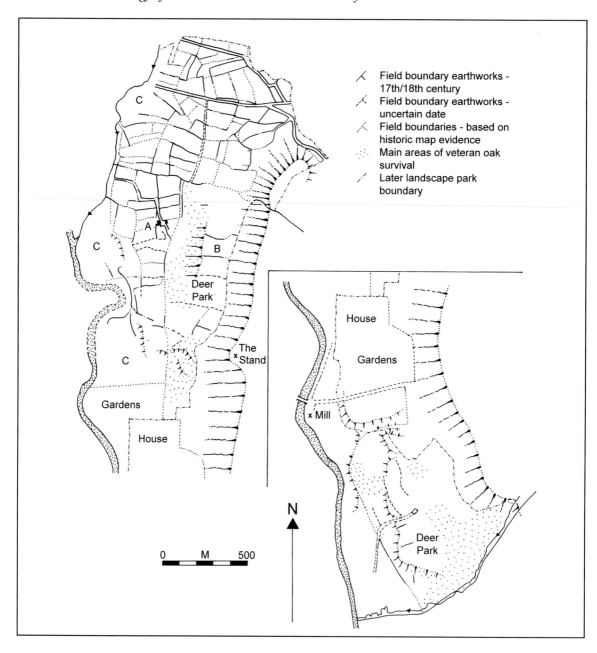

common throughout the Peak and beyond. In some areas, the boundaries are gently curved in a reverse-S and such fields can be long and thin. As noted in Chapter 4 these areas have once been parts of medieval open fields where the originally unfenced strips were later 'fossilised' by the building of permanent boundaries around parcels of strips. In contrast, many fields across the Estate are roughly rectangular in shape. Again some may be medieval in origin, used as private grazing pastures, but many are post-medieval in date. A proportion

FIGURE 49. Surviving earthworks of post-medieval field boundaries within the Park east of the River Derwent (A: farmstead, B: Enclosures within the deer park, C: Insufficient data).

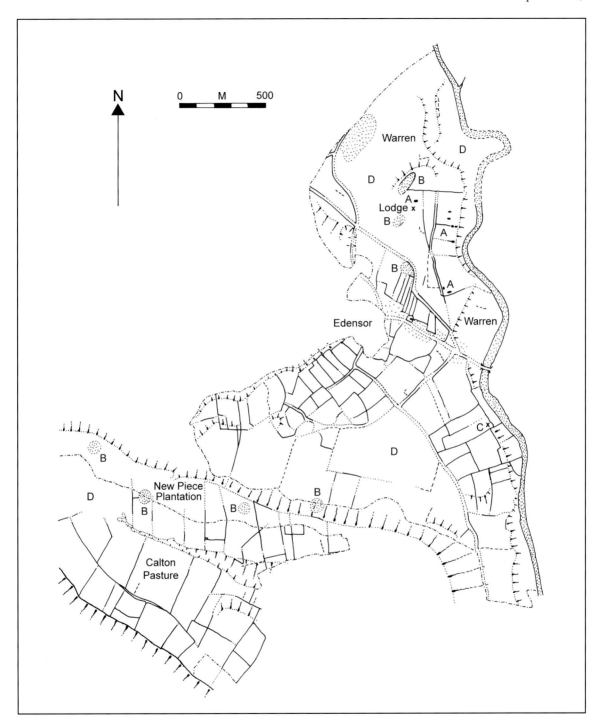

FIGURE 50. Surviving earthworks of post-medieval field boundaries within the Park west of the River Derwent, New Piece Plantation and Calton Pasture (A: Pillow mounds, B: Early-18th century plantings, C: Site of a small stable, D: Insufficient data) (For a key see Figure 49).

of these fields have ruler-straight edges. This is a clear sign they have been planned on a map before being built. It is known that a few of these are late 17th century in date, but most belong to the 18th or 19th century.

Enclosure of the medieval open fields around the villages into bounded fields presumably started well before the Cavendish family arrived at Chatsworth and certainly continued up until the early 19th century before it was complete. Similarly, the enclosure of medieval wastes and commons in places west of the Derwent was not complete until sometime between the 16th and 18th centuries. East of the Derwent many of the high commons were never enclosed, while some more favourable areas were improved in the late 18th and 19th centuries.

While much enclosure in post-medieval times was achieved gradually in piecemeal fashion, with field shape and pattern reflecting this, other enclosure was planned on a larger scale. This applies particularly at former commons, sheepwalks and the warren. Such changes were often instigated by the Estate or in the case of parts of Beeley Township as part of an 1832 Parliamentary Enclosure Award. A period of significant change is demonstrated on estate maps of 17th to early 19th century date, but by the mid 19th century, virtually the whole of the present pattern of fields on the Estate had been established; changes since then have been less and in modern times the trend has been for boundary loss.

Space does not permit a detailed area-by-area description of the Estate's post-medieval farming landscapes and how they changed through time. Much of this detail is illustrated in the accompanying figures; the different dates used here reflect the available estate maps for each area. What follows picks out only specific highlights.

The Park and Calton Pasture: 'Fossilisations'

When the landscape park was created in 1758–60s and extended in the 1820s archaeologically important field layouts were swept away but remain visible in earthwork form. Estate maps present snapshots in time and while Senior's early 17th century plans are invaluable, for this part of the Estate there are no further maps for the mid 17th to mid 18th centuries. Thus, we are fully reliant on the extensive earthwork evidence that survives today to identify radical agricultural changes which included much new enclosure of the landscape in this period.[41] These post-medieval field boundaries were normally defined by hedges and are seen today as low banks, lynchets and drainage ditches.

On the Chatsworth side of the river, there are extensive earthworks north of the House in Chatsworth and Baslow Townships.[42] Amongst the old field boundary banks there are earthworks of a farmstead that was in use in the same period.[43] South of the House the remains of similar field boundaries are more fragmentary.[44] In contrast, field boundary earthworks are at their most extensive west of the Derwent around Edensor where they often run together

FIGURE 51. Edensor and the Western Shelves in the early 17th century (A: Bubnell, B: Edensor, C: Pilsley, D: Birchill, E: Cracknowl Pasture) (For a key see Figure 36).

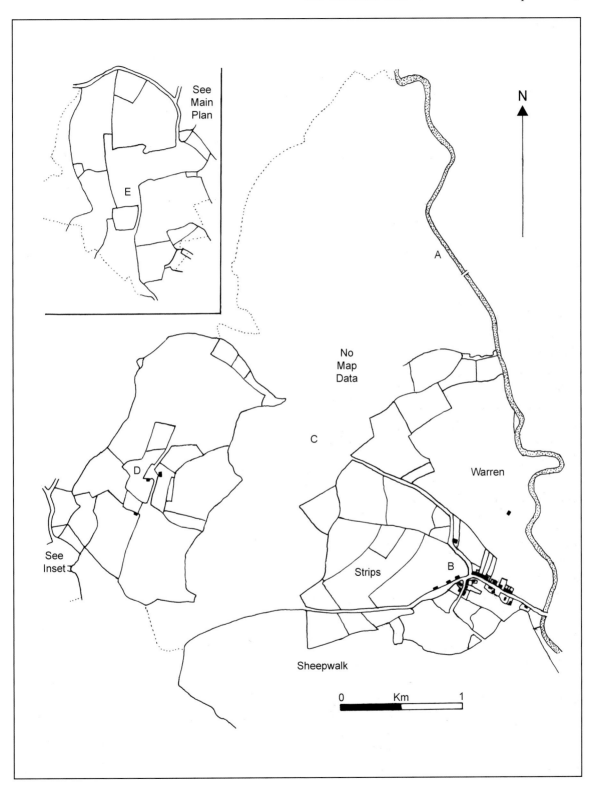

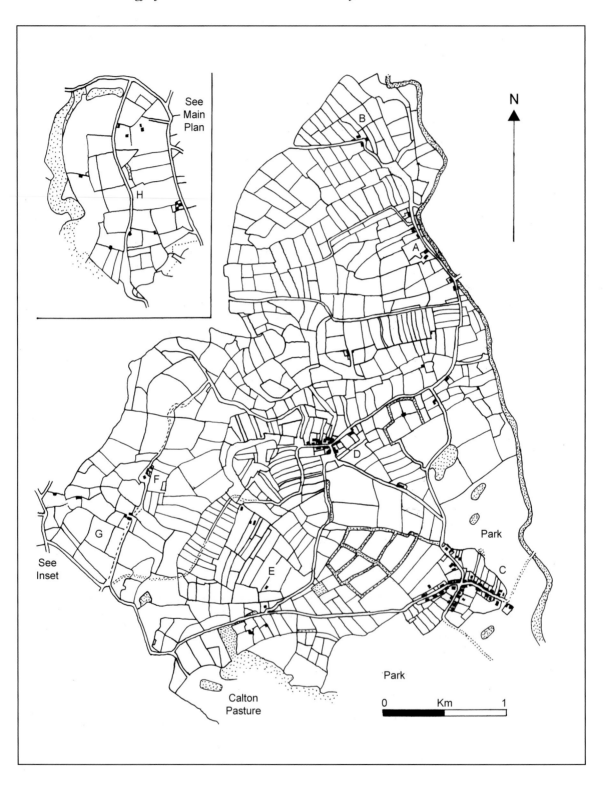

FIGURE 52 (*opposite*).
Edensor and the Western
Shelves in the late 18th
to early 19th centuries
(A: Bubnell, B: Bramley,
C: Edensor, D: Pilsley,
E: Handley Bottom, F:
Birchill, G: Birchill Flatt,
H: Cracknowl Pasture)
(For a key see Figure 36).

seamlessly. Here they represent a complex palimpsest of medieval and post-medieval features. Around the village there are many small fields, while there were larger fields on higher ground to the south-west.[45]

Today's open sheepwalk of Calton Pasture, divided today only with wire fences, has earthwork evidence which shows that it was previously fully enclosed into a series of hedged rectangular fields.[46] These again were created sometime between the mid 17th century and earlier 18th century, taken in from what was open Estate grazing. The fields were removed in the 1760s as part of the grand scheme instigated by the 4th Duke and Brown, which included the creation of the landscape park, the planting of New Piece Plantation and an 'outer park' at Calton Pasture.

The enclosed farmland

FIGURE 53 (*below*).
This enclosed farming
landscape at Handley
Bottom has rectangular
and less-regular fields
defined by hedges, many
of which have grown out
and been replaced by
wire fences.

West of the Derwent, the fields in Bubnell Township are varied in type. They include a ruler-straight field system west of Bramley, present by 1799 and probably created as estate planning by the Dukes of Rutland. Elsewhere there are less regular fields, with traces of 'fossilised' strips in places. Significant 20th century boundary removals have to an extent disguised traditional patterns.

Around Edensor the character of enclosure has changed markedly from the large irregular fields shown on Senior's survey of 1617 to the north and west

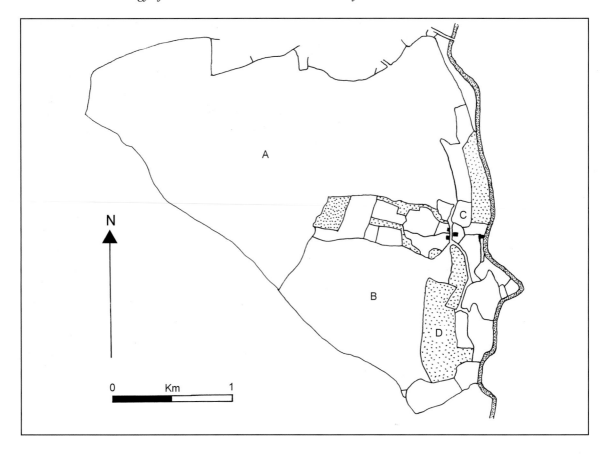

FIGURE 54. Calton Pastures and Calton Lees in 1617 (A: Sheepwalk, B: Calton Moor, later known as Lees Moor, C: Calton Lees, D: Lindup Wood) (For a key see Figure 36).

of the village. The overall subsequent trend was for them to get smaller. Some boundaries are ruler-straight while others are set within ha-has. Pilsley is a township of contrasts; there is good medieval cultivation-strip 'fossilisation' with sinuous wall lines found around the village and ruler-straight hedged and fenced boundaries at Handley Bottom and in smaller areas elsewhere. Today Birchill has large prairie-like fields created in the first half of the 20th century, with a central access track, created for the development of the large dairy unit here. The track allowed easy daily movement of cows between the milking parlour and the grazing pastures. The hedged boundaries at Birchill Flatt contrast with the rectangular limestone-walled fields nearby at Cracknowl Pasture. Fields already existed at Cracknowl in the early 17th century, but these were subsequently subdivided; when the walls were first built is unclear.

Further south, in the Calton Lees valley there are small rectangular enclosures of post-medieval date, some of which around the settlement itself were already present by the early 17th century but have now been much changed through time. Below, in the Derwent Valley bottom, most of the traditional boundaries are now removed. On the former Lees Moor there is a small area of later enclosure now subsumed in woodland, while parts of Lindop Wood are, with

Stand Wood on the other side of the valley, the largest long-standing areas of woodland on the Estate.

East of the Derwent, the fields above Stand Wood and Bunkers Hill Wood, which fill the old deer park, have a distinctive ruler-straight layout with shelterbelts dating to the late 18th century, with the Estate-farmsteads of Park Farm and Park Gate Farm to either end. Later in the 19th century a series of layout alterations led to the decorative shelterbelt design eventually losing its integrity. Above Bunkers Hill Wood there is a narrow strip of walled fields in the uppermost part of the old park. This carefully designed layout, with a central walled access lane, was created in the mid-19th century, perhaps as lambing pastures.

In strong contrast, the fields around Baslow Near and Far Ends are mostly irregular and some may have medieval origins. Jack Flat Farm, now abandoned, was probably originally created as an intake from the wastes and commons of Baslow. Many of the fields on the Robin Hood shelf have been radically altered, and new areas improved from moorland, in the 19th century. A series of maps from 1799 onwards show the transformation from an enclosed landscape with relatively irregular fields of unknown date, including a roughly-oval area of fields which look in plan like a typical moorland intake, to one with rectangular fields. These changes are typical of large estate management, where relatively expensive field layout changes were executed.

FIGURE 55. Calton Pasture and Calton Lees in 1785 (A: Calton Pasture, B: Calton Lees, C: Lindop Wood, D: Calton Houses, E: New Piece Plantation) (For a key see Figure 36).

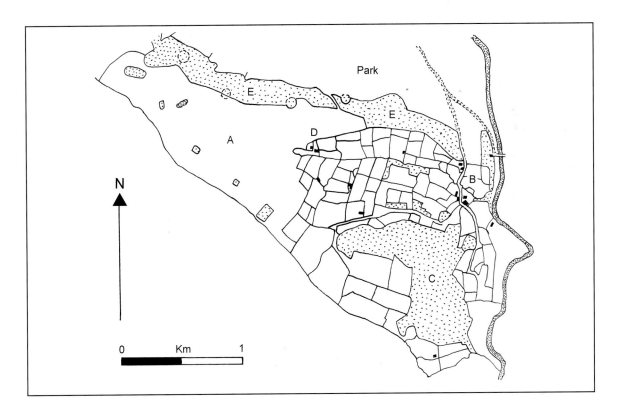

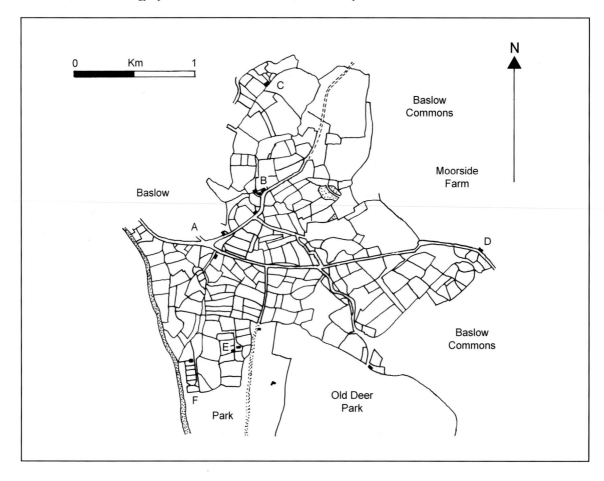

Further south, around Beeley village, today's rectangular fields defined by hedges and walls have only a few traces of medieval strip 'fossilisation'. Much enclosure had taken place by the end of the 17th century, and when first mapped in 1785 the 'fossilisation' pattern was already only partial.[47] These patterns became less clear in the 19th and 20th centuries with gradual changes to and removal of boundaries. On the main upland shelf at Beeley Hilltop and Fallinge, and further east at Harewood Grange, there are irregular clusters of walled fields, some of which have early origins. The field layouts were altered in the 19th centuries with the addition of, and replacement with, straight boundaries. In contrast, around Moor Farm and Hell Bank Plantation there are straight-sided fields that had been taken in from commons by 1836, after having being 'privatised' by the 1832 Beeley Enclosure Award;[48] some have now been subsumed within the modern plantation.

FIGURE 56. The Core Estate part of Baslow in the late 18th century (A: Baslow Near End, B: Baslow Far End, C: Jack Flat Farm, D: Robin Hood, E: Unnamed farmstead in Chatsworth Township, F: Kitchen Gardens) (For a key see Figure 36).

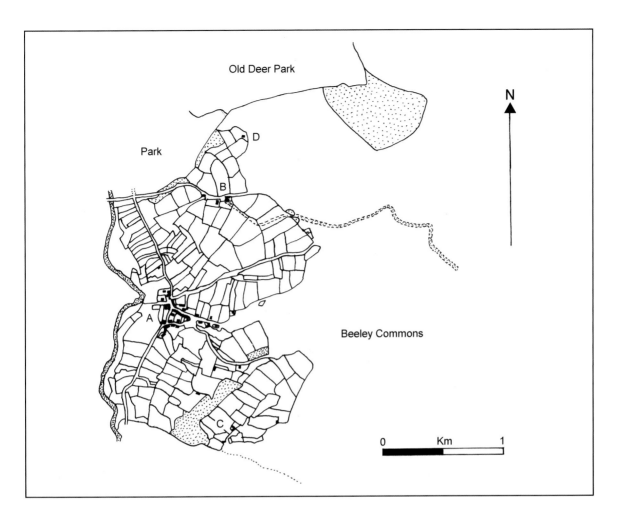

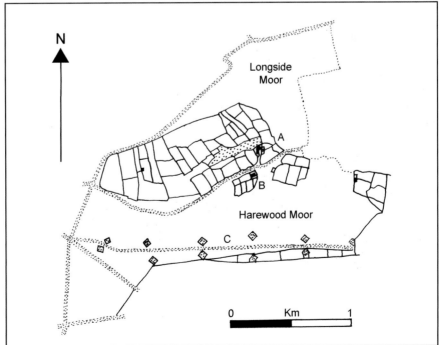

FIGURE 57 (*above*). Beeley in 1785 (A: Beeley village, B: Beeley Hilltop, C: Fallinge, D: Doe Wood Farm) (For a key see Figure 36).

FIGURE 58 (*right*). Harewood Grange in 1814 (A: Harewood Grange, B: Harewood Grange Farm, C: the mid 18th century drive) (For a key see Figure 36).

Dividing the farmland: walls and hedges

In the Peak District field walls are commonplace and hedges occur locally. Such boundaries are often taken for granted, but they have great value as features that frequently have great time depth. The field patterns they form, often most clearly seen from the air or on a map, are one of the main components that visibly define the historic landscape character of swathes of the Core Estate landscape. Boundary 'furniture' adds to local character.

Drystone walls

Walls dominate the enclosed farmland of the Core Estate.[49] Generally they are built upon footings of large stones, with the un-mortared stonework above faced on both sides, slightly battered inwards, with a rubble core. One to three courses of through-stones tie the two faces together and the whole is topped with coping stones, often roughly shaped half-rounded blocks or slabs. At the base the walls are usually between 60 and 70cm wide, and they are often between 1.25m and 1.50m high. Notable exceptions are walls bounding plantations, which are often higher, probably to prevent deer or stock jumping into the woods. At these, the face of the wall on the wood side is very often rough with protruding stones, whilst that on the outer side has a smooth batter.

In 1813 Farey described the drystone walls at Peak farms as having ring boundaries that were five feet (1.5m) high with a 9 inch (0.23m) coping of stones on edge, whilst internal walls were 7 inches (0.18m) lower.[50] These of course were the ideal and no doubt in practice there was variation. The cost of walling in Farey's day was between 6 and 10 shillings per rood of seven yards (6.4m) in length. This included getting the stone, carting it and building the wall.

Variation in the shape and size of the stones used in walling is largely dictated by very local geological characteristics, which in turn influenced the waller's building style. Normally the Core Estate walls are in gritstone or sandstone, where some are built of blocky, rectangular stones whilst thin, platy stones dominate others; both are usually crudely coursed. At Cracknowl Pasture limestone is the local bedrock. Here the walls are, because of the nature of the limestone, built of very irregularly shaped stones, often with little rubble infill between the two outer faces. The majority of walls across the Estate have relatively angular stone that has been quarried, although in some cases, as at Harewood Grange, it is rounded and has been surface-gathered. Occasionally, stone salvaged from redundant walls or from demolished buildings has also been used.

The presence of large boulders or upright stones at the base of walls is not necessarily an indication of their antiquity, as has been postulated for walls elsewhere,[51] but rather the existence of uncleared ground at the time they were created. Often it was easier to build the wall over and around a large boulder than attempt to remove it or break it up. In other cases, placing a large stone in a wall was a convenient way of placing it out of the way of cultivation; at initial clearance such stones would be plentiful. Not surprisingly, the greatest occurrence of upright stones on the Core Estate is in walls at the 'moor-edge' farms below Gardom's Edge and at Harewood Grange.

In some parts of the Estate, as at Beeley Hilltop for example, the drystone field walls are flanked with mature trees spaced at intervals along their lengths. Up until recent decades, these were routinely planted to provide timber for the Estate and tenant farmers.

While some walls on the Estate may have medieval origins, many are of 17th to 19th century date. However, individual walls cannot easily be dated with any precision from their appearance. The biggest barrier to this is that walls are constantly collapsing and being repaired or rebuilt as an on-going part of farm management. Therefore, while a wall line and sometimes its footings may be ancient, much of what we see comprises 19th and 20th century repairs and rebuilds.

Hedgerows

Field hedges were once commonly used to enclose fields in parts of the Estate such as the lower slopes of the sheltered Derwent Valley. In Chatsworth Park there is extensive earthwork evidence for the many fields swept away in 1758–60s and in the parkland extensions on the early 19th century, which show that the pre-park boundaries were virtually all hedges not walls.

An 1855 Estate map of Beeley distinguishes between hedges and field walls.[52] This allows comparison with today and shows not only that hedges have later been replaced by walls on Derwent Valley land, but also that live fences sometimes also existed on higher ground, as for example at Beeley Hilltop where walls now predominate. In some parts of the Peak District, as across the limestone plateau, it is beginning to be suspected that hedges were often the norm and that walls only became commonplace from the later 17th century onwards.

Today hedges are still to be found relatively frequently around Beeley, often planted when medieval cultivation strips were enclosed. Others occur at Calton Lees, Handley Bottom, Birchill Flatt and Bubnell. The most common location for hedges still in use today is bordering turnpike routes and other late 18th and early 19th century roads.

The hardy common hawthorn is the most common hedging shrub, with ash, hazel and to a lesser extent blackthorn inter-mixed. Sessile oak, elder, alder, midland hawthorn and rose also occur. The oak and ash also occur as standard trees. The road approaching Chatsworth Park through Beeley has the greatest mix of hedge species although hawthorn again dominates. Here there are stretches of almost pure blackthorn, snowberry and wild privet, perhaps planted for effect, as well as elm and hazel. Regularly spaced along these hedges are mature sycamores and limes.

Details in stone: field barns, wall furniture and water for stock

One of the key characteristics of the Peak District's traditional agricultural landscape is the barns found scattered through the fields. Unfortunately, field barns are now redundant and have no place in modern farming methods and the cost of upkeep is often prohibitively expensive. A significant number have gone, frequently others are ruined or derelict, while only a minority are kept in good repair or have been converted to camping barns.

Built into many of the walls enclosing the farmland at Chatsworth and elsewhere in the Peak are features relating to the management of those fields, for example gateways, sheep throughs, smoots (rabbit holes), stiles and water troughs. The location and function of the boundary often determines the type of features or 'furniture' built into it, although throughout the Peak District many of the traditional features are now redundant and over recent decades they have disappeared at an alarming rate as walls are rebuilt or removed. When gateways are enlarged to accommodate modern machinery, one gatepost is often removed and sometimes left lying nearby. Dating boundary furniture can be difficult, especially as it is known that, for example, gateposts have been reused, although it is suspected that much is of 18th and 19th century date.

Other important features within fields are freestanding water troughs and dew ponds. These again are probably mostly 18th and 19th century in date.

Field barns

These buildings were once a vital part of the farming economy, providing places where farm animals, normally cattle or sheep, could be fed, milked and sheltered. They enabled stock to be kept in the fields rather than returning them to a main farmstead for milking or over-wintering. Some are substantial two-storey buildings with haylofts above and stalling below, while others are smaller one-storey sheds and byres. Larger buildings commonly have associated walled yards and at some sites two or even three outbuildings were placed together to form working farm units which were effectively farmsteads minus a dwelling. Field barns were sometimes located in fields at a distance from village farmsteads, where it was more convenient to have a building amongst the fields. In other cases, the field barn was the only farm outbuilding owned or rented by a smallholder.

The numerous field barns on the Core Estate vary in size and condition, and most date from the 19th century, although some were here in the late 18th century and may be significantly earlier.[53] Over 140 past and present field barns have been identified, but only 61 of these are upstanding and in a relatively intact if sometimes dilapidated state. The Estate has repaired several in recent years, and a couple at Pilsley have been converted to camping barns.[54]

Field barns are typically built of uncoursed gritstone with varying amounts of ashlar stonework at quoins and surrounds to openings. There are virtually no

decorative features, except where large ashlar blocks are used for lintels. Thin sandstone slabs or blue slates were the most common original roofing materials. Some field barns retain internal wooden fittings such as mangers and stalls.

While some field barns were for Estate use or on land farmed from the main village farmsteads, in a significant number of cases, as classically illustrated with the barns immediately west of Edensor, they were built on land held by smallholders who had no main farmstead. In the fields on the south-facing slope near the village and below the 1739 Bakewell to Chesterfield turnpike road, there is a significant arrangement of 13 field barns, unfortunately now with only seven surviving in reasonable condition; in the 19th century virtually every field had a building.[55] While the fields are earlier, presumably laid out when the park was created in the 1760s to compensate for the loss of fields and traditional grazing rights, the barns were mostly added in the 1830s–50s. These may well have been built by the Estate as part of the improvements at Edensor when the model village was created.

In contrast to the majority of field barns, which are plain functional buildings, there is a minority with designs or architectural detail indicating likely construction by the Cavendish Estate for in-house use. The atypical and now dilapidated stables complex at Farlow Paddocks was home to the Estate's shire stallions in the late 19th century.[56] The importance of shire horses to the estate economy and the pride taken in these is reflected in the quality of the buildings' details. Access by tenants to good quality stallions meant that the farm workhorses in the neighbourhood came from good stock. Another example of more complex livestock buildings with yards lies high on the northern top of Cracknowl Pasture and comprises a well-planned but plain estate-type building that was probably built in the 1830s–40s.[57] This retains its mangers and internal wall partitions that create feeding corridors with openings to the mangers.

On the riverside meadows south-east of Calton Lees there is an exceptional 18th century seven-bay, open-sided, hay barn.[58] It has gable walls of coursed gritstone with stepped brick piers and a roof of stone tiles and was presumably built for storage of large crops of hay cut from the river meadows here. This building, together with a handful of others at Estate farmsteads noted above, is highly unusual in a Peak District context.[59] Their rarity must be partly explained because of the upland nature of the region, while the presence of examples on Chatsworth Estate may well also reflect both the necessary money to build them and the Estate's desire to follow what was regarded as progressive agricultural practice in the 18th and 19th centuries.

Gateposts

There is much variation in the types of humble gatepost used across the Estate[60] – it is a rewarding diversion to look out for these as you walk around.

Traditionally, gritstone was the most commonly used stone for gateposts on the Estate, even at Cracknowl Pasture where the walls were of limestone. This was easier to shape and decorate. They vary considerably in size and pattern of decoration and have often been reused, as shown for example by common evidence of several phases of holes for hinge pegs on single stones.

Unlike many gateposts at the boundaries of the parkland and others nearby, where patterned posts with symmetrical rounded heads predominate, the most-common type of gatepost in the farmland elsewhere was the roughly-dressed undecorated post. These had irregular, square or round heads, and may or may not have been tapered along their length. A square-headed post is usually used for the gate hinges, whilst a slightly slimmer round-headed post takes the latch. If a stone gatepost is carefully dressed or carries a pattern, this usually covers the three outer faces with the one abutting the wall headers left undressed. The simplest patterning comprises roughly chiselled stipples or diagonal hachures, where numerous short diagonal cuts were made on the surface of the stone. This pattern is also commonly seen on many dressed details in field barns. The pattern of the hachures may be in one direction only, or may be varied to form either a long herring-bone pattern down the face of the post or a patch-work of hachures going in alternate directions. Other posts have a 'ribbon edge' running around the outer edges of the post. This ribbon is either plain or smooth with no decoration, or has traces of narrow horizontal lines. Within the area framed by the ribbon edge, a pattern of either vertical, diagonal or herringbone lines is usually carved. A further complexity to the design can be a horizontal ribbon decoration added where the curve of the top begins.

The most highly decorated posts were not erected by the Estate, but by early 19th century Turnpike Trusts. With symmetrically rounded tops, these posts have neat parallel vertical or diagonal lines across the three outward faces, with a ribbon pattern to the edges. There is also another small group of highly decorated and ornate small posts associated with footgates alongside a water pipe laid down the Derwent Valley by the Derwent Valley Water Board in the early 20th century. These have ribbon-edge patterning enclosing a stippled interior and have rounded heads.

At Dunsa, pyramidal tops decorate posts to either side of the entrance drive to the Estate farmstead. Two plainer Estate gateposts have been found above Calton Lees and in Stand Wood, which unusually are dated, with inscriptions of 1757 and 1758. At the edge of the Estate at the east end of Harewood Moor, a pair of massive gateposts flank the former drive built in 1758. These asymmetrical posts with ribbon edging framing hachured dressing stand over 2m high. They made a statement: you were entering a Duke's domain at this point.

Many further examples of relatively plain but finely-dressed gateposts of normal size are found across the Estate and probably mostly date from the second half of the 18th and 19th centuries. The use of these decorated gateposts is prevalent around Edensor and the walls bordering Paddocks Plantation. By far the greatest concentration of roughly decorated gateposts is in Handley Bottom and in fields around Ballcross Farm. In contrast, very few decorated posts occur on farms edging the moorland, such as at Moor Farm at Beeley, Yeld Farm and Yeldwood Farm at Baslow Far End, and Fallinge Farm, Park Farm and Harewood Grange on the eastern gritstone upland above. Here roughly dressed posts predominate. While these occur commonly across much of the Estate they are most frequent in boundaries enclosing land that was moorland prior to the 19th century. Elsewhere, these posts also dominate the fields at Bubnell, Bubnell Cliff and Bramley Farms, all of which were part of the Rutland Estate prior to 1870.

Early gateposts are characterised by roughly hewn stones with one, two or three holes either going right through or part-way through the post. They are no longer common but are found across the enclosed farmland of the Estate, sometimes moved from their original locations.[61] These circular or square holes took poles instead of hinged gates, used to block the entrances. Writing at the beginning of the 19th century, Farey described poles as the long-established method of closing gateways in the region and one that was still commonly in use.[62] On some posts, originally paired with a stone with full holes, the holes do not go right through the stone but are deep enough for wooden poles to rest in. Simple loose-rail gates with 'holes and eyes' were not suitable for cattle as they could easily push against the rails. Thus, an alternative design with deeply curving grooves was often employed in the region, which made it harder for cattle to knock the rail out of place.

Creeps and smoots

Movement of stock around fields is allowed not only by gateways but also by sheep throughs, sometimes also known as creeps or hog holes. These were described in the early 19th century by Farey, as follows:

> 'In building walls between fields, holes are often left large enough for a sheep to pass through, and are closed afterwards by a flat stone, set up against them; which can then be removed whenever the sheep but not the cattle are intended to have the range of two fields.'[63]

In recent decades sheep throughs often have not been rebuilt after wall collapses; it is suspected they were once very common. However, there are some fine examples still remaining across the enclosed farmland in the Core Estate.

Across the Peak District smaller holes were constructed in walls, normally at ground level, to allow rabbits or water to pass through. Holes are necessary if the wall is constructed across a slope where water is liable to dam up behind and then subsequently de-stabilise it. Rabbit holes, called 'smoots', were used to catch these animals with a snare or trap.

Stiles

The majority of stiles are found on public footpaths. There are two traditional forms made of stone at Chatsworth, the 'step-over' or 'step', and the 'squeeze through' or 'squeezer'. The former comprises between two and four long stones placed through the wall. The latter comprise either two upright flagstones or stone posts set to allow a person to step through while preventing livestock

FIGURE 60. The Estate has gateposts in a variety of styles. These include posts with holes for bars rather than gates, as near Pilsley (centre), and carefully dressed posts as at Beeley Warren (left) and near Calton Lees (right).

doing the same. The modern practice is to replace or supplement these with foot-gates to allow disabled access.

Water troughs

A regular supply of fresh water is important for livestock welfare and the troughs and dew ponds found around the Estate are testament to this.[64] Water troughs carved in gritstone occur across the Estate, with over 150 recorded, but these are most frequent on the farmland around Pilsley and Edensor. Out in the fields they are usually located by sources of spring water or at convenient places where drained water can be collected. However, they are also commonly associated with field barns and farmsteads. Across the Peak District there were probably once significantly more troughs than there are today; many have unfortunately been taken and reused as garden ornaments, while others have been broken up or become silted and buried.

As landscape features, water troughs reflect an important part of the story of agrarian change, linked with the enclosing and managing of fields for stock. While sheep can often survive well with only relatively small amounts of standing or running water, cattle need a regular large supply. Keeping cattle in earlier centuries was facilitated by access to rivers and natural meres within the commons as part of a regular cycle of herding between grazing and

FIGURE 61. Water troughs in the park have stonework designed to guard against undue erosion and to protect the inlet pipe.

watering places. With the enclosure of wastes and commons in the 18th and early 19th centuries, the traditional practices must have become difficult if not impossible to maintain and the use of both troughs and dew ponds became more necessary.

John Farey wrote in 1813 that the:

> 'making of drinking places for cattle is much attended to by the Farmers of Derbyshire and hewn stone cisterns are placed in most cattle yards and in a large proportion of the fields, where the springs on the side of the Hills admit of supplying them, even the commons were early supplied with these, in many situations; the sides of the public roads were also well supplied with this essential convenience.'

Troughs are also fine examples of the now near-lost practice of carving gritstone into utilitarian artefacts. On the Estate they are commonly about 1.0m long by 0.5m wide and 0.5m deep, often with an overflow lip on one of the ends, hewn out of solid freestone blocks of gritstone. However several significantly larger and a few smaller examples also exist. They are commonly only roughly hammer-dressed or have rough diagonal hachures, although some have smooth outer sides.

In Chatsworth Park and at Calton Pasture, on land managed directly by the Estate, the troughs are often quite sophisticated. Covered stone gutters feed water into the troughs and vertically placed gritstone flags flanking these on the upslope side, to prevent cattle damaging the inflow pipes. There are also cobbles downslope to prevent undue erosion. Generally water troughs in the enclosed farmland were simpler, as is normal in the Peak District, consisting of one, or less commonly two or even three troughs, fed by a simple inflow pipe and often without any of the surrounding features. Sometimes they are placed through a wall, thus providing water for stock in either field.

Dew ponds

Across the Peak District where springs were not common, because of geology or topography, a standing water supply for livestock was provided with the creation of circular dew ponds lined with stone and puddled with clay and straw. These are probably mostly of 19th century date. While found elsewhere, they occur most commonly on the limestone ground. A good example of this in the Core Estate is provided at Cracknowl Pasture, where there are at least 13 examples, most still surviving but in some cases now dry.[65] High on the Calton Pasture gritstone ridge in an area with no obvious natural water supply, fields near Ballcross Farm have been provided with two dew ponds.[66] A few further examples of dew ponds exist across the Estate, in areas where it seems springs/troughs could have provided viable options.[67]

Gardens for all: village allotments

A rare survival of low earthworks at abandoned allotment gardens is to be found at Pilsley just beyond the east end of the village.[68] Most of the now grass-covered garden plots and access paths are clearly visible. This allotment was created sometime shortly before 1836 and abandoned in the 20th century. Other allotments of similar date also once existed at Edensor and Beeley, but there is little trace today.

Sheep, grouse and peat: the township moorlands

The extensive Estate moorlands are not natural wilderness but have long been maintained. There has been livestock grazing over many centuries and, over the last 200 years, the careful burning of heather to make the moors suitable for the rearing and then shooting of grouse. The peat found on the wetter areas was in one case dug for domestic fuel. Traditionally these areas have also had industrial uses, as places where stone was quarried and lead smelted and this will be returned to in Chapter 7.

The loss of common rights on what are now Estate moorlands was formalised by a series of Parliamentary Enclosure Awards, for Darley in 1769, Ashover in 1783, Baslow in 1826, Brampton in 1831 and Beeley in 1832.

Grazing

Although long important, using the moors for stock rearing has by its very nature left only minor recognisable features within the archaeological landscape. These include four 'sheep lees', where short isolated sections of drystone wall were built that provide shelter for sheep and helped with their gathering using dogs; usually they are associated with small folds.[69] There are also a small number of simple folds and shepherds' shelters.[70]

Grouse shooting

The killing of grouse became a popular sport in the first half of the 19th century and on the Peak's eastern moors both the Dukes of Devonshire and Rutland used their extensive estates for this. Above Padley, the 5th Duke of Rutland built Longshaw Lodge, probably in the early 1820s, and developed the Longshaw Estate.[71] His prime reason for this was his interest in grouse shooting. Further south, the Enclosure Awards of the 1820s and 30s may well have been instigated by both Ducal families to formalise their rights over the moors and to exclude others, in part in order to protect game birds.[72]

The majority of the moorlands on the Estate have lines of shooting butts.[73] These display varied construction, some square, others more circular, some drystone-walled, others built of turf. In other cases just timber was used and today there are now only ephemeral traces. The number of butts in a line also varies, with up to 12 having been recorded. On Gardom's Edge, an area owned and shot by the Dukes of Rutland until the sale of their Longshaw Estate in 1928, there are the footings of a small shooting cabin.[74] Such cabins littered the Peak's grouse moors and here shelter was provided, refreshments were served and game stored until the end of the day's shooting.

Peat cutting

One small peat cut has been located, sited on Harewood Moor.[75] Peat cuts are rare on the Peak's eastern gritstone moors, although common around Edale and the Upper Derwent, and on the Staffordshire moorlands.[76] The example at Harewood Moor was probably for domestic use, presumably for Harewood Grange Farm which lies immediately below, and possibly also for Harewood Grange itself. When peat first started to be cut here is unknown. However, it is likely to have ceased sometime in the late 18th or early 19th century at latest with the advent of better roads and the resulting access to cheap local coal.

Boundary stones

A fine series of boundary stones survives associated with the present boundary of Beeley Parish.[77] To the north-east there are three to four stones of relatively

FIGURE 62. The ancient boundary stone close to Umberley Well, at the heart of the Chatsworth moorlands, placed at the junction of three townships.

early date, on the lower dip slope of Harland Edge running to the head of Umberley Brook, following the boundary with Brampton to the point where that of Baslow is met.[78] The stone at the junction is noted in surviving accounts of the 1614, 1625 and 1721 perambulations of bounds of Baslow.[79] There are also two 19th century stones, each carved with 1856.[80] The stones have various combinations of initials indicating the townships involved, including the initials 'W' for Walton, which once had rights over what is now the Brampton moorlands.[81] The Beeley boundary continues north-westwards across the upper end of Gibbet Moor to a stone next to the boundary of Bunkers Hill Wood,[82] also dated 1856 and in this case clearly a replacement stone; there is documentation of a stone at about this spot since at least 1625.

The south-eastern boundary of Beeley, on Harewood Moor, is again marked by a series of stones within the area surveyed. All four have been incorporated into a later boundary wall and are of the same design as each other.[83] Each is marked with a 'B' for Beeley and an 'A' for Ashover. The stones, which are in a late style, were presumably erected when this boundary was formalised, presumably in the 18th century, either for the Ashover Enclosure Award of 1783 or earlier.

Training for war and the use of clubs

The Chatsworth moorlands were used for military training during the 1939–45 war.[84] This was also the case beyond the Estate boundary, on Gardom's Edge and Big Moor to the north.[85] There is a local tradition that American troops trained here, said to be the Airborne Division, but this seems unlikely as there is no record of it in the Division's archives.[86] It is also said the Home Guard trained on these moors, but some of the features found, such as heavy-gun emplacements on Gardom's Edge, indicate activity on a significantly larger scale than the Guard would have been involved in.

The main military focus on the Core Estate was the open moorland of Gibbet Moor, where there are earthworks at a military command post, temporary mortar/machine gun platforms, and a lookout post comprising a prominent earthen mound with central hollow.[87] The first feature, of some rarity, comprises an oval area measuring 43 × 15m, which is defined by concentric shallow trenches at either end, and three regularly-placed rectangular foxholes along both sides. There are three further foxholes beyond to the downslope side. In another training episode, Gibbet Moor was used for target practice, probably from the gun platforms on Gardom's Edge; large shells are still occasionally found buried in the peat and 'bomb disposal' are called.

In times of peace a different type of weapon has been used. The rocky slopes east of Yeld Farm at Baslow Far End contain the rare remains of a long-disused golf course.[88] This was part of the facilities provided by the Baslow Hydro, a large hotel/hydropathic establishment in the village, opened in 1881 and demolished in the mid 1930s.[89] There is no trace of its first golf course in what are now plantations on the other side of the main road. This course was complemented in 1900 by the New Golf Course, which is said to have stayed in use until 1939, although the Hydro closed nearly a decade before. The course had nine holes and the rectangular well-made platforms of six greens survive, together with five sets of tees with much smaller earthworks. The greens were on one occasion reported to National Park Authority archaeologists as unusually well preserved prehistoric house sites! Few would guess that this unlikely spot once was a place of organised recreation.

CHAPTER SEVEN

Wealth from the Earth: Two Thousand Years of Industry

The Peak: an industrial landscape

Many who live and visit the Peak District National Park appreciate it for its scenic beauty. Only a few realise that until recent times there were whole swathes of landscape which from a modern perspective would be classified as industrial wasteland. Now the 'scars' are largely unobtrusive and the industrial remains are some of the most fascinating archaeological relics, telling of past endeavours that enrich the Peak's landscape.[1]

Amongst the most important of the traditional industries, some dating back many hundreds of years, are mining for lead, copper and coal, smelting the metals, and quarrying of sandstone and limestone. Millstones, troughs and gateposts were made in the thousands. Limestone was burnt to produce lime in huge quantities. Woodlands were carefully managed for charcoal and kiln-dried wood, both for smelting and other industrial purposes. Water-powered mills ground corn and produced textiles and pigments.

The Cavendish family had a hand in most of these industries, exploiting the resources on their land from the 16th century onwards. Within the Core Estate there are important archaeological remains of quarries, coal mines and lead-smelting sites. Elsewhere in the Peak District and north-east Derbyshire important coal and metal mines, and limeburning complexes, contributed significantly to the wealth of the Estate. One place of particular importance was Ecton Hill between Wetton and Warslow, where mines provided the Estate with huge profits in the second half of the 18th century. The impacts all these industrial ventures had on the landscape and its people contrast strongly with the idealised landscape created around Chatsworth House.

The importance of heavy metal: the mining and smelting of lead

Lead mining has been an extremely important industry in the Peak District since the Roman period, if not before.[2] Mining was extensive in the medieval period and production was at its highest in the 17th and 18th centuries. Lead long vied with iron as Britain's major export behind wool and the Peak District was one of the major lead orefields. The Cavendish family owned important mines,

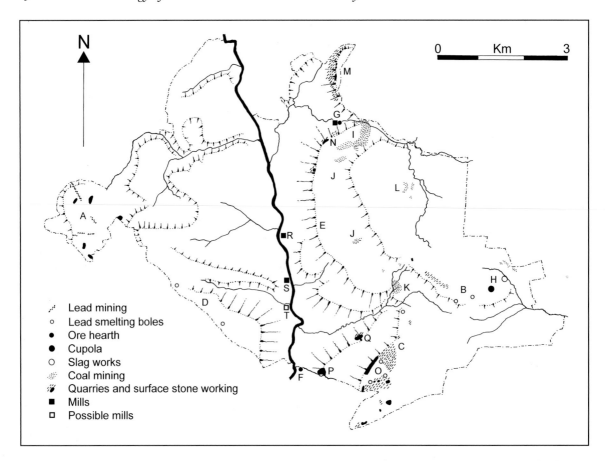

FIGURE 63. Industrial sites in the Chatsworth landscape (Places mentioned in Chapter 8 – A: Cracknowl Pasture lead mines, B: Harland Edge lead smelting boles; C: Beeley Moor lead smelting boles, D: Calton Pasture lead smelting boles, E: Chatsworth Park ore hearth, F: Smelting Mill Brook ore hearth, G: Heathy Lea Mill ore hearth, H: Harewood Cupola and slag mill, I: Baslow Colliery, J: Chatsworth Old Park Colliery, K: Beeley Moor Colliery, L: Gibbet Moor coal trials, M: Gardom's Edge quarries, N: Dobb Edge and Under Pasture Edge quarries, O: Fallinge Edge quarries, P: Burntwood Quarry, Q: Lime Tree Quarry, R: Chatsworth Old Mill, S: Chatsworth New Mill, T: Calton Lees Mill).

notably at the extremely rich copper and lead mines at Ecton.[3] They also held or in some cases rented the mineral rights over large parts of the orefield, which brought in significant income. However, features related directly to lead mining on the Core Estate, which is well beyond the focal mining areas, are only found on Cracknowl Pasture; this is the only part where the ore-bearing limestones occur at surface.

While many old lead workings have been reworked for other now-important minerals such as fluorspar, barytes and calcite over the last hundred years, the traditional laws do not apply. These minerals, known to the old miners as 'gangue', were originally mostly discarded as worthless. The old lead miners' waste hillocks are nowadays usually fully levelled after gangue extraction has been completed. Other workings and spoil mounds have often been ploughed-over and shafts filled-in for agricultural purposes. A recent review showed that only about a quarter of the surface features of this important aspect of our heritage now survive in reasonable condition.[4] These surface remains left by centuries of lead mining are far more than interesting archaeological relics. They have important geological interest and have internationally rare ecological communities, with for example heavy-metal-tolerant flowering plants such as leadwort and mountain pansy. The mining remains are also a visible reminder of the social and industrial history of the Peak District and make a valuable contribution to its historic landscape.

The archaeology and historical context of lead mining

We know very little about Roman lead mining, our main evidence being from inscribed lead ingots found in the region and beyond. From the medieval period onwards, and probably at earlier dates, much small-scale lead mining was carried out by miner/farmers, while larger mines were mined by full-time miners. Early mines are likely to have been either surface opencasts into vein outcrops or relatively shallow underground workings, dug using simple tools. In exceptional circumstances, as at the easily worked 'pipe' deposits on Masson Hill at Matlock Bath, extensive underground mines existed by 1470.[5]

By the end of the medieval period most rich deposits were starting to become exhausted above the water table,[6] and from the 17th century onwards, deeper and much larger mines were developed. This required investment capital and such mines were often controlled by the landed gentry, noble houses such as the Cavendish family and an emerging group of wealthy industrialists. Alongside the larger ventures, miner/farmers continued to supplement their income from agriculture by mining smaller veins at slack times in the agricultural year. Many miners had smallholdings that were essential when mining was proving unprofitable. Such mining continued to use the simplest of extraction techniques and underground workings were usually relatively shallow.

By the 17th century effective ways of preventing flooding of the workings were needed and drainage levels known as soughs started to be driven into workings at depth from nearby valleys.[7] In a few instances water-wheels, at surface and underground, were also employed for pumping. Another approach adopted at large mines in the 18th and 19th centuries, once the technology became available, was the installation of steam-powered pumping engines. Engines were also used for winding ore up engine shafts at the largest and deepest of mines.

One technological development, which was eventually adopted in mines of all sizes, was the use of gunpowder. This was first used in the 1660s and became common in the early 18th century.[8] Powder allowed the hard limestone in which minerals lay to be removed effectively, and enabled narrow but sometimes mineral-rich deposits to be effectively mined for the first time.[9] It also speeded up extraction generally.

FIGURE 64. A stone setting on Harland Edge, thought to mark the edge of a lead smelting bole.

Preliminary 'dressing' of ore was usually carried out at the mine before the resulting concentrate was removed to smelters, usually located elsewhere.[10] Initial dressing was often done underground as this meant less haulage to surface, and this was particularly useful when surface water was scarce but was more abundant at depth. At surface, dressing floors are common, usually sited by the shaft top; there are usually waste hillocks of broken and crushed material nearby. Much ore dressing was traditionally done by hand, breaking the mineral down with hammers, to facilitate the removal of the gangue minerals. This work was often done by women and children. It is a moot point as to which was worse, the hard and dangerous work underground, or the sheer tedium and discomfort of breaking rocks outdoors in all weathers.

The most common surface archaeological evidence for lead mining comprises opencast workings, shaft tops and waste hillocks often situated along extensive veins, called 'rakes', which run for long distances across the landscape. Smaller veins, known locally as scrins, also have similar but less massive remains. Elsewhere shafts drop to 'pipe' workings that often do not outcrop at ground level. A fascinating variety of other surface features exist, including horizontal mine entrances known as adits or levels, sough entrances, engine houses and a variety of other buildings at large mines, small multipurpose sheds known as 'coes' at smaller mines, dressing floors and ponds, circular platforms at the sites of gin engines, and circular beds of stone or iron where ore was crushed.

The Cracknowl Pasture mines

Within the Core Estate, on Cracknowl Pasture, there are typical examples of smaller-scale mining remains surviving in reasonable condition, with small waste hillocks and hollows following vein workings.[11] One vein running south-west/north-east may well have produced lead in moderate quantity from underground workings, but elsewhere on the Pasture the small workings are probably little more than surface trials. Nothing is documented of the names and dates of these mines other than a brief reference to the delivery of timber to mines at Cracknowl in 1754–55.[12] On the main vein, a field boundary present in the early 17th century appears to respect the mining remains, suggesting the first lead extraction was much earlier.

Lead smelting

The moorland parts of the Core Estate were extensively used for early smelting, although the visible remains of this are now slight. Similarly, a 17th century ore hearth smelter at Heathy Lea east of Baslow has gone, although the overgrown remains of part of its millpond dam remains. A later cupola smelter and nearby slag mills, north of Harewood, have been reduced to foundations with piles of slag nearby.

Much smelting of lead took place in the Derwent Valley, on the eastern moors and Coal Measure foothills of the Peak District. This divorce from the limestone plateau orefield took place for a number of reasons. Routeways to traditional markets for lead have always gone eastwards, it being shipped via river ports on the Trent, Idle and Don, down the Humber to Hull for distribution further afield.[13] Many smelters were sited on the way eastwards, close to the coal or wood sources used as fuel. Until the late 16th century the main method of smelting was in simple bole hearths, which required high locations such as the eastern moors or the gritstone scarps immediately west of the Derwent, in order to take advantage of the wind in creating suitable draught for reaching the required smelting temperature. From the 16th to 18th centuries a new smelting method was employed. These 'ore hearths' harnessed water power to drive bellows, and smelt sites migrated to valleys. From the 1730s onwards however, the cupola furnace was employed, using coal as fuel. Many cupolas were built on higher land, close to coal sources.

Bole hearths

Bole hearths were used for smelting lead throughout the medieval period and possibly before, but gradually went out of use through the 16th century.[14] By this time some boles were in regular use by professional smelters and had become proto-industrial sites. Even these boles were often little more than large bonfires in which the ore was heated, making their traces hard to identify during field survey. Sometimes the presence of a bole is indicated by the place name, discarded slags, scorched stones and earth, and slight platforms or hollows. At one particularly informative site, gullies and hollows at Totley Bole Hill west of Totley have been interpreted as being where the ore was drawn off and collected.[15] Different evidence has been found on the Core Estate upon Harland Edge and Beeley Moor where there are sometimes short low walls or lines of stone, some of the stones heat-altered, together with small quantities of ore, slags, and burnt soils nearby.[16] The exact purpose of these 'walls' is unknown. Many further sites no doubt remain to be identified in places where today's vegetation remains unbroken. One excavated bole on Beeley Moor had been inserted into the side of a Bronze Age barrow.[17] In two barrows on Calton Pasture, 19th century antiquarian excavations found pieces of galena and part-smelted lead within disturbed areas of the mounds.[18]

The identified boles on the eastern moors concentrate on prominent scarp crests. The sites identified are also close to hollow-ways that were no doubt used both for transporting ore from the west and taking smelted lead eastwards.

Slags from medieval boles often contain pieces of unsmelted or part-smelted galena, and gangue minerals, that could be re-smelted to produce further lead. These re-smelters were known as blackwork ovens and were fired using charcoal rather than the timber used in boles. Slags from blackwork ovens are much cleaner and one identified site set back from Harland Edge has produced such better-refined material, in very low hillocks, indicating that this may well be a secondary smelting site.[19]

Ore hearths

Today there is little to see of the ore hearths that once existed near Chatsworth. While most of these were operated with waterwheels, this was not always the case; some early examples had foot bellows. One such experimental smelter was built in 1571 somewhere within the deer park east of Chatsworth House.[20] This used timber from the park but operated only until 1573–74. A water powered ore-hearth, of late 16th to early 18th century date, stood south of Smelting Mill Brook between Beeley and Little Rowsley.[21] Another, dating to the early 17th century, was located at Heathy Lea Mill.[22] Here nothing remains of the hearth itself, the building having been rebuilt in the 19th century for other milling purposes. However, upstream and shrouded in woodland, what was probably part of its mill pond dam still survives.

Harewood Cupola

The only 18th to 19th century smelter on the Estate was the Harewood Cupola.[23] Extensive foundations and part-robbed waste hillocks remain, with the outlines of a range of buildings and a yard still clear. This cupola was built in 1752 and continued in use until at least 1814 and perhaps into the late 1830s; by 1847 it was certainly ruined.[24]

The slag mill, used for re-smelting the cupola slags, was sited a short distance away by Hipper Sick, where there are surviving foundations of a small building and a head-race.[25] While the cupola was sited to be adjacent to a major routeway, the slag mill was placed next to the stream in order to utilise this to power the bellows used to achieve the necessary temperature for re-smelting. Documentary research suggests that it may have built initially as a red lead mill,[26] at a slightly earlier date than the cupola.[27]

Digging the black stuff: the local coal mines

The extensive coal-mines just beyond the Peak District to the east and west were long vital to Britain's economy before their decline in the second half of the 20th century and the premature closure of many in the 1980s. What few people realise is that coal was also mined in the Peak District uplands on the eastern and western moorlands.[28] While these mines were relatively small in scale, it is ironic that far more archaeological remains survive here than in the flanking lowlands where social and political pressures led to the obliteration of most of the relics of this once-iconic industry.

The Core Estate includes the southern half of one of the largest and for many now-forgotten coalmines on the eastern moors, that at Baslow Colliery. These archaeologically important remains include many mounds of waste rock from shaft sinking, together with the sites of buildings and drainage soughs. Similar but less extensive mines existed within Chatsworth's old deer park and on Beeley and Gibbet Moors.

Coal mining on the eastern moors of the Peak District has exploited several relatively thin seams from medieval times onwards.[29] There are a number of mines with good survival of surface features from Ringinglow and Stanage Edge in the north to Beeley in the south.[30] While never as productive as the seams further east in the Coal Measure foothills around Sheffield and Chesterfield, the eastern moors mines were however conveniently sited for local markets to the west, the coal used industrially for firesetting in lead mines, lead smelting and lime burning, and also for domestic purposes.

Two outcropping coal seams within the Core Estate on the gritstone uplands east of Chatsworth were certainly worked, though even here the mineral was thin and in parts not economically viable. Although there were soughs draining workings at Baslow Colliery to some depth, the coal was not rich enough to justify deep workings with large shafts as was common in the richer mines to the east from the 18th century onwards, where large steam engines operated pumps and winding ropes. The Baslow Seam, a good quality but thin bed of house coal, was mined at the Baslow Colliery at Robin Hood, further south at Chatsworth Old Park Colliery and on the moorland beyond at Beeley Moor Colliery. The

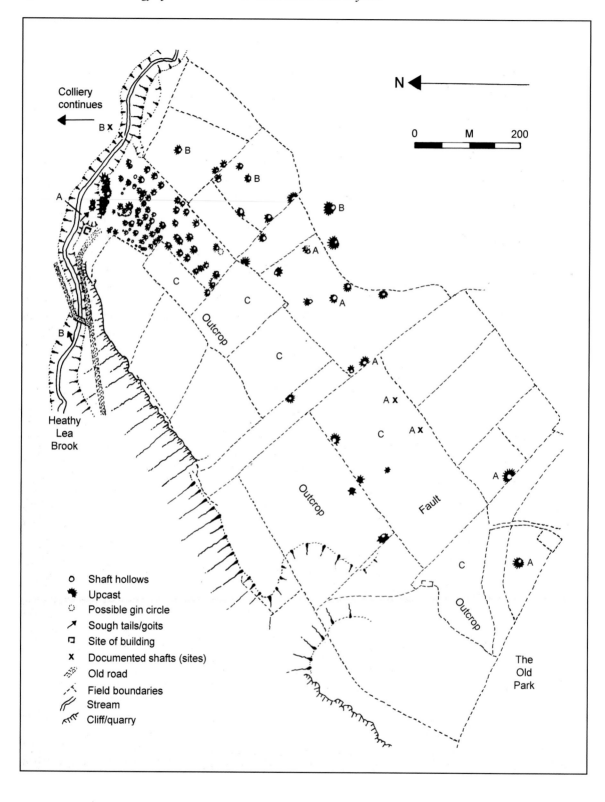

FIGURE 65. The southern part of the Baslow Colliery (A: Entrance and shafts at Boler's sough, B: Adit entrance and shafts at Deep Level, C: Improved land where further mining features may well have been destroyed).

Belperlawn or Soft Bed coal was worked at a small mine, comprising what may be little more than trial shafts, on Gibbet Moor.

Baslow Colliery

This disused coal mine has the most extensive set of surviving surface remains on the eastern gritstone moors of the Peak. It was centred on the hamlet of Robin Hood and ran north and south on land once owned by the Duke of Rutland. Only the southern half lies within the Core Estate, while the northern half is mostly on Moorside Farm.[31] On the Estate there are remains of about 80 opencast pits and closely-spaced shallow-shaft hollows with waste hillocks close to the coal outcrop south of Heathy Lea Brook. A further 25 to 29 more widely-spaced larger hillocks for deeper shafts lie further south and south-west, sunk to extract the coal as it dipped south-eastwards under the rising slope of the shelf.[32] Some shafts are in particularly close proximity to each other, suggesting more than one phase of working in the same ground. On a large flat-topped platform above the stream there once stood what was presumably the mine office and/or a workshop, and this was probably the surface focal point of the mine in its later years. From here there was easy access just down the valley to

FIGURE 66. A deep hollow at a collapsed coal mine shaft, at the Baslow Colliery south of Robin Hood.

the mid 18th century turnpike road. At between one and three places in the brook, ochre deposits indicate where now-flooded and collapsed drainage levels and seam workings came to surface.

This mine may well have been worked from medieval or early-post-medieval times but nothing is recorded of its early history. The first known documentation is for 1764–65, when the mine was worked by Edward Boler.[33] By then it clearly was already a long and extensively worked mine. A drainage sough running deep underground to follow the seam had reached the northern boundary of Chatsworth's old deer park and an agreement was made to extend it south-westwards and create Chatsworth Old Park Colliery.

Baslow Colliery was worked until at least the early 1830s, but may have been closed soon afterwards. A mine plan dated 1832 shows the extent of workings at that date.[34] The far part of the 1764–6 sough is drawn, as is another later sough at greater depth named 'Deep Level'. The tail of this lower sough was adjacent to the Heathy Lea Brook and what is almost certainly its walled outlet leading to the stream is still visible. One reason for the commissioning the 1832 plan may have been to assess the mine's viability. The 6th Duke had acquired the land here in the 1820s and it may be that after a period of assessment, and removal of easily worked reserves, it was decided to close the colliery. The mine was reinvestigated in about 1912 but found to be an unprofitable proposition.[35] However, there is a local tradition that the colliery was reopened briefly during the 1914–18 war to provide coal for the Great Conservatory in the gardens of Chatsworth House.

Chatsworth Old Park Colliery

Today there is little to see at surface of this once-important area for coal mining within the old deer park and the farmland created after its demise. All that survives is one or possibly two shaft hillocks in the southern part of the old park.[36]

The earliest recorded coal mining 'at Chatsworth' dates to the early 17th century. Mining at this time must have been relatively intensive, as Estate accounts record that over £110 was invested in the mining in 1623–25 and coal was sold for over £82.[37] Whether this represents a loss is unclear, as some of the coal may well have been used on the Estate rather than being sold. Smaller coal outputs are recorded between 1656 and 1659.[38] Eventually this mining presumably ceased after the seam was followed to a depth where workings flooded.

The coal seam was again trialed in 1759–60 when about ten shafts were sunk, including one that was abandoned because it was too wet.[39] However, no further work appears to have been done for a further five years.

From 1764–65 the Baslow Colliery drainage sough was extended from the Duke of Rutland's land under the Duke of Devonshire's old deer park following the seam in the unworked coal at a deeper level in the dipping seam than the older workings. Here it was mined as Chatsworth Old Park Colliery, given a separate name to reflect the different land ownership.[40] However, it was still worked by the Baslow miners under Edward Boler and was in effect part of the same operation. This sough dewatered all remaining coal that lay upslope of the level, making it available for extraction. At the insistence of the Estate, the shafts were filled and hillocks removed as they became redundant.[41]

In the mid 1760s the new landscape park in the valley below was reaching completion and the Estate was presumably particularly interested in finding new uses for the old park. However, it seems likely that the mining here was a relatively short-lived venture. It was confined to the northern part of the old park, extending only 350m south-westwards from the park boundary, and the mine was noted as already disused in 1811.[42] It may be that it was found that much of the coal further south had already been extracted, or that the seam thinned and was uneconomic.

Beeley Moor Colliery

This colliery on moorland at the east end of Beeley Warren has the remains of 10 opencast pits or hollows at very shallow shafts, with the hillocks of a further 21 to 23 somewhat deeper shafts to the north and east, sunk to extract the coal as it dipped under the rising slope.[43] Further upslope from the outcrop there were two still deeper shafts, each with the recognisable site of a horse-powered gin engine on the flat tops of their spoil heaps.

Documentary evidence identifies at least five potential phases of activity at this mine.[44] The right to mine coal on Beeley Moor was sold in 1559–60 for £1 2s 3d a year.[45] As the features noted above are the only identified coal-mining remains in Beeley parish it seems likely that extraction was taking place here at this time. This is one of the earliest references for coal mining in the region, making the remains at Beeley Colliery of particular interest and importance.

In 1725 an article of agreement was drawn up between the 2nd Duke of Devonshire and George Savile of South House Grange, Derbyshire, as the result of recent disputes over coal mines opened within the lordship of Beeley. This gave each a half share of royalties and excluded any mining under the deer park. This suggests mining was again taking place, presumably at Beeley Colliery, at around this date. However, it probably ceased soon afterwards, for surviving Estate accounts, which exist intermittently from 1729 through to the 1770s do not record any income or rent from coal mining in Beeley.

The colliery was again recorded in 1811 as having recently been worked for coal and still producing 'crow stone'.[46] This is a hard stone, more commonly known as ganister and usually found immediately under coal seams, which was used as road metalling and in crushed form for crucible making.[47] It seems probable that a phase of substantive coal extraction at the colliery took place in the late 18th century, and that this tailed off in the early 19th century. After abandonment, which probably took place in about 1814, later trials were

FIGURE 67. One of the discard
domed millstones, with a piece
broken from it, at Gardom's E
Behind to the right there is a
discarded rough-out.

undertaken in about 1835, possibly also in 1864–65, and again in the 1870s or
early 1880s. None of these succeeded in finding workable reserves that would
have proved financially viable.[48]

Gibbet Moor

At surface there are between 10 and 16 shaft hillocks here, mainly in two north/south lines running at right angles to the bedding.[49] The close proximity of some shafts to each other suggests the area has been explored at least twice. Farey does not record a colliery in this vicinity in his extensive list of early 19th century mines and the remains are perhaps likely to have been short-lived trials.[50]

Using coarse stone: gritstone quarrying

The Peak District has long been an important source of coarse gritstones and finer sandstones, used for building and the manufacture of objects such as millstones, gateposts and troughs.[51] The Core Estate has a number of important quarries, including those producing millstones from the medieval period to the early 19th century. They include vertical quarry faces cut into the natural cliffs and many smaller delves amongst the boulders below. These evocative sites, all for removing Chatsworth Grit, tell much of the process of quarrying and include broken and abandoned domed millstones, some of which were left where they were being dressed as if the quarrymen were coming back the next day but never did. The Gardom's Edge quarries are particularly important as the extensive remains span several centuries of work. They have still-visible access and stone-rolling tracks with nearby ruined work sheds and were one of the main sources of millstones from the Peak District.

There are also several large quarries of 18th to 20th century date, further south on the Estate, centred on Fallinge Edge and a second scarp below. These all provided good quality building stone but again also contain broken products, including stone troughs and cylindrical millstones/pulpstones, as well as having access trackways, ruined buildings and tramway beds.

Millstone making

The making of millstones was one of the main traditional industries of the Peak District and the quarries around Baslow, particularly at Gardom's Edge, were one of two main production centres.[52] Stones of identical form, with one flat face and the other domed, were made from at least the 14th century into the early 19th century. The quarries at the other centre, at and around Millstone Edge above Hathersage, have subsequently been extensively reworked, making those at Gardom's Edge of particular archaeological importance.

Although some millstones were undoubtedly taken downslope from the eastern moors quarries into the Derwent Valley for local use, the majority were taken to the scarp tops and transported eastwards across the moors, to inland ports at Bawtry and Stainforth to be distributed to other regions of Britain.

Domed millstone production reached its peak in the 16th and 17th centuries. One wonders how often the presence of grit in bread led to teeth being broken. As the eating of white bread became more common, the use of Peak stones declined as the grit from these turned the product an unappetising grey colour. From the 19th century into the early 20th century, Peak stones continued to be made for processing animal food and more importantly as pulpstones used to crush wood pulp for the manufacture of paper; many were exported to Scandinavia. These stones were not domed but instead often cylindrical with two flat faces.

Millstone makers at Baslow are recorded from the 14th century onwards and documentation suggests production here had tailed off by the end of the 16th century.[53] However, the archaeological field evidence suggests significant later working also took place. It is likely, from their character, that some of the larger Gardom's Edge quarries are of 17th or 18th century date and working was certainly taking place at around this time a little further south.[54] Estate accounts show that a quarry in Chatsworth Park was leased by John Rotherham between 1695 and 1745 for millstone production.[55] However, the millstone quarries visible today on Dobb Edge and Under Pasture Edge above the northern end of the Chatsworth Park cannot be those referred too, as the Estate did not acquire this area from the Duke of Rutland until the early 19th century. It is possible that Rotherham's stone quarry was fully backfilled with waste material from sinking coal mine shafts in the second half of the 18th century. A draft agreement to set up Chatsworth Old Park Colliery, dated 1765, specifies that this was to happen at a quarry in the northern part of Stand Wood.[56]

Gardom's Edge

The quarries on Gardom's Edge are particularly extensive and of great archaeological importance as the largest intact area of domed-millstone production site in the region.[57] Here there is both a series of face-quarries spaced along the Chatsworth Grit outcrop of Gardom's Edge, each cut into the cliffs at the scarp, and also evidence for working the extensive boulder-strewn area below.[58] The latter include extensive areas with stone breakage, ranging from individual small boulders that have been split, to large pits with associated spoil heaps, where massive boulders have been broken and removed. Running from both the face-quarries and the delves below are complex arrangements of access cart-tracks.[59] There are also three or four narrow millstone-rolling tracks, which descend down the steep slope from quarries to cart-tracks.[60]

The main quarry trackways are carefully arranged to facilitate co-ordinated extraction from the quarry delves and some, or possibly originally all, of the face-quarries above. They indicate that stones were taken both to the top of Gardom's Edge for transport eastwards and downhill into the Derwent Valley. The movement of dressed stones off the rocky slopes must have presented a major problem, and a well-organised exploitation of the Edge is suggested by the trackway layout. It is not known if these trackways were built as a co-operative project by the millstone masons, who worked individually and were paid for each pair of stones produced, or whether the owner of the land or other financial backers organised their construction. Planned production at this scale may well be a post-medieval characteristic and suggests undocumented quarrying after the 16th century. A number of small quarrymens' sheds are sited adjacent to the trackways and these may well also be post-medieval in date, as building in stone was normally the reserve of the elite and Church before the 17th century in the Peak District. One of these sheds has been excavated and shown to have probably been a smithy.[61] The dating evidence presents something of a conundrum, for the bulk of the workings are associated with the trackways and sheds, while the documentary evidence indicates extensive medieval work which remains difficult to recognise in the field.

The multiple working areas across the Gardom's Edge quarries as a whole undoubtedly reflect the activities of a number of master masons. However, it is unclear how many faces and delves were in operation at any one time. Amongst the quarries and boulder-strewn areas there are a large number of unfinished and broken millstones, together with some finished examples that were never removed. The domed stones are usually of between 1.3 and 1.8m diameter, with one flat face and one domed; finished examples usually have a central hole. Several stones are inscribed with mason's marks. Millstones were abandoned at all stages of production, from rough-outs where only the approximated shape has been defined, to others where virtually all the fine dressing had been done when the stone cracked or a flaw became apparent. Some stones are still placed on their chock stones indicating these have been left at the place where dressing was taking place. Rejects were often rolled away, presumably because they were in the way. In the case of chocked examples on the dressing floors of the main face-quarries, these stones were probably being made at the time the quarries closed.

In the face-quarries the only discarded products observed were domed millstones. However, in the delves below there are also other products. In the upper delves these are rare, but include three small flat-sided stones, either quernstones or small grindstones.[62] Similar stones have been produced in Britain from Roman times onwards. In the lower delves, other products include two broken stone troughs, two gateposts, and two cylindrical millstones/pulpstones.[63]

Dobb Edge and Under Pasture Edge

South of Gardom's Edge, on the other side of Heathy Lea Brook, there is a second smaller area where millstone manufacture took place. The focal point was at Dobb Edge, later subsumed within Chatsworth Park in the 1820s, but old workings continue north-eastwards into now-enclosed farmland at Under Pasture Edge.[64] The quarries appear to have been disused by the end of the 18th century. There are seven conjoined face-quarries at Dobb Edge as well as smaller delves, while at Under Pasture Edge there are only shallow delves and split boulders; perhaps these are early in date. In both areas there are a number

of domed millstones abandoned at various stages of production, including one unfinished stone chocked for dressing under each Edge. Finished stones from these quarries would have been easily transported eastwards or westwards via the major hollow-way nearby that runs between the two.[65]

Fallinge Edge and environs

In the southern part of the Estate, focused on Fallinge Edge, the extensive quarries into Chatsworth Grit are probably of 18th and 19th century date. There is a series of large vertical-faced quarries along the scarp and on the moor behind, together with smaller peripheral workings.[66] On lower land at the shelf scarp below Fallinge, there are two large quarries cut into Ashover Grit at Burntwood and Lime Tree.[67]

The quarries are often served by access cart-tracks and some have quarrymen's sheds and loading platforms. In one case there is a tramway network within the quarry and at another an unfinished tramway running across the moor. Judging from discarded items, the main products in some face-quarries and delves may have been cylindrical millstones and pulpstones, although other items such as troughs and gateposts were also made. Some large quarries however, have no discarded products. These, and perhaps some of the others, may well have concentrated on high-quality building stone.[68]

It is probable that some of the quarries on Fallinge Edge, or possibly those set back from it, are those recorded by Farey in 1811 as 'flagstone' quarries on 'Beeley Moor'.[69] He also records a 'grindstone' quarry at 'Beeley'; this may well be Burntwood Quarry. Quarrying at the southern part of the Estate became a long established tradition and continued into the 20th century.[70] For example, Wragg's Quarry behind Fallinge Edge was in use in the mid to late 19th century and the nearby Bond's Quarry was active in the late 19th and early 20th century. Burntwood Quarry, after a period of probable closure in the 1830s, was re-opened in the mid 19th century and developed into a particularly large quarry. It continued in use into the first half of the 20th century.

The power of water: mills

There are many mills and their sites, mostly now converted to other uses or demolished, beside the rivers and larger streams of the Peak District. Corn has been ground in these since at least medieval times and in more recent centuries textiles have been produced at often-large industrial sites of late 18th and 19th century date. Other mills have been used for such things as fulling, pigment grinding and lead smelting. The region is well known for its place in the early development of large textile mills by Richard Arkwright and others, at places

FIGURE 69. The main access track, running up a large spoil heap, into the Dobb Edge millstone quarries.

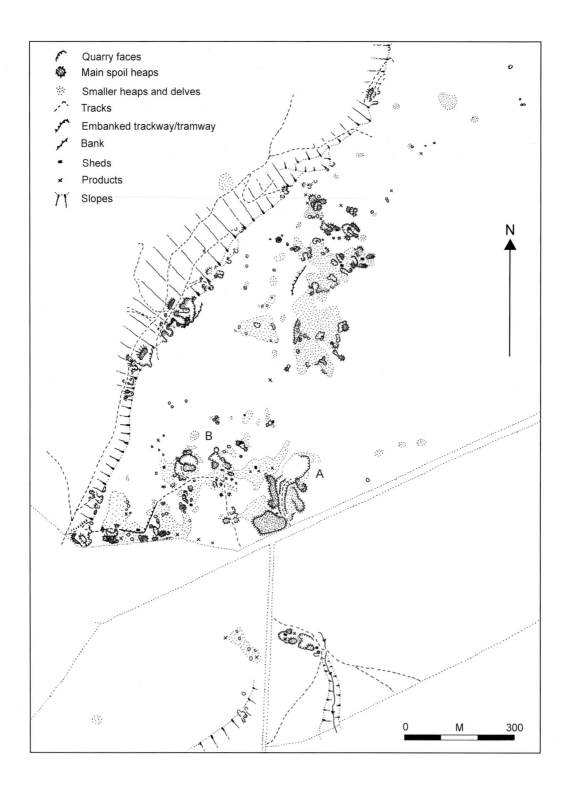

N

like Cromford, Matlock Bath, Cressbrook and Litton.[71] The two standing mill buildings in the Core Estate are less ambitious structures.

There has been a water mill at Chatsworth since at least the 14th century. A building stood on the east bank of the Derwent a short distance downstream from the House in the 17th and 18th centuries but was demolished with the creation of the landscape park. It was replaced in 1759–60 by the mill at the southern end of the park, designed by James Paine in a classical style. This was conceived as an eye-catching statement of the sophistication and wealth of the Dukes of Devonshire, visible at close quarters by those entering the park from the south and seen in the distance from the House and gardens as a key feature in the landscaped backdrop.[72] This functional as well as decorative building is now a picturesque ruin, abandoned when the roof was destroyed by a falling tree during a storm in 1962.[73] A short distance further south there may have been a mill east of Calton Lees. Senior shows a building by the confluence of the stream and river; this had gone by 1785 but the small wood here was known as Mill Wood.[74]

The only other standing but disused mill on the Core Estate, at a private secluded site amongst woodland, is Heathy Lea or Marple's Mill.[75] This substantial but plain and somewhat stern functional building with attached dwelling dates from 1867, and nearby are outbuildings, millpond and race. The mill at first processed flour but later was used as a sawmill. It replaced a 17th century lead smelting mill and what may have been a subsequent building shown on estate maps drawn in the first half of the 19th century, which presumably milled flour.

FIGURE 70. The stone quarries at and near Fallinge Edge (A: Wragg's Quarry, B: Bond's Quarry).

CHAPTER EIGHT

Lines Between Places: From Packhorse Routes to Tarmac Roads

....

Stuck in the mire: packhorses, moorland hollow-ways and sunken lanes

Until the 18th century the main road network in the Peak District, as with the rest of the country, bore little resemblance to what exists today.[1] Not only were there no cars, but only carriages, carts, livestock and people on horse or foot, but also few roads had good surfaces suitable for quick travel and many took different routes to those that came later. Until the advent of purpose-made turnpike roads, paid for by tolls, travel was slow and difficult as roads were often rutted quagmires, particularly in winter.

Despite the problems encountered before the 18th century, people have always travelled, many from settlements to fields and pastures, others between home and places further away. In medieval times and before, the problems were probably not as severe as later, as heavy and damaging usage was not as great. However, in post-medieval times, with ever increasing amounts of raw materials being extracted from the ground for distant sale, and the movement of more manufactured goods to consumers, this stretched the capacity of traditional routeways to breaking point. The mature development of industrialisation from the later 18th century onwards was only possible with radical road improvements. Main arteries were made into turnpike roads, sometimes taking new routes, while in places like Chatsworth estates improved the local infrastructure and built drives to country houses. Today, County Councils maintain the roads, while evidence for 'lost' traditional routeways can sometimes be traced as earthworks.

In the Peak District the archaeology of pre-19th century communication routes largely takes the form of hollow-ways, and such features are particularly common on the gritstone moorlands of the region.[2] Within the Core Estate, on Gibbet Moor, Harland Edge, Beeley Warren, Beeley Moor and Bumper Pieces they often form impressive but redundant features. Ancient routeways are also traceable in enclosed farmland, either as earthwork features, or still in use as surfaced roads and green lanes. Sometimes they are deeply cut into the surrounding land with high sides, created where the fields to either side restricted the route and funnelled all traffic down one line. Where routeways were not bounded by fields, as on today's moorland, they often comprised a series of

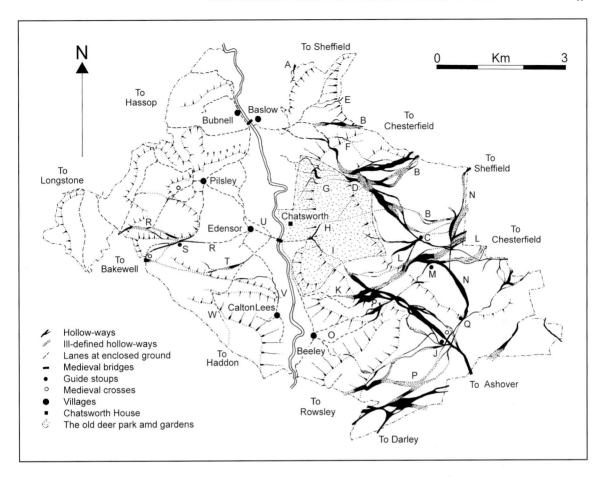

FIGURE 71. Pre-18th century hollow-ways and lanes crossing the Chatsworth landscape (A–W: see text).

braided hollows where alternative routes were taken to avoid boggy ground in earlier hollows. Early roads across moorland are often only intermittently traceable, normally most obvious on steeper slopes, because here there was much erosion by water once the vegetated surface was broken by traffic. In places the routeways comprise many semi-parallel braids, with depths varying from the barely perceptible to several metres.

In some cases exceptionally deep 'cart-ways' exist, as at an example close to Harland Sick.[3] At the Gardom's Edge scarp, where hollow-way erosion was severe, many stones have been moved from underfoot into adjacent piles.[4] Clearing of material from major 'trenchways' by local parishioners, as part of agreed parish duties to maintain highways, had taken place since 1555 and continued until such routeways were superseded by turnpike roads.[5]

Taken together, the traditional routes form a complex network of interconnected ways running between settlements and their fields and commons: from village to village in the Derwent Valley and to market centres such as at Bakewell beyond: and from industrial production centres and consumers in the Coal Measure foothills to the east, centred on Sheffield and

Chesterfield. Some are parts of long-distance routes, such as saltways, which cross the Peak District from lowlands to east and west. Many routes may well have medieval or earlier origins, although this is often difficult to document with any certainty. Much of the commercial traffic transported goods by strings of packhorses although wagons could be used on some routes, if with difficulty. Exports included lead, millstones and other quarried objects, and agricultural produce such as cheese. Imports included manufactured items from potteries, ironworks and other workshops.

Hollow-ways on Chatsworth Estate's eastern moors

Survival of disused routeways is good east of the Derwent, particularly on slopes up to and across the eastern moors, where erosion has given them greater definition.[6] The major examples follow two main trends, north-east/south-west and south-east/north-west, leading to important population foci in these directions. The other main controlling factor locally was the positions of long-established bridges over the Derwent, which existed at Baslow, Chatsworth, Rowsley and Darley.

Several through-routes ran eastwards from the medieval Baslow Bridge, coming from Hassop, Bakewell and places beyond. One major example ran up Baslow Bar, where a small part lies within the Core Estate (Figure 71: A), bifurcating more than once on the moorland above to Sheffield, Dronfield and Chesterfield.[7] Another was a major braided hollow-way running south-east towards Chesterfield (B).[8] Various alternative branch routes could be taken from this and some linked with other 'roads'. For the stranger the choice of ways must have been confusing and there is a stoop, the local term for a guidestone, high on Gibbet Moor near Umberley Well (C).[9] Some braids are early, as they are truncated by the boundary of Chatsworth deer park (D).[10] This major routeway, as well as being used for much general traffic, may also have been a saltway, transporting rock salt from the Cheshire Plain, via Leek and Bakewell, to Chesterfield and beyond.[11] Other routes from Baslow Bridge leading to Chesterfield were more minor, although one is exceptionally deep and cut down to solid bedrock, as it ascends to the crest of Gardom's Edge (E).[12] Another may have led from coal pits south of Robin Hood (F).[13]

A number of routes ran eastwards from Chatsworth Bridge, coming from Edensor, Hassop and Bakewell. Several of these probably went out of use when Chatsworth old deer park was created and they are not shown on Senior's map of 1617. Others continued to be used until the bridge was demolished in the mid 18th century. One important route snakes up the Stand Wood scarp slope within the northern end of the deer park to join the main road from Baslow to Chesterfield (G).[14] By 1617 a more southerly branch had been adopted (H). This has a hollow-way running diagonally up the scarp slope but is otherwise now untraceable in the old park, indicating it took relatively little traffic, perhaps all on Estate business.[15] Another major braided route, shown by Senior in the deer park but which has earlier origins, heads south-west towards Ashover (I).[16] It passed a medieval cross, medieval lead smelting boles, the Beeley coalmines and an early 18th century guide stoop (J).[17] This route had continuing importance from the 16th to 18th centuries as it provided the way to the Cavendish family's other main seat in the region at Hardwick Hall. In 1710–11 the braided way was improved as a coach road, but lost some of its importance in 1739 when an early turnpike was created, which came out of the valley following a different route. Both were finally closed in 1759 as part of the preparations for creating the landscape park. Another major pre-turnpike route from Chatsworth Bridge followed the Derwent Valley southwards for a distance before rising to Beeley Hilltop and the moors beyond (K), passing a medieval cross on Beeley Warren.[18] A short distance further on, travellers could either turn south-eastwards along the route noted above to Ashover, or go ahead to Chesterfield (L).[19] Behind Harland Edge at the junction with a route from Beeley, there is an early 18th

FIGURE 72. This deep hollow-way at the northern end of Chatsworth Park was once one of the main routes from Baslow to Chesterfield.

century guide stoop (M), which gives one of the destinations as Sheffield, indicating travellers could also pass north-eastwards along a hollow-way from Darley Bridge which ran close by (N).[20]

Relatively minor routes ran onto the moors from Beeley and stand in contrast to the others (O). They may well have been primarily for local traffic as there was no bridge over the Derwent here. One started as a deeply sunken lane through fields, but became a braided hollow-way once unenclosed ground was reached.[21] This joined other routes to Chesterfield and Sheffield. Another sunken lane left Beeley more to the south-east, giving access only to fields and the common beyond.[22] A further now-modified route going through the heart of Beeley village ran along the bottom lands of the Derwent Valley. This lane again gave access to the village fields and presumably also once ran on to Chatsworth and Edensor in the north and Little Rowsley in the south.[23]

On the southern parts of the Estate moorlands there are further widely braided routes (P) that came from Bakewell, Youlgreave and Winster, using Rowsley Bridge or in one case Darley Bridge, heading towards Sheffield and Chesterfield.[24] They passed medieval lead smelting sites on Fallinge Edge and Harland Edge.[25] At the junction with the road from Chatsworth to Ashover there is a guide stoop where the traveller could turn (J), while a second stoop a short distance further on indicates the branch to Sheffield (Q).[26] One braid here, which runs close to the medieval cross of Harland Sick, is unusual in that it is causewayed where it crosses marshy ground.[27]

Ancient routes west of Chatsworth

The evidence for ancient routeways is more fragmentary west of the Derwent.[28] Perhaps the most important has braided hollow-ways at slopes, on a route from Bakewell to Edensor (R).[29] Despite these steep slopes, it was marked on a map of 1778 as a coach road.[30] At a branch point to Pilsley and Baslow, there is a fine surviving guide stoop between Edensor and Ballcross (S).[31] From here the route continues in a sunken lane heading into Edensor.[32]

Further stretches of hollow-way exist at Ballcross and these are probably on an alternative course of the route from Bakewell (T).[33] One part of this branch ran further south, bypassing Edensor and going straight to Chatsworth Bridge.[34] Its course within the park cuts through medieval ridge and furrow and was probably in use during later medieval/early post-medieval times when this area had become an open sheepwalk. The area was enclosed again in the late 17th or early 18th century, by which time the route was out of use, except near the river where it was adopted as an access lane between fields. Another route similarly skirted Edensor village to the north side, which can still be traced in part as a hollow-way in the park (U).[35] This is the 'public road' to 'Pilsley and Baslow' recorded as closed in 1759 when the park was created.[36]

Other vestiges include a sinuous hollow-way on the 'dead-end' route between Edensor and Calton (V), which in 1617 ran at the edge of the open sheepwalk.[37]

A second route went to Haddon (W). This is shown on an estate map of 1773 running out of the park onto Calton Pasture, where there is a now-disused lane that passes through the postulated medieval settlement of Calton.[38] No doubt important messages were carried this way between the two ducal families of the region.

Laying firm foundations: turnpike roads and estate drives

In the Peak District the first turnpike routes were created in the early 18th century but only became common in the 1750s.[39] These good roads were set up by private trusts, made possible by Acts of Parliament. They were paid for by levying tolls and were a long-term investment by the trustees, for the cost of construction was only recouped years later. In order to make them work, an infrastructure of bridges, toll bars and toll houses was built. Milestones were also added, different trusts having stones of their own design. From the 19th century cast-iron mileposts were used. Where the roads crossed open ground, at first many were not walled out, but eventually boundaries were added. This was partly to prevent people entering and leaving at will and thus avoiding tolls, but also to facilitate management of moorlands which were privatised from common land in the 18th and early 19th centuries. Many of these turnpikes are used today as public roads. Most of their bridges still take traffic, although some have had to be strengthened or widened. Some milestones and posts stand by roads, largely ignored by motorists who drive too fast to read them. The toll bars have gone, but some toll houses have been converted to ordinary dwellings.

The 18th century turnpikes often followed earlier traditional routes. Where these crossed enclosed farmland, the new roads mainly kept to somewhat sinuous pre-existing lanes; it is only where they crossed moorland that new straight routes were created. On the moorlands, earlier, widely-braided hollow-ways can be seen following roughly the same line, but with one particular track adopted, straightened and surfaced as the new road. However, in places the turnpikes themselves have been later re-routed, leaving grassy terraces along their old lines.

The first main wave of turnpike building took place in the second half of the 18th century, but afterwards it was realised that some parts of the routes were not ideal in that they contained steep gradients that were difficult for heavily laden wagons to negotiate in winter when covered by snow or ice. The first turnpikes had, where crossing moorland, been built in long straight stretches to save on cost. This eventually led, often in the early 19th century after initial costs of road building had been recouped, to re-routing short stretches along new and more sinuous lines to reduce gradients. In some instances more radical changes took place, as for example the moving of the road from Baslow to Chesterfield in the 1820s with the enlargement northwards of Chatsworth Park, or the building of entirely new routes across the moorlands to create better links to the burgeoning industrial centres to the east.

Turnpike roads on the Estate

The earliest turnpike route to cross the Core Estate, built well before a regional network of such roads was built up, was the Bakewell to Chesterfield road authorised in 1739 that went via Edensor.[40] However, this turnpike was closed for public use in 1759 with the creation of Chatsworth Park and two local alternative east/west routes were developed. One, authorised in 1759, ran through Hassop to Baslow and then eastwards on to Chesterfield.[41] The other, of 1760, passed through the southern edge of the Core Estate, coming westwards from Chesterfield then branching on the moortop to bridges over the Derwent both at Rowsley and Darley.[42] Both were in effect branches of the Chesterfield to Matlock Bridge turnpike network created in the same year. Traditional hollow-way routes across moorlands were adopted in both cases. Another short stretch of turnpike crossed the western end of the Core Estate going from Hassop to Bakewell.[43] More generally however, in the enclosed areas of the Estate, many of the long-established access lanes continued in use.

By the early 19th century the turnpike roads built about 40 years before were still in use but by now the other moorland hollow-way routes were probably largely redundant. At this time new turnpike roads were built across the moors

FIGURE 73. 18th and 19th century turnpike and other roads, drives and lanes crossing the Chatsworth landscape (A–U: see text).

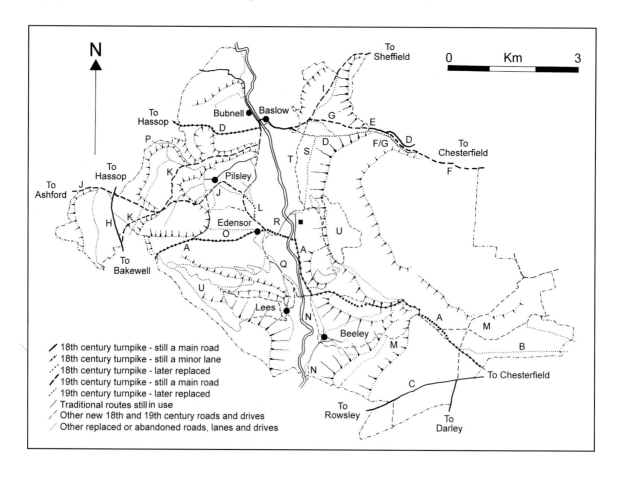

- 18th century turnpike - still a main road
- 18th century turnpike - still a minor lane
- 18th century turnpike - later replaced
- 19th century turnpike - still a main road
- 19th century turnpike - later replaced
- Traditional routes still in use
- Other new 18th and 19th century roads and drives
- Other replaced or abandoned roads, lanes and drives

to Sheffield and Chesterfield.[44] West of the River Derwent, the villages of Baslow, Pilsley and Edensor were linked by new roads to Bakewell, Ashford and places further west.[45] These turnpikes took new routes across farmland rather than following the earlier roads they replaced. The early route past Ballcross and that from Bubnell to Hassop both had steep slopes which the new roads were designed to avoid.

Looking at these routes in more detail, while many are still the current roads crossing the Estate, interesting 18th and 19th century features survive, particularly where they have been diverted or abandoned.[46] The Bakewell to Chesterfield Turnpike (Figure 73: A), authorised in 1739, ran over high land at Ballcross on its way from Bakewell, then followed the now quiet back lane that comes from the west into Edensor. After crossing the bridge over the Derwent, it probably ran along what is now a private drive in the park east of the river from Chatsworth House to the later Beeley Lodge and then turned up the now little-used walled lane past Beeley Hilltop and on to Gladwin's Mark.[47] High on the moors it was joined by a private Estate drive built in 1758, which crosses Harewood Moor from Chesterfield (B). This moorland route, still used as an Estate trackway, originally had small walled plantations spaced in pairs along its length.[48] It was built for use by the Cavendish family and their visitors, as part of a direct route to and from Chatsworth, via that part of the 1739 turnpike that ran through Beeley Hilltop. The usefulness of this turnpike as a public route through to Bakewell was negated once the 1760 Rowsley Bridge to Stone Edge Turnpike had been built (C).[49] Thus, the whole route would have effectively become largely private shortly after the construction of the moorland drive and this may have been anticipated. Perhaps one aspect of this drive's design was visual theatre, increasing the impression of the vast extent of the Estate and contrasting the wildness of the place, tamed somewhat by the flanking plantations, with what was to come once the splendours of the park and gardens of Chatsworth were reached. However, the visual effect of the plantations was ruined once the parish boundary wall between Beeley and Ashover was built, leaving five of the plantations to the south of the drive behind the wall.[50] This wall was certainly there in 1831 and may have been built in 1783 at the time of the Ashover Enclosure Award.[51] Thus, it may well be that the 1758 drive was only short-lived as a prestige access route; perhaps its upkeep was prohibitive or the planned impact did not live up to expectation. Driving here would have been a bleak and lonely experience in a winter storm, with serious danger of the route becoming impassable.

The original line of the 1759 Chesterfield to Baslow turnpike road (D) mostly matches the present road from Old Brampton to Robin Hood. West of Robin Hood, it ran over the impressive but now collapsing Millstone Bridge over Bar Brook (E), to follow a straight route along what is now an Estate trackway. It then passed through the northern part of Chatsworth Park where its course can be traced as a slight linear terrace.[52] A route eastwards (F) from the southern end of Millstone Bridge was created with the building of the new Baslow to

Chesterfield Turnpike authorised in 1812; this again can be followed in part as a trackway.[53] This new turnpike route complemented but never fully superseded that of 1759. Radical changes came in the 1820s when all the public roads south of the Bar Brook stream were diverted except for Estate traffic, with the creation of the northern extension to Chatsworth Park and the building of the present road network north of the stream from Robin Hood to Baslow (G).

The 1759 turnpike from Hassop to Bakewell in the western part of the Core Estate linked Sheffield with Bakewell and Ashbourne (H). Modern roads still follow the route, except for a short original stretch visible as an earthwork adjacent to Hassop Roundabout, which was abandoned and moved to the current line when the 1812 Ashford to Edensor Turnpike was built.[54] A new and more direct turnpike route between from Baslow to Sheffield was authorised in 1803 (I); this is the present main road.[55]

West of the Derwent, the construction of the 1812 turnpike from Edensor to Ashford (J), combined with the building of the earlier 1801 road from Baslow to Bakewell (K), led to the rationalisation of traditional local routes on Birchill Flatt and south of Pilsley.[56] The old routes had largely gone by 1831. Around Pilsley however, their lines can still be seen in parts as terraces, hollow-ways and banks at boundary lines.[57] Part of the 1812 turnpike road north of Edensor

FIGURE 74. This grassed-over but originally carefully engineered terrace was for a short time, in the 1820s–30s, the main road from Edensor to One Arch Bridge and Beeley beyond.

(L) was re-routed in 1830–31 as Chatsworth Park was enlarged here; traces of the earlier alignment are still visible as an earthwork.[58]

Other well-built roads around Chatsworth, while not turnpike roads, were added in the early 19th century, presumably at the instigation of the Estate. The most ambitious of these is a network of new roads, here by 1824, that run across the moors east from Beeley, linking it with Harewood Grange and places beyond (M).[59] The new road coming out of Beeley to the moors superseded earlier lanes that were subsequently abandoned. The traditional valley route through Beeley was also replaced sometime between 1791 and 1814 by the present main road (N).[60] This followed a new line from the lodge at the southern end of the park, skirted the village to the west and avoided the river flood plain further south.

West of the Derwent, several further changes and additions were made by the Estate in the early 19th century, some planned in the mid 1820s as part of a major restructuring of roads and drives in the park and beyond.[61] One of these improvements was an ambitious new drive up an avenue from Edensor (O), running to the ridgetop to the west, but never finished.[62] Another new route across Estate land was created in the 1830s (P), which may well have been a private carriage drive to Hassop Hall from the 1801 turnpike to Bakewell; part of this has now been abandoned but can still be traced and is a public footpath.[63]

Estate Drives and Parkland Roads

Some of the most radical and most often modified routes on the Estate were those created from 1759 onwards in the landscape park. These mid 18th to mid 19th century developments have been described recently in some detail elsewhere and only a brief outline is given here.[64] Many of the abandoned public roads and private drives dating to this period still have well-preserved earthwork remains.

When the new park was first laid out, several old roads were closed or rerouted in 1759. A new public road (Q) up the valley from Beeley to Edensor was made possible with the building of One Arch Bridge at the southern end of the park. This took traffic through the park on the other side of the river to the House. The other radical change was the demolition of the old Chatsworth Bridge and its replacement further upriver by the Three Arch Bridge in order to bring a new private drive (R) to the House. This swept diagonally in front of the House, showing off its grand architecture and fine setting to best effect. Another private drive (S) led northwards from the House to meet the Baslow to Chesterfield turnpike just beyond the then northern limit of the park.

In the 19th century major changes were made. Parts of the public road from Beeley to Edensor were moved slightly in 1818–19 to create a more sinuous route through the park. Other changes associated with the expansion of the park in the 1820s and the resulting diversion of roads have been noted above. At the same time a new drive (T) was built to the Golden Gates at the new boundary

FIGURE 75. There are several early 18th century guide stoops on the Estate, as for example west of Edensor (top left), south of Harland Sick (top right), the south end of Harland Edge (bottom left) and near Umberley Well (bottom right).

of the park, giving access to the turnpike roads from Baslow to Sheffield and the newly diverted one to Chesterfield. Other changes in the 1820s–30s were made in association with the partial demolition of Edensor village.

Another important development was the creation of the scenic drives (U) from the House up onto Calton Pasture to the west and into Stand Wood to the east, which were discussed in Chapter 5. These were first created in the mid 1820s and 1839 respectively, but were redesigned on a grander scale in the 1850s as Serpentine Drives with carefully engineered carriageways that zigzag up the parkland slopes.

Negotiating the countryside: stoops, mileposts and bridges

FIGURE 76. The packhorse bridge over Bar Brook near Cupola Cottage.

We turn lastly to what can be termed road 'furniture'. This includes fine pre-turnpike guidestones at hollow-ways, later stone milestones and cast iron mileposts alongside turnpike roads and several post-medieval bridges.

Associated with the moorland hollow-ways there is an exceptional group of four guide stones, known locally as stoops, centred on Harland Edge.[65] These

are important because they indicate the destinations of long abandoned routes, the way on shown by three-fingered hands pointing to market centres, often spelt differently to today's standardised norms. All four stones are probably of early 18th century date, as an Act of Parliament of 1697, enforced locally in 1709, required that such stones be set up by road commissioners.[66] A fifth stoop survives next to a junction of lanes west of Edensor and this is actually inscribed 1709.[67]

Two medieval cross bases have been discussed above in Chapter 4 and could have served as route markers at a much earlier date than the stoops. A simple clapper bridge across the Umberley Brook Leat at the heart of the moors acts as a focal point for several routes and thus may be an original feature placed here when the leat was dug in 1719.[68] The Three Men cairns, placed on top of a prehistoric barrow on the crest of Gardom's Edge next to a deep hollow-way, appear on the 1879 Ordnance Survey map and there are associated local traditions dating well back into the 19th century, if not before.[69] One tale states the cairns were built to commemorate the deaths during a snowstorm of a packhorseman and his two sons; another says a cleric and sons.[70] There is also a record of three clergymen travelling from Eyam to Yorkshire on 22 April 1740 who were caught in a snowstorm with the result that two died.[71] This may be the incident commemorated.

Only one 18th century turnpike milestone survives, placed against the road crossing the Core Estate at the southern end of Beeley Moor.[72] Adjacent to this is a later cast-iron replacement. All the surviving mileposts at the 19th century turnpikes that cross the Chatsworth Core Estate are of the cast-iron drum type.[73] These are usually painted white, with black lettering, and can be spotted while driving through the area.

There are four bridges of note within the Core Estate. The elegant One Arch and Three Arch Bridges across the Derwent are associated with the creation of the landscape park from 1758–59 and were designed by the architect James Paine. The third bridge is the massive but now ruined Millstone Bridge over the Heathy Lea Brook gorge.[74] This was built for the new 1759 turnpike road and was subsequently widened. Although built at around the same time as the other two, this is a much plainer and more utilitarian structure. Crossing Bar Brook near Cupola Cottage there is a modest packhorse bridge just wide enough for such traffic.[75]

CHAPTER NINE

The Woven Strands: The Past in the Present

Chatsworth: lost worlds and the archaeological legacy

This chapter provides an overview of the key archaeological sites that survive today on the Estate. Often ancient features within a backdrop of parkland, fields and moors sit cheek by jowl with later creations. The resulting rich historic character of the landscape is celebrated.

While many ancient features have been identified in this survey, they all exist in the present and are part of today's landscape. Looking at individual sites is rewarding and important examples pertinent to particular periods or types of activity can be very instructive. However, the site-specific approach is also limiting because it hinders understanding of how people in the past have moulded and used the whole landscape over several thousands of years.

It is this landscape in its entirety that presents an historical record of our forebears and which impacts on how it is used by today's farmers and its other custodians as well as by those who visit fleetingly to feast on its visual appearance. Every building, wall, field, moor and trackway is part of an integrated whole, each part with a story to tell, which when put together make up a truly rich land influenced by the lives of past people over many generations. Even on the moors, the ecology is not one that would be here if left to nature; every part of the landscape contains plants and animals that live within a landscape with habitats shaped by people. Much of the natural forest and wood pasture which once largely covered the area had been removed by 2000 years ago and this process had started several millennia before.

Thus, this chapter draws together much more than a list of individual features of archaeological and historic importance. The type, range, diversity and degree of preservation of features define both the historic character and the depth of visible history for any particular part of the Chatsworth landscape and the region as a whole.[1] It is this landscape character and the rich diversity of features within it that draws people to visit the Peak District time and again, even when they do not always recognise the impact past generations have had. While many come to Chatsworth for the House, park and gardens, there is far more for those who have learnt to read the landscape.

The influence of the past can be felt as part of an aesthetic appreciation of landscape. Also, the Chatsworth countryside can be understood intellectually, the historic landscape read as a book with its own structure and syntax. A deep

FIGURE 77. One of the more unusual disused buildings on the Estate, standing west of Bubnell and thought to have been a lock up.

FIGURE 78. The Derwent Valley near Beeley, with the Calton Lees valley behind, where the historic landscape has had fields and woodlands for several centuries, the details of which have been modified through time by the Estate.

understanding of the complex meanings within landscape can go far beyond academic interest, but can instil a strong love of the countryside and a desire to see it maintained for future generations. Through understanding we can enhance our respect for this landscape from realisation of the depth of human transformations over time that have given us this special place.

The underlying bones of the Chatsworth landscape are the local geology and geomorphology, but clothing it is a mosaic of vegetation, interspersed with buildings, walls and roads, the pattern shaped by people over the millennia. The landscape throughout history has provided the setting for, and is a record of, the long interaction of human communities with their environment; sometimes harmonious, sometimes not. As we have seen throughout this book, the Chatsworth Estate is enriched by its sharply contrasting historic landscapes. These range from the soft, tree-framed, undulating pastures of the 18th and 19th century parkland, to the hedged and walled fields of the enclosed farmland with its clear signs of medieval origins and later change, and to the sweeping starkness of the open moorland with its many low piles of cleared stones and ritual monuments left here by farming families in prehistory.

A lack of understanding of the historic character of any given area of countryside, combined with an aggressive agricultural management policy can significantly alter the look of a place and detract from its overall landscape quality. This has happened over large tracts of lowland Britain, due to the perceived needs of modern agriculture and other socio-economic changes. In many cases elements of local distinctiveness have disappeared and dull uniformity has started to dominate. At Chatsworth, as with many parts of the Peak District, we are lucky that the farmed landscape has escaped the most sweeping of modern changes. Thus, we have traditional landscapes of great character that are all the rarer for changes elsewhere. We are fortunate that the opportunity to maintain these vibrant landscapes into the future in a sustainable way still presents itself; this is one of the great challenges for present and future generations.

In the following sections, each of the three contrasting historic landscapes at Chatsworth and their surviving archaeological sites will be reviewed in turn.

House, elegant pleasure grounds and the 'fossilised' past

When asking people what their first impression is of Chatsworth or what they remember about its landscape, for most it will probably be the grand house in its garden and parkland setting, with the Derwent flowing by, framed by the surrounding tree-clad hills. The Cavendish family have long influenced the character of the gardens and landscape setting beyond. They inherited a deer park and built a mansion and formal gardens in the 16th century, with each subsequent generation making further changes, culminating in major 18th and 19th century transformations. Sometimes described as 'the Jewel of the Peak', Chatsworth House and its gardens, park and the model village of Edensor, make an outstanding and unique contribution to the diverse historic and aesthetic qualities of the Peak District landscape. As a radical transformation that only one of the richest families in the land could achieve, they stand in strong contrast with the farmed 'vernacular' landscapes around them.

What is not immediately obvious, except to landscape archaeologists, is that the parkland is carpeted with a rich and diverse mosaic of archaeological features. These tell of what went before as well as the development and modification of the designed landscape. The extensive pre-park earthworks were 'fossilised' when the sweeping grassy swathes were created and have not suffered the ravages of more modern agriculture.

Essentially the gardens and landscape park at Chatsworth are parts of a post-medieval landscape contrived and shaped by polite views on what is aesthetically pleasing, following the fashion of the time, be it formal or picturesque. This idealised landscape was achieved using profits derived from farming the agricultural land and exploiting the mineral wealth on Estate properties across the Peak District and beyond.

The gardens are a rich mixture of features dating from the 16th to the 20th centuries, with lawns and formal walks near the House, leading to wooded slopes above dominated by the grand statements made by Paxton and the 6th Duke in the first half of the 19th century. Formal features dating to the 17th and 18th centuries include the fine Cascade, the Canal Pond and various buildings and fountains. Early gardens existed north of the House within what is now the park and at Queen Mary's Bower there are rare earthwork survivals of features finally abandoned in the early 19th century. High above in Stand Wood is the fine hunting tower, dating to the late 16th century, which once lay at the heart of the old deer park. Returning to the gardens, later formal features include the grand early 19th century raised terrace outside the west front of the House and the embankments that surrounded Paxton's now-demolished 1830s Great Conservatory. These contrast with the sinuous walks through the extensive upper gardens that link rockworks, a grotto and an arboretum.[2]

Amongst the many designed landscape details in the park, 18th and 19th century highlights include the two fine bridges over the river, the stable block, the ruined mill, the model village of Edensor, the aqueduct in Stand Wood, various lodges, numerous disused roads and drives, ha-has, weirs, kitchen gardens, an icehouse with adjacent ice pond, a game larder and a deer barn. Hidden in the upper part of Stand Wood are ponds and impressive lakes, fed by long leats, which provided the water for the fountains. In the 19th century these reservoirs were transformed into decorative features in their own right, linked to the House and park by carriage drives, with designed vistas ornamented by features such as Swiss Cottage. Similar drives went to Calton Pasture to take in the views and Russian Cottage. Together, all these tell of grand schemes to create idealised landscapes punctuated by designed buildings. Each Duke stamped his mark according to what was fashionable at the time.

There is little to see of those parts of the village of Edensor removed in the early 19th century, while elsewhere in the park the medieval settlements on the

FIGURE 79.
Archaeological features
of different dates and
types are often found
cheek by jowl within the
designed landscape, as
here on Calton Pasture
with a post-medieval
water trough below a
prehistoric barrow.

east side of the Derwent have gone without trace. A solitary house against the
site of the old village street at Edensor bears witness to what was removed, and
its vernacular style suggests the village looked much like others in the valley,
before the model village with its flights of architectural fancy was created.

Underlying the formal parkland landscape are the extensive and important grass-covered earthworks of the medieval to mid 18th or early 19th century agricultural landscapes that preceded it. The gentle regular undulations of ridge and furrow, the lines of old hedge banks and the curving courses of pre-park lanes and later abandoned drives add to the texture of the parkland pasture. Some of the earthworks reflect the layout of the large medieval open fields of Edensor and smaller strip layouts on the east side of the river. Many of the mature trees in the park, often oaks, lay within hedges present when the parkland landscaping started. This counters the commonly held notion that 18th century parks took decades before the tree plantings reached maturity and the original concept could be appreciated to the full. At Chatsworth, as at parks elsewhere, a 'ready-made' parkland was achieved by using pre-existing trees.

In the eastern parts of the park one of the highlights is the exceptional veteran oak trees, a vestige of woodlands that lay within the late medieval deer park on the slopes above riverside fields. In parts these overlie earlier cultivation strips. North-east of Edensor, there are several small and easily overlooked mounds which tell another fascinating part of the story, for these were made to house rabbits in the now long-gone warren, which was another prominent feature of the Estate landscape before it was transformed by Brown and Millican.

New Piece Plantation was planted as a designed backdrop to the landscape park at the time this was created. Beyond this woodland, in the 'outer park' at Calton Pasture, boundary earthworks for rectangular fields that pre-date the mid 18th century are also extensive. There are also significantly earlier remains which include strip lynchets and the earthworks of a small deserted settlement probably of medieval date.

Amongst the pre-park field boundary earthworks in the park, in its flanking woodlands and on Calton Pasture there are also several old roads, including deep and braided hollow-ways and the terrace of a disused 18th century turnpike, while high in the north-east corner of the 19th century park there are important examples of millstone quarries on Dobb Edge.

The only pre-medieval features in the park are three prehistoric barrows to the west of the river. These are a rare survival for the Derwent Valley and complement the many barrows long known on nearby higher ground. The Chatsworth Park barrows bear witness to ancient farmers who occupied this valley, where extensive medieval and later agricultural activity has destroyed all other surface traces of their presence.

Taken together, the extent and range of surviving pre-park features is outstanding and puts into perspective the earth moving and engineering works which took place in the late 18th and early 19th centuries, undertaken for the 4th, 5th and 6th Dukes of Devonshire. Contrary to commonly held views, these works only affected small areas of the parkland, when compared to the entirety of Chatsworth Park which has many earlier features still in evidence. The only large area of the parkland where features are under-represented is in its north-western part. Here extensive ploughing took place as part of the 1939–45 war effort. Luckily earthworks across the rest of the park escaped.

Farms, fields and woods: the Chatsworth enclosed farmland

Chatsworth Park sits within a wider farmed landscape of equal historic importance, with a different but equally complex palimpsest of survivals from the past. The strong contrasts between the two areas throw each into clearer perspective. In historic landscape character terms, the farmland is essentially post-medieval enclosed countryside, dominated by long lines of drystone walls, dotted with field barns and scattered farmsteads. Set within the farmland are the villages of Pilsley, Beeley and Edensor, parts of Bubnell and Baslow, and the hamlet of Calton Lees. These settlements have long been important focal points for the communities that inhabit the farmed landscape with its pastures and arable fields. There is a mix of cottages and farmhouses, both juxtaposed with agricultural outbuildings, including barns, cowhouses, stables and pig sties. With the exception of the medieval church at Beeley, the standing buildings date from the 17th century onwards when stone took precedence over wood.

Complementing the villages are a number of scattered farmsteads, again now with buildings that are no more than 400 years old, some replacing antecedents that go back to medieval times. In the valley areas these sites with early origins include Birchill and Bramley. On the fringes of the eastern gritstone moorlands scattered early farmsteads were the norm and on the Estate these include Fallinge and Beeley Hilltop. The latter has one of the many minor halls erected by gentleman farmers in this period that have survived in the Peak District. Harewood was a medieval monastic grange and there are boundary earthworks defining a large enclosed area at the eastern edge of the moors.

Most other farmsteads on the Estate are post-medieval creations. Yeld, Parkgate, and Park Farms are particularly good examples of post-medieval estate farmsteads. Cracknowl Cottage is an unspoilt 17th century cottage in an isolated location. In contrast, architect-designed houses include Park Lodge and Dunsa House. Station Farm, adjacent to Hassop roundabout, was built in the 1860s as an inn when the adjacent Matlock to Buxton Railway was created. Again in contrast, high to the east, Parkgate Farm is probably on the site of an earlier packhorse inn known as The Horns Inn.

It is the variously designed fields with their walls and less-commonly hedges, together with occasional boundary trees, shelterbelts and plantations, that visually dominate the enclosed landscape beyond the settlements, forming a diverse tapestry.

Field shape is sometimes dictated not only by the landform but also by the way today's field boundaries fossilise the pattern of medieval open field strip cultivation that preceded enclosure. More commonly, fields are roughly rectangular or irregular in outline and these were normally created in later medieval and post-medieval times. In some instances, normally dating from the 18th and 19th centuries, field boundaries are distinctive in that they are ruler-straight. These were planned on a map before being laid out, reflecting both developing cartographic skills and more importantly changing attitudes to land. The mix of different field types varies from place to place, each with

FIGURE 80. The farmed landscape includes many agricultural buildings, including this fine 18th century hay barn near Calton Lees.

its own distinctive character. Contributing to this local variation is the size and type of stone used in the walling and coping, as well as subtle variations in stiles, gateposts and other boundary features.

There are a significant number of field barns for livestock on the Estate, including examples still standing, if sometimes in disrepair. A similar number again are now very ruined or have been removed. Many of the surviving buildings are small structures, some with hay storage above, others just simple byres. At a smaller number of places, more than one outbuilding is placed together. Associated yards are common. One exceptional complex is that at Farlow Paddocks, developed in the second half of the 19th century to house the 9th Duke's heavy horses. On the river meadows south-east of Calton Lees there is a highly unusual, large, open-sided hay barn built in brick in the 18th century.

Turning now to archaeological earthworks of redundant features within the present day fields, there is further evidence for open field cultivation in the form of broad ridge and furrow, and strip lynchets on sloping ground. They complement those in Chatsworth Park noted above and are found for example at Edensor, Pilsley, Baslow, Beeley and Beeley Hilltop. While the use of such cultivation strips has origins in the medieval period, in some cases these traditional farming practices continued in fragmented form into the 17th, 18th and even the early 19th centuries. Thus, the actual surviving earthworks are often hard to date precisely. At Birchill, historical map evidence suggests open fields once existed but were probably out of use by the beginning of the 17th century at the latest; the small size of the hamlet at this time allowed radical creation of new rectangular land parcels without 'fossilising' traditional land rights by following strip boundaries. A similar situation may well have existed at Cracknowl Pasture. Again rectangular land divisions were present by the early 17th century, but here there is surviving earthwork evidence for earlier medieval strip cultivation, some or all presumably associated with the settlement of Holme.

A very different type of agriculture is represented by the earthwork remains of the disused Pilsley allotment gardens created shortly before 1836. Regionally earthwork remains are rare for this interesting form of garden agriculture.

The enclosed farmland also encompasses rare survivals of prehistoric activity, mostly in the form of a few large and durable prehistoric monuments that have survived the ravages of later agriculture. Mostly these comprise large round barrows, found within later fields where more ephemeral prehistoric surface structures have been ploughed away. There are several examples on Calton Pasture and others near Pilsley and on Cracknowl Pasture. An exceptional site is the small later prehistoric 'hillfort' at Ballcross.

At Beeley, an interesting discovery was made in the 1990s when a Bronze Age cremation urn with burnt human bones and grave goods was discovered near the Derwent. This discovery illustrates that important archaeological sites do exist which present no surface clues as to their existence.

One unusual field monument from the medieval period is the cross base on the crest of a small prehistoric barrow west of Pilsley; only one other example of this interesting combination of monuments is known in the Peak District, at Wind Low near Wormhill. Another rarity is the survival of tees and greens at an abandoned early 20th century golf course amongst the fields above Baslow Far End.

Some woodlands in the enclosed farmland zone have been in existence since at least the early 17th century, but the amount of tree cover on the Estate was increased markedly with new plantations in the 18th and 19th centuries. While most were planted as a long-term economic crop, they were frequently also designed as visual statements to be seen from roads running through the Estate. In the vicinity of Dunsa and Pilsley, these views are emphasised by 19th century ha-has. The planting of trees has continued through the 20th century and there is more woodland now than at any other time in the last 400 years.

Buried deep in Paddocks Plantation, there is a large disused boundary bank and ditch for an ornamental oval copse, perhaps designed by Kent in the 18th century. In the 1820s a long avenue defined by shelter belts flanking a drive, the latter probably never finished, was created running almost due west from Edensor, aligned from the main apartments of the House and running to the skyline. Little of the original layout has survived as the visual appearance of this part of the Estate was radically re-designed later in the 19th century, although two large banks that flanked the central road survive on the hillside. Exceptionally large sweet chestnut trees nearby may be the vestiges of an early

18th century avenue on the same alignment. The line of these avenues was re-established in the late 20th century by cutting a broad 'ride' through Paddocks Plantation, although the visual effect of this is markedly different from the original concept.

Industrial remains also exist, which are of medieval and post-medieval date and are varied in character and scale. While most of the Estate has no limestone bedrock, the exception is Cracknowl Pasture and here there was small-scale lead mining. What appear to have been medieval lead smelting bole-hearths were inserted within two of the barrows on Calton Pasture. Heathy Lea Mill, although rebuilt as a corn mill and later used as a saw mill, may well have had its origins as a 17th century lead smelting ore-hearth. Part of what is probably the original mill pond dam is a rare survival. There are small millstone quarries at Under Pasture Edge above Heathy Lea Brook, on land that was later enclosed into fields. Relatively large 19th century gritstone quarries at Burntwood Quarry and Lime Tree Quarry lie on the enclosed scarp between Beeley and Fallinge.

One particularly important industrial site is Baslow Colliery, about half of which lies within the Estate. While this mine was only relatively small compared with many on the Coal Measures to the east, extensive surface earthworks survive as the site has not been redeveloped. Although many of the visible features here, mostly shaft mounds, are probably of 18th and 19th century date, they may well also include significantly earlier workings.

Routeways have evolved in the Derwent Valley over many centuries and some of the roads and lanes in use today have medieval or earlier origins. Others are new creations of the 18th and 19th centuries. As new routes were created, older ones were sometimes abandoned. Thus, there are earthworks of disused remnants of a complex network of roads and lanes. Associated with one long-used road is an early 18th century guide stoop midway between Edensor and Ballcross. Some of the routeways leading up to the eastern moors, as at those below Gardom's Edge, those in the old Chatsworth deer park and others in the Beeley area, are characterised by deep hollow-ways eroded by the passage of many people, packhorses and wagons. There is also a narrow packhorse bridge crossing Bar Brook near Cupola Cottage.

Some traditional routeways became redundant or lessened in importance in the late 18th and early 19th centuries with the building of the turnpike network. While these new roads are largely still in use today, there is an abandoned stretch adjacent to Hassop Roundabout and another south of Heathy Lea Brook at Robin Hood. The turnpike routes have surviving mileposts. Near Robin Hood the disused Millstone Bridge, an impressive example of a 1759 turnpike feature, still spans Heathy Lea Brook but has serious structural defects.

The barren wilderness: the Chatsworth moorlands

In contrast to the valley landscape, the wide, open, and sometimes apparently featureless sweep of the eastern moors superficially seems timeless. People often regard these moorlands as natural in character. However, nothing could be further from the truth. This landscape has changed radically through time and because it has been primarily used for upland grazing throughout historic times, it contains extensive remains of prehistoric activity. These present evidence for settlement and cultivation of these once tree-covered upland areas at a time when the climate was better and before soils deteriorated. In some places, sustained farming probably took place for well over a thousand years. Numerous low piles of stones are not naturally placed but provide evidence of people clearing ground for cultivation. Other piles are monuments marking where farming families buried their dead. Larger stones, set upright, mark places for rituals concerned with rites of passage and the seasons. Thus, today's moorlands have significant reminders of long-gone ways of life poking timidly through heather- and grass-covered peat.

On the eastern gritstone moors of the Peak District, of which the Chatsworth moorlands are the southernmost third, an exceptional amount of archaeological features dating to the last two millennia BC have survived. Taken together, these prehistoric remains are some of the most intact in northern England. Because there are large continuous expanses of moorland, where destruction by later activity has been minimal, this gives the rare opportunity to study how prehistoric peoples organised themselves across the landscape and how they used different parts of the land. There are scattered house sites amongst what were once hedged or fenced fields. The circular buildings were built of wood, with roofs of turf or thatch, and typically now little remains. The ancient field boundaries are sometimes visible today as low earthen banks and as linear heaps of clearance stone that were piled against them. There are also large numbers of clearance cairns, where prehistoric people piled stone as they prepared ground, both for cultivation and to improve the quality of pasture. The main focal areas for prehistoric fields, as at Gardom's Edge, Gibbet Moor, Beeley Warren and Beeley Moor, have associated ritual monuments, including small stone circles, ringcairns and stone settings, as well as larger barrows.

There are also much smaller cairnfields on the Chatsworth moorlands, mostly on less favourable ground and, in some cases at least, presumably made over a shorter period. Beyond the cultivated land there are extensive areas with only scattered prehistoric features, often of a ritual nature, including large barrows and a number of scattered or clustered small cairns that may well also be funerary. These areas were probably extensively used in prehistory for unenclosed grazing.

Most of the prehistoric agricultural remains are hard to locate as they are low and the vegetation is commonly thick, although perhaps the easiest place to search these out is Beeley Warren. Amongst the most obvious ritual monuments are barrows such as that on the crest of Gardom's Edge underlying the Three Men cairns, and the unusual Hob Hurst's House on Harland Edge. The evocative Park Gate stone circle on Beeley Warren, with its stones peeping above the long grass, is also worth the walk. An unusual feature, only part of which lies on Chatsworth Estate moorland, is the massive Later Bronze Age enclosure on Gardom's Edge. Its bracken-shrouded bank can be followed for much of its length. Many other prehistoric monuments on the Chatsworth moorlands are of great interest to the archaeologist, but are low and hard to find unless the heather has been recently burnt.

Although bleak, these moors have also been utilised throughout the historic period, albeit on a less intensive scale than the enclosed farmland. If sheep had not continuously grazed them over the last two millennia then they would have reverted to woodland. Extensive quarries with a scattering of discarded products such as millstones and troughs, former coal mines and lead smelters, and a multitude of criss-crossing hollow-ways are a testament to the continued exploitation of the moorland in medieval and post-medieval times. The archaeological features that remain from these activities are vital parts of the moorland landscape, albeit often contributing in a more overgrown and thus visually less obvious way than in the enclosed farmland.

FIGURE 81. Although much of the archaeology on the Chatsworth moorlands is prehistoric, this is a standing stone with a difference, erected in the early 18th century to guide travellers crossing the bleak moors on their way to Sheffield.

Medieval features include cross bases and boundary stones. Hollow-ways form a complex network of medieval and later routeways from the Peak District villages to the industrial production centres and markets to the east. These routeways, for example around Beeley Warren, often comprise broad bands of braided hollow-ways, eroded by the passage of people, packhorses and wagons,

moving sideways to avoid hollows that were already boggy. On slopes water erosion has often deepened them significantly. These routeways and their associated guide stoops became largely redundant in the later 18th century with the building of the turnpike network that is largely still in use today. After the moors were privatised and became Estate property, lines of butts were added, used for grouse shooting in the 19th and 20th centuries.

In the Baslow area there are remains of millstone making of exceptional importance, dating from the medieval period onwards. The production of these, along with lead mining, were the main medieval industries of the region and the quarries at Gardom's Edge were at the heart of one of two main centres in the Peak. These are fascinating places to explore, with working areas, unfinished and discarded millstones, access trackways and ruined quarrymen's sheds. However, visitors need to take care because of the precipitous quarry faces and much loose rock on steep slopes.

Quarries are also extensive further south, on Beeley Moor and Fallinge Edge, and again interesting broken products such as troughs, pulpstones and millstones litter the landscape. The moorland just east of Beeley Warren has extensive surviving low shaft-sinking waste heaps at the Beeley Colliery, which was worked from the 16th to the 19th centuries.

Other features of interest include the 18th and 19th century leats that feed the header lakes for the water features in the gardens at Chatsworth House, with the Emperor Stream on Gibbet Moor being particularly impressive. The spectacular designed landscape which lies out of sight in the valley below, sent out tentacles to even the remotest moorland part of the Estate.

CHAPTER TEN

A Sense of Place: Visiting the Chatsworth Estate

Chatsworth: a place of many interests

This chapter is devoted to eight walks that allow the visitor to the Estate to easily explore some of the archaeological highlights and gain a flavour of its varied historic landscapes.

Access to the Chatsworth land varies from place to place. For the House and gardens there are set opening hours and a charge is made. Visitors are allowed to walk freely over much of the park and the moorlands are mostly Open Access Land. However, in the enclosed farmland, please remember that access is restricted to roads and public footpaths.

Wherever you visit, please respect the countryside and remember that it is a working landscape. Similarly, some of the archaeological sites are Scheduled Monuments and it is an offence to damage them in any way. Digging holes, even the small ones dug by metal detectorists, on any known archaeological feature does harm.

For each walk its starting point, distance and grade of difficulty are given. Some are over rough ground so remember to wear appropriate clothing and footwear. Unfortunately, space does not allow for detailed route descriptions to be given and you will have to rely on the detailed maps provided and the Ordnance Survey, 1:25000 scale, White Peak Area map. For each site, a cross-reference is given to where it is discussed in previous chapters.

The House and gardens

Much has been written elsewhere about what there is to see at Chatsworth House and its gardens (and above pp. 4–5, 69–75, 94–9). Undoubtedly they should be the focus for anyone's first visit to the Estate. Guidebooks are available on site and details are not repeated here. For those wanting a detailed history of the gardens and parkland beyond, we recommend – *Chatsworth: A Landscape History*, by John Barnatt and Tom Williamson, published by Windgather in 2005.

The House and gardens are open from March to December each year; details of opening times and entrance charges can be found at their website – www.chatsworth.org. There is extensive car parking close to the House.

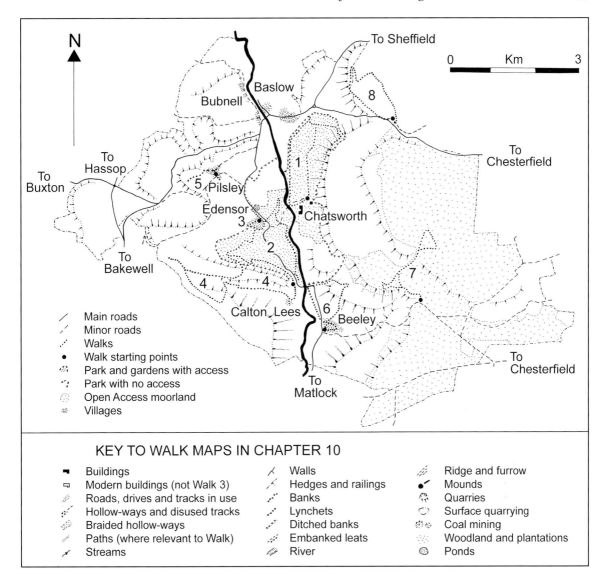

N

To Sheffield

0 Km 3

Baslow
Bubnell

8

To
Chesterfield

To
Hassop

To
Buxton

5 Pilsley
Edensor
3
Chatsworth

2

4 4
Calton Lees 6
Beeley

7

To
Bakewell

To
Chesterfield

To
Matlock

	Main roads
	Minor roads
	Walks
•	Walk starting points
	Park and gardens with access
	Park with no access
	Open Access moorland
	Villages

KEY TO WALK MAPS IN CHAPTER 10

◄	Buildings		Walls		Ridge and furrow
	Modern buildings (not Walk 3)		Hedges and railings	●	Mounds
	Roads, drives and tracks in use		Banks		Quarries
	Hollow-ways and disused tracks		Lynchets		Surface quarrying
	Braided hollow-ways		Ditched banks		Coal mining
	Paths (where relevant to Walk)		Embanked leats		Woodland and plantations
	Streams		River		Ponds

FIGURE 82. The locations of suggested walks 1 to 8 across the Chatsworth Estate, together with roads and access areas.

Chatsworth Park

The parkland is full of wonderful things to see. Two walks are given, one on either side of the river.

Walk 1 (Figure 83): This starts from the car park (charge made) adjacent to Chatsworth House (SK 261 703) and takes you north towards Baslow (alternatively start at Baslow Nether End, where there is a car park (pay and display) and bus stops, and take the public footpath to the park to join the walk part way round). The parkland walk is wholly within the part where visitors are welcome to roam at will. The suggested route is about 5 miles (8 km) long and

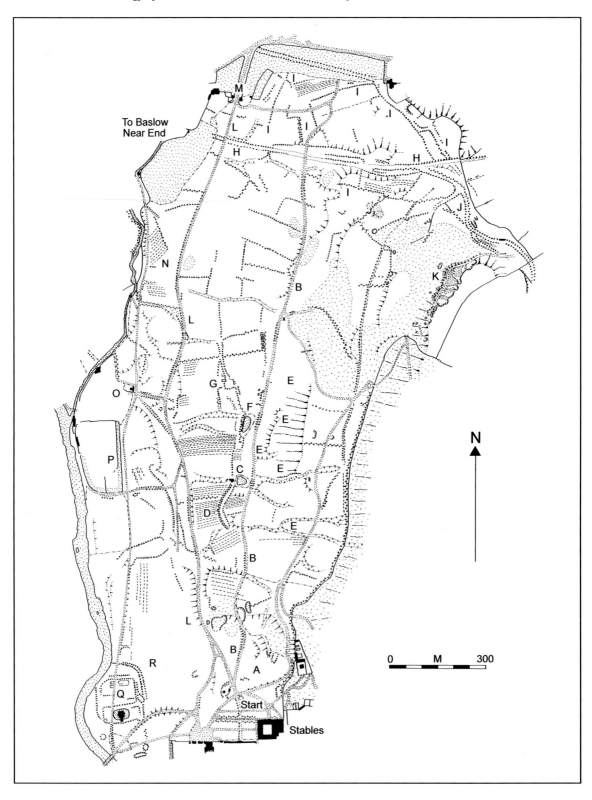

is mostly easy walking across grassland, but with one optional steeper gradient over rougher ground.

Close to the car park north of the House and stables there is a clump of veteran oaks (A), a relic of the woodland growing here since at least later medieval times inside the old deer park (pp. 75–6). The trackway (B) running just below the clump was the main drive going northwards when the landscape park was first laid out in 1758–60s (p. 157). A few minutes walk brings you to a pond (C), created in about 1760. Below are the dry earthworks of a shallow crescentic pond where, in winter, water was let in overnight to form ice. This was stored in the adjacent underground icehouse (p. 81). The ice pond earthworks cut through low ridge and furrow (D), perhaps last cultivated when the medieval settlement of Langley was still occupied (pp. 52, 58–9).

Running north, on the upslope side of the old drive, there are many veteran oaks (E), once in the old deer park, some formerly pollarded others stripped for deer fodder. Double back to the downslope side of the drive to a second pond (F), said to be at the site of clay pits dug for the bricks used in the late 1770s to build the New Inn at Edensor, now the Estate Office (p. 85). A short distance further north, amongst low field boundary banks for hedges swept away in the 1820s (p. 82), there are the slight and hard-to-identify footings of a farmstead (G) built in the 17th or 18th century (pp. 106, 108, 114).

Eventually, after passing several clumps of trees, the old drive (B) crosses the site of the 1759 turnpike road from Baslow to Chesterfield (p. 155), intermittently just visible as a slight linear terrace (H).

One option is to follow this upslope to the east, where it eventually leads to a gate in the park wall. On the way many of the scattered trees in the park here (I) lie on slight remains of further old hedge banks, the hedges grubbed out in the 1820s when all the fields here were removed as the park was enlarged (p. 82). On the right an earlier routeway (J), with probable medieval origins and replaced by the 1759 road (p. 150), should be followed up the steepening slope to where there is a deep hollow-way winding sinuously. Near the top, a traverse south-westwards across rough ground leads to old millstone quarries on Dobb Edge (K), hidden from the rest of the park below by woodland. These quarries are probably of 17th/18th century date and there are several unfinished and broken millstones to find (pp. 143–4); take care – there are vertical faces, loose waste heaps and a multitude of boulders to trip over.

Returning down the old 1759 road this eventually meets the 1820s main drive (L), running from the wrought-iron Golden Gates, made in the late 17th century and once standing in pride of place outside the House. They were re-erected in their present position in the 1840s, flanked by lodges designed by Wyatville (M), to control access to the House on the drive passing through the dense tree screens which isolated the idealised landscape from the main 19th century roads and workaday farmland beyond (pp. 82–3, 85, 156).

After turning and starting to head back towards the House, at the lower edge of the park, shaded by tall parkland trees, there is a small surviving area

FIGURE 83. Walk 1: Chatsworth Park – north-east (A–R see text) (for Key see Fig. 82).

of medieval ridge and furrow (N) which was once part of the open fields of Baslow (pp. 58–9). The footpath running south from here passes White Lodge (O), built in 1855 on the access drive to Paxton's house (now demolished) and his plant nurseries (p. 85). Further on is the high brick wall (P) of what were the kitchen gardens created in the 1760s at the same time as the park, when the clutter of outbuildings and other functional appendages around the House were swept away (pp. 71–2).

Just before Queen Mary's Bower is reached, there is a rare survival of geometrically arranged earthworks (Q), which are all that remain, in modified form, of 16th century formal gardens to the north of Chatsworth House (p. 70). Here there were once six large ornamental fishponds, together with orchards, linked by a grid of paths. While much of this was swept away for Brown in the 1760s, one small area, partially hidden by trees and called the Rookery Gardens, survived into the 1820s. However, this was dismantled at around the time the Bower itself was restored by the architect Wyatville, leaving only the earthworks we see today.

Nearby a relatively small area of the parkland is atypical in that it is devoid of archaeological features (R). This is the site of a 17th century ornamental canal that was infilled in the 1760s (pp. 70–71), but which was similar in size to that south of the House where the 19th century Emperor Fountain still jets water high into the air. There are local traditions of vast earthmoving undertaken for Brown, but other than here and at the river below the House, this is not true (p. 82).

Walk 2 (Figure 84): This starts from the car park (charge made) at the southern end of the park, next to the Garden Centre at Calton Lees (SK 258 685) and takes you north to beyond Edensor. The whole walk is again within the public areas of the park where visitors are welcome to roam at will. The suggested route is about 4.5 miles (7 km) long and is easy walking across grassland with several short but moderate gradients.

Just inside the park, close to the river, the ruin of the 1760s mill (A) was designed by James Paine as one of several eye-catching architectural highlights decorating the park (p. 84). South from here there is the low causeway (B) of a disused public road, running from One Arch Bridge by Paine (C), built when the old road to Chatsworth on the other side of the river was closed as the park was created (pp. 155, 157). The road was diverted again to today's route in 1818. The imposing weir (D) was created in 1838, on the same site as one built at the same time as the mill.

Following the path along the top of the steep slope above the river, you pass low earthworks (E) at the sites of hedged field boundaries removed in about 1760, together with traces of ridge and furrow (pp. 54–6, 108–11). A second weir (F) was created by Brown, when the river upstream was widened by digging away its banks, to make it lake-like in front of the House (p. 82). The effect

FIGURE 84. Walk 2: Chatsworth Park – south-west (A–V see text) (for Key see Fig. 82).

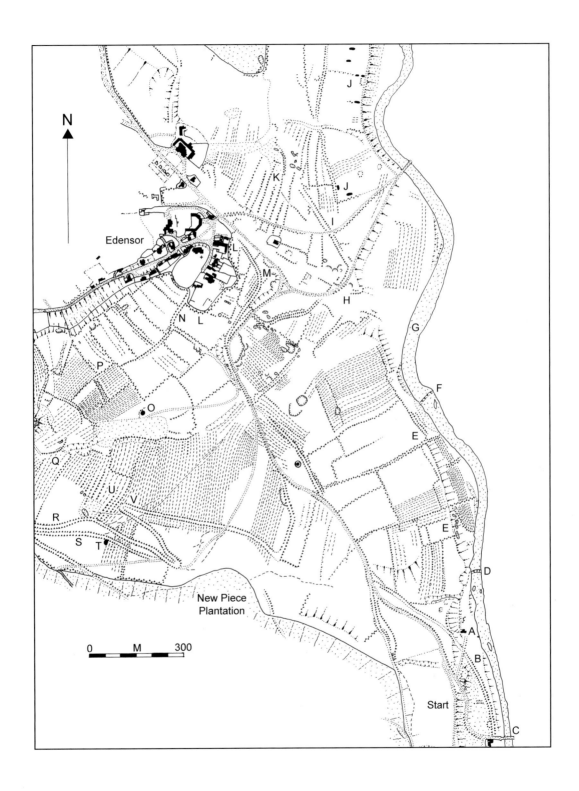

Edensor

New Piece
Plantation

0   M   300

Start

has now been lost due to silting. Similarly, nothing remains of the medieval Chatsworth Bridge and nearby mill (G), which Brown had removed (p. 72).

From here the old road ran north-westwards to the bottom end of Edensor village (H). With the exception of one cottage further up the street, all was demolished here in the late 1810s to early 1830s (pp. 86–7); there is now little to see. An old sunken lane (I) rose up the low ridge behind the village that blocked the view of Edensor from the House and ran along the edge of the warren until imparkment took place (p. 152). Between here and the river there are several low oval mounds (J) where the rabbits were reared (p. 78).

Heading south-west, well-defined medieval strip lynchets (K) on the slope above the site of the old village street may well be original toft boundaries (pp. 49–51). Skirting the late 1830s to early 1840s model village (described below), and its walled ha-ha (L), there is a mid 1820s road terrace (M). This road was abandoned only a few years after it was built, once the demolitions at old Edensor were completed (pp. 86–7). Behind the village there is the sunken course of Jap Lane (N), with old flanking hedgerow trees, which until the 1820s was the main road into Edensor (p. 157).

Further to the south-west is the finest of the prehistoric burial mounds in the park (O), a remarkable survival in a small corner of land not cultivated in the medieval period (p. 26). A short distance away there is a particularly fine

FIGURE 85. The landscape park behind Edensor has much earthwork archaeology, but it is also a working landscape where Estate stock are grazed.

group of oaks (P), the oldest of which lie on old hedge banks defining pre-1760 fields that still contain ridge and furrow (p. 107).

Uphill there is a great deal of medieval ridge and furrow (Q) that once lay within Edensor's extensive open fields (pp. 55–6). Above, is the heavily engineered 1850s Serpentine Drive (R), running close to the less ambitious 1820s drive (S) which it superseded (pp. 157–9). Following this earlier drive eastwards, you pass a second prehistoric barrow (T), truncated on one side by strip cultivation. Downhill from here the medieval cultivation strips are well defined (U) and there is a particularly impressive bend on the 1850s drive (V). Nearby there are linear hollows at the site of an earlier routeway dating to the late medieval period when this area was an open sheepwalk (pp. 152).

A walk south-eastwards leads back towards the car park; many of the pre-park earthworks gradually become less well-defined in this direction.

Walk 3: Edensor Village (Figure 86)

This gentle stroll takes in the model village. It can be included in the last walk described, or done independently. Please respect residents' privacy by staying to footpaths and roads. There is a limited amount of roadside parking below the churchyard at the green just inside the village curtilage (SK 251 699).

Edensor was a large settlement before the Norman Conquest and continued to thrive through the medieval period and beyond (pp. 49–51). However, much was demolished in the late 1810s to early 1830s and soon afterwards the upper part was transformed into a model village (pp. 86–9).

The green is an ideal place to start viewing the eclectic architecture of the model village, mostly designed by Paxton and Robertson in the late 1830s and early 1840s (p. 85). By the gates is Castle Lodge (A), built in the 'Norman' style in 1842. When this was first created it lay within a tree screen that separated the village from the park, except at the gates. To the east of the green there is the impressive Italianate Villa, with a Norman arch at the 'well' nearby (B). On the opposite side of the green are what remain of the outbuilding ranges designed by Decimus Burton of what initially was a model farm (C). Hidden behind in private grounds is Edensor House (D), originally the farmhouse but significantly enlarged in the mid 19th century and thereafter for many years the home of a succession of the Estate's land agents. On the green itself there once stood the village school, demolished in 1950.

St Peter's church (E) was an afterthought, replacing a more modest medieval building with squat tower. The present building, over-large and ugly, was designed by Sir George Gilbert Scott and built in 1867–70. Within there is an impressive early 17th century monument from the old church, dedicated to William, 1st Earl of Devonshire, and his elder brother Henry, both sons of 'Bess of Hardwick'. In the churchyard there is a medieval cross base with a modern shaft and sundial, and amongst the many graves is that of Joseph Paxton and at the top end the Cavendish family plot.

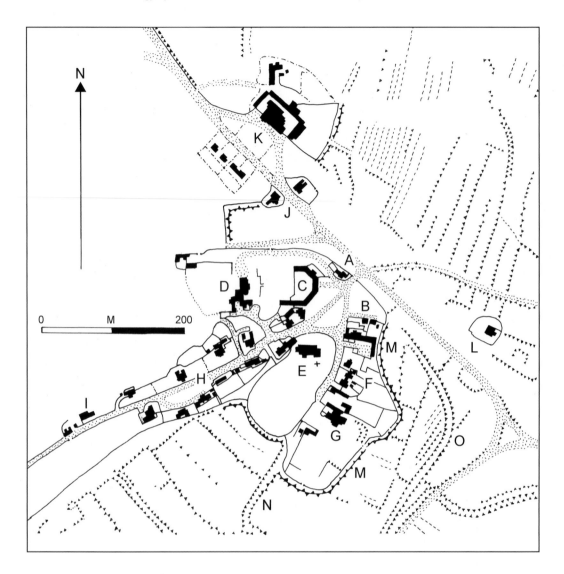

Many of the close-packed buildings (F) on the short lane to the south of the church were already present in the 1830s, the main ones of which were remodelled. What is now the post office was once a farmhouse. The row of cottages with four dormer windows was not built until 1868. At the top of the lane there is a large old vicarage (G) hidden within its private grounds.

A walk up the lane north of the church passes a whole range of new and re-faced dwellings designed by Paxton and Robertson (H), where the well-spaced buildings are carefully orchestrated to show off the variety of architectural styles employed. Near the top of the street there is also Moor View (I), designed by Romaine Walker in Arts and Crafts style and added in 1912.

Outside the village gates, flanking the main road, there are two lodges (J) designed by Wyatville but not built until 1837–39. Beyond is the 20th century

FIGURE 86.
Walk 3: Edensor Village (A–O see text) (for Key see Fig. 82).

FIGURE 87. Edensor: the Norman arch at the 'well' near Italianate Villa.

Teapot Row. Opposite this is the Estate Office (K), built in brick as the New Inn in the late 1770s (p. 85) and not altered during the restructuring of the village 60 years later.

In the opposite direction, down the road, is the solitary survival of a cottage in the old eastern half of the village (L), built in a plain vernacular style. Nobody knows for sure why this was left when all else was swept away in the early 19th century.

Skirting the village on its south side, there is a fine walled ha-ha (M), built when the village was remodelled, while at the back there are earthworks marking the sunken line of Jap Lane (N), which before the 1820s was the main way into Edensor from the south. There is now no way through, the old route blocked by a high boundary wall to the old vicarage garden. Nearby there is the terraced causeway (O) of the new road which replaced Jap Lane in the mid-1820s. This in turn was replaced a few years later by the present road when the demolitions at Edensor were complete.

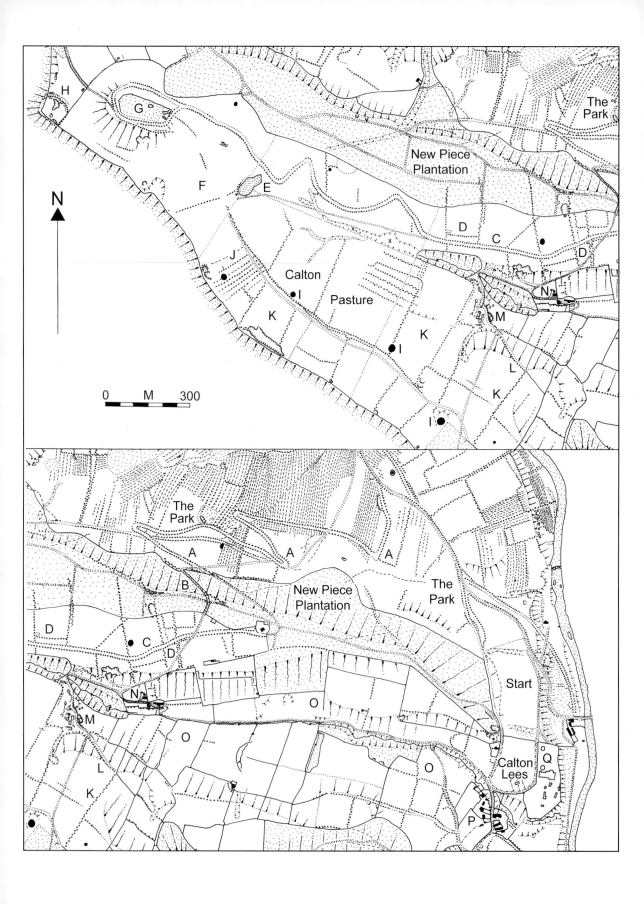

Walk 4: Calton Pasture and Calton Lees (Figure 88)

This walk, using public footpaths, goes first up to Calton Pasture and then down through farmland to Calton Lees. It starts from the car park (charge made) at the southern end of the park, next to the garden centre (SK 258 685). Once beyond the park, please stay on the footpaths. The suggested route is about 6 miles (10 km) long and is relatively easy walking with occasional moderate gradients.

Start the walk in the park, keeping left of the road and slowly rising to eventually join the old Serpentine Drive (A), a grassed-over terrace which was engineered in the 1850s to take carriages up through the park onto Calton Pasture and Moatless Plantation in order to show off the Estate and its grand landscape views (p. 159). While a straight line can be taken to the public footpath into New Piece Plantation (B), which follows a later Estate trackway through the wood, it is worth first following the more gradual gradients of the sinuous carriage route to savour the fine views of the park that the Dukes' guests would have enjoyed.

The plantation (B) was part of Brown's 1760s design, created as a scenic backdrop to the park, which ever since has been managed and replanted by the Estate for its timber and game cover (p. 90). At the top of the diagonal route up the steep slope the path enters Calton Pasture, an 'outer park' or sheepwalk also created in the 1760s (p. 81). Take the footpath which runs westwards heading along the ridge; this again follows the 1850s Serpentine Drive (C). If you look carefully and the grass is not too long, there are occasional low banks and lynchets to be seen at right-angles to either side (D), which mark the positions of the rectangular 17th or early 18th century fields that were swept away in the 1760s (p. 107).

After passing through a gate in the next fence, the path takes a relatively straight line ahead, while the old drive can be seen taking a more winding course to the right. The pond (E) is an ornamental feature probably added in Brown's time and was perhaps also used for waterfowling (p. 80). The vestigial clump of trees (F) a short distance to the west is the sole survivor of four small decorative plantings on the Pasture created in the 18th century (p. 91).

Following the path westwards leads to Moatless Plantation (G), recently replanted, on the highest point of the Pasture. This was the destination of the Serpentine Drive and its line can still be made out surrounding the summit. Coaches ran here to take in the fine vista across this part of the Estate and the distant views beyond. In the first field to the west (H), are the earthworks of the later prehistoric Ballcross 'hillfort' (pp. 35–6); there is no public access to the site.

After retracing your steps towards the pond, follow the public footpath along the southern ridge. This part of the pasture has four prehistoric barrows (pp. 25–9), all somewhat damaged but easy to make out because of the fences that surround them; three are close to the path (I). Before the first of these is reached, visible if the grass is low, are slight strip lynchets (J), thought to be medieval in

FIGURE 88. Walk 4: Calton Pasture and Calton Lees (A–Q see text) (for Key see Fig. 82).

date (p. 61), together with further parts of the later rectangular field layout (K) removed in the 1760s. Unfortunately, all these low earthworks were damaged several years ago by ploughing when the Pasture was reseeded.

The woodlands ahead are one of the largest areas of forestry on the Core Estate. Some are ancient, such as Lindop Wood which flanks the Derwent Valley, already there when Senior mapped the Estate in 1617 (p. 112). Later estate maps illustrate complex changes and enlargements which gradually enveloped what had once been unenclosed sheepwalks and was later enclosed farmland.

From close to the near corner of the wood take the footpath going northwards downhill. As the walled wood in the valley bottom is approached, an old trackway (L) between Chatsworth and Haddon is joined (p. 153). This runs through low earthworks which define small rectangular buildings and yards (M), which are thought to be at the site of the original medieval settlement of Calton (pp. 53–4).

The trackway down the valley soon passes through Calton Houses (N), where there are two 18th century dwellings and derelict 19th century outbuildings. The valley has a complex arrangement of walled and hedged fields (O), which have been slowly created and changed over the last few hundred years; many have now been removed. The picturesque hamlet of Calton Lees (P), first recorded in 1205, has fine vernacular buildings of 18th and 19th century date, including the stylish Calton Lees House (pp. 52, 102).

Follow the road past Chatsworth Garden Centre (Q) back to the car park.

Walk 5: Pilsley (Figure 89)

This short walk of about 2 miles (3 km) takes in the village and makes a relatively short excursion to a burial mound in farmland nearby. There is usually some roadside parking in the village (SK 241 710). Please respect residents' privacy. Stay on the public footpath on the walk to the barrow. The walk to this is relatively easy going.

Pilsley is hidden away on a small gritstone shelf above the Derwent Valley and was first recorded in Domesday Book in 1086. The main street, aligned east/west, was probably first laid out when the village was created as a planned settlement, with crofts and tofts all along the north side of the street (pp. 50–1).

The small picturesque village has a fine collection of old farmhouses, cottages and outbuildings, mostly in typical Peak District vernacular style and dating to the 18th and 19th century (p. 100). At the centre is the 18th century Devonshire Arms (A). The school (B) is by Paxton and was built in 1849, while Top House on the opposite side of the road into the village is also attributed to him and was probably built slightly earlier. The nearby village post office/shop was formerly also a bakery.

Going east down the original main street, Duck Row (C) is a fascinating collection of cottages built at different times in different styles, two with 18th

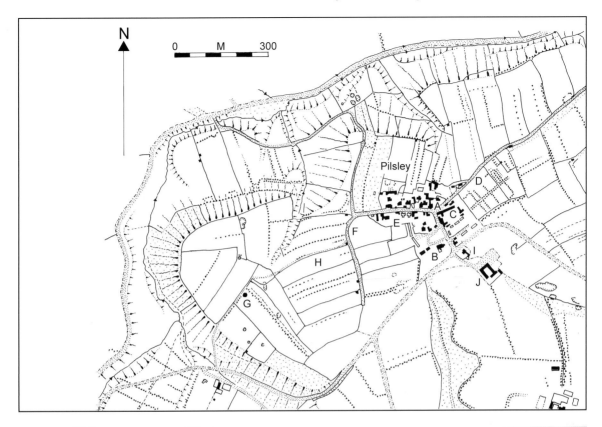

FIGURE 89. Walk 5:
Pilsley (A–J see text)
(for Key see Fig. 82).

FIGURE 90. The medieval
cross base on the
prehistoric round barrow
near Pilsley. On the
day the photograph was
taken the grass was so
long that the mound was
barely visible.

century datestones. The cottage with a bay window is said to have once been a coaching inn. Just beyond the eastern end of the village, to the right of the lane on the rough ground (D), low earthworks, usually overgrown in summer, and old fruit trees, are all that remain of the village allotment gardens laid out in the early 19th century (p. 125). At the roadside the second small gate gives access to an old village well.

Going west along the main street (E), you pass: the village hall on the left, formerly a chapel built in the early 19th century: and on the right Top Farm and outbuildings set back from the road: and at the top end Top House and Bradley House, once also a farmhouse, with mullioned widows and later details.

From the west end of the village, following the narrow field lane round to the left, you pass a first and come to a second very dilapidated small 19th century field barn (F) (pp. 118–20). Just before this, branching right down across the fields, a footpath takes you to a small but very interesting round barrow (G) (pp. 25–9). This mound is sited on flat shelf land and is presumably of prehistoric date but unusually has a medieval stone cross base on its summit (pp. 46–8). The mound is barely recognisable in long summer grass so look out for the stone. There is a local tradition that long ago a farmer removed this cross base to use it as a trough, but after a run of bad luck he replaced it. A local who dug in the mound is said to have died soon afterwards.

As you turn back, note that several of the walled fields you have passed through (H) are narrow, or contain low lynchets and banks where walls have been removed, all of which 'fossilise' medieval cultivation strips that once were within one of the open fields of Pilsley (pp. 57–8).

After retracing your steps to the village centre, a short walk to the south takes you past Pilsley House (I), designed by Paxton in Italianate Style (pp. 84–6), to the Chatsworth Farm Shop (J), originally built in 1910 as part of the Stud Farm for the 9th Duke's prized shire horses (p. 104).

Walk 6: Beeley (Figure 91)

This walk takes in Beeley village and its surrounding landscape using public footpaths, including the hamlet at Beeley Hilltop. There is usually some roadside parking in the village (SK 266 675). Please respect residents' privacy. Stay on the footpaths on the walk to Beeley Hilltop and back. The suggested route is about 3 miles (4.5 km) long and is mostly easy walking but with a long steep ascent to Beeley Hilltop.

Beeley was first recorded in Domesday Book in 1086 but may well be significantly older. The village has a complex and somewhat irregular plan, which suggests a long history of gradual development (pp. 50–1, 100–1). This continued into the recent past, when the Estate made radical changes to the road layout in the late 18th or early 19th centuries. New routes allowed travellers following the Derwent Valley to bypass the village, and to follow a newly created road onto the moors to the east, which replaced two traditional ways (pp. 152, 157).

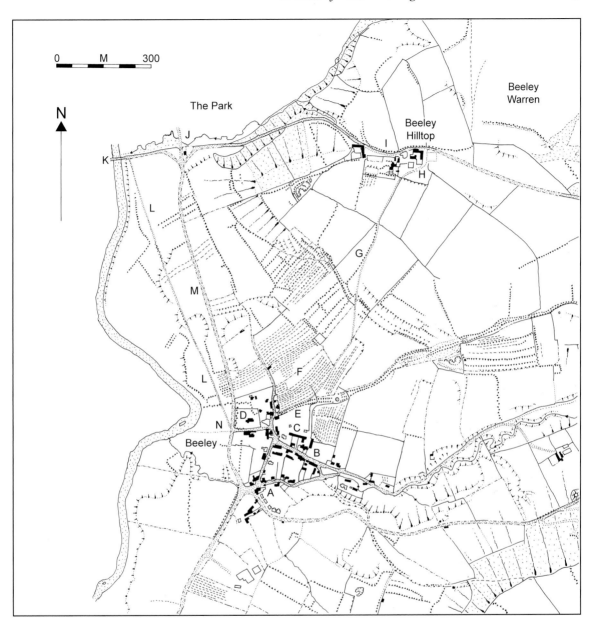

FIGURE 91. Walk 6: Beeley (A–N see text) (for Key see Fig. 82).

A good place to start a walk round the village is outside the Devonshire Arms (A), known to have been here since the 18th century. Nearby the curious Victorian Y-shaped set of cottages is one of the few architect-designed buildings in the village, said to be by Stokes, who was Paxton's son-in-law. A walk up the brook-side lane going eastwards takes you past several unpretentious properties, mostly of 18th and 19th century date. Doubling back at the first left turn soon leads to the Old Hall on the right (B) and Norman House Farm on the left, both substantial stone farmhouses with 17th century details. Further down the street, set back, there is the impressive 18th century Duke's Barn (C). In front, by the road, the old schoolhouse and accompanying schoolmasters dwelling are probably both by Paxton.

St Anne's church (D) is medieval in origin, with a largely rebuilt nave but an original squat tower and details elsewhere from the Norman period onwards.

A short distance up Pig Lane, the main road to Chatsworth until this was diverted about 200 years ago, a footpath leads off eastwards. This follows beside a deep hollow-way (E), which was the main route into the village from Chesterfield and Sheffield until the village roads were reorganised. To the north there is low ridge and furrow (F), one of the many vestiges which can still be found today of medieval farming in Beeley's three large open fields (pp. 56–7). After the first field, the path veers away from the old hollow-way and ascends steeply up the valley side. From the top of the steepest section there is a fine view back over Beeley and its complex farmed landscape (pp. 114–5). What you see today reflects landscape evolution extending over a thousand years, with medieval strip cultivation and later walled and hedged field boundaries that have been created, modified and in some cases become redundant or been removed over more recent centuries.

As the slope lessens, a high lynchet (G) close to the path is the site of an old field boundary which became redundant when the field layout was re-organised in the late 19th century. The curve of the lynchet suggests the old boundary 'fossilised' open cultivation strips used in the medieval period.

Beeley Hilltop (H) is a working farm with large modern sheds as well as modified earlier outbuildings (pp. 53, 103). The hall is a fine example of a 17th century residence built for the Greaves family, who then were lords of the manor of Beeley. The high and finely built lane-side wall immediately west of the house now encloses a small paddock, where out of view there are three small terraces within, evidence of once small formal gardens here.

The lane (I) running past the hall was probably improved as the first turnpike road in this part of the Peak, which was created in 1739 and ran between Bakewell and Chesterfield (p. 155). This became redundant only about 20 years later, except for Estate traffic, when Chatsworth Park was created and a new turnpike network was built across the moors.

At the base of the hill stands Beeley Lodge (J), built in 1861 at one of the private entrances into Chatsworth Park (p. 85). There is a high deer-proof wall at the edge of the park. The old deer park boundary followed this line in 1617 and may have been established here many decades prior to this. However, the wall has probably been rebuilt several times (p. 75).

Ahead along the main road lies One Arch Bridge (K), designed by James Paine to take the road going northwards when this was diverted to the other side of the river when the park was created in 1758–60s (p. 157).

Immediately before the bridge a footpath leads south through the large riverside meadow (L). This area was divided into several fields until the early

19th century, when the hedged boundaries were removed and one large grazing area was created for the Estate working horses, which were proudly 'displayed' to travellers who were using the adjacent new road (pp. 101, 157). Earlier field boundaries can still be traced in parts as low earthworks. Some of these defined fields that extended north-eastwards until the new road (M) was built through them two centuries ago.

Just before the village is reached there are two small metal domes (N), which are inspection hatches for the early 20th century pipeline from the Derwent and Howden Reservoirs to Derby, Nottingham and Leicester.

Walk 7: Beeley Warren and Harland Edge (Figure 92)

This Open Access Land walk across moorland takes in extensive prehistoric remains, old coal mines and major pre-turnpike routeways. Use informal roadside parking at the junction of the minor road from Beeley to Holymoorside with a green lane at the top of Hell Bank Plantation (SK 287 681). Please use designated access points at boundaries. The suggested route is about 4 miles (6 km) long and is moderate walking over rough ground with one steep uphill gradient. Locating features of interest needs map-reading skills. Check the weather forecast, it is easy to get lost if visibility is poor.

The rough lane (A) is probably part of the particularly early turnpike from Bakewell to Chesterfield created in 1739. A road on roughly the same line had first been made into a coach road for the Estate in 1710–11, which took the Cavendish family across the moors towards Hardwick, their other main seat in the region. The turnpike was closed for through traffic in 1759 (pp. 151, 155).

Eventually, at a high gate, follow an Estate trackway (B) onto Beeley Warren. The trackway is probably the 1710–11 road, whereas that of 1739 continues downslope as the walled lane. Once the crest of the moorland shelf has been reached, the trackway passes through a prehistoric field system (C), with small clearance cairns and low field banks, which can be found, with perseverance, amongst the moorland vegetation (pp. 19, 22–3). To the right the banks, in part now bracken-covered, define small parallel-sided fields that have not been farmed for well over 2000 years. For the real enthusiast there are many traces of prehistoric agriculture and small monuments elsewhere across Beeley Warren, especially on the low ridgetops, again often found as much with the feet as the eyes.

On the left, shortly after a bend in the trackway, there is the base-stone of a medieval cross (D), now lying on its side in a bracken-free area (p. 63). From here there are fine views over the Derwent Valley with its long-used farmland around and above Beeley and to Chatsworth Park further north (pp. 46–8, 62–3). The cross stood at the head of a major hollow-way system (E) that wound its way up the now bracken-covered scarp slope (pp. 149–52).

A short distance beyond the cross base, there is a mound (F) in the bracken, disturbed by removal of its interior for stone and more recent bulldozing for

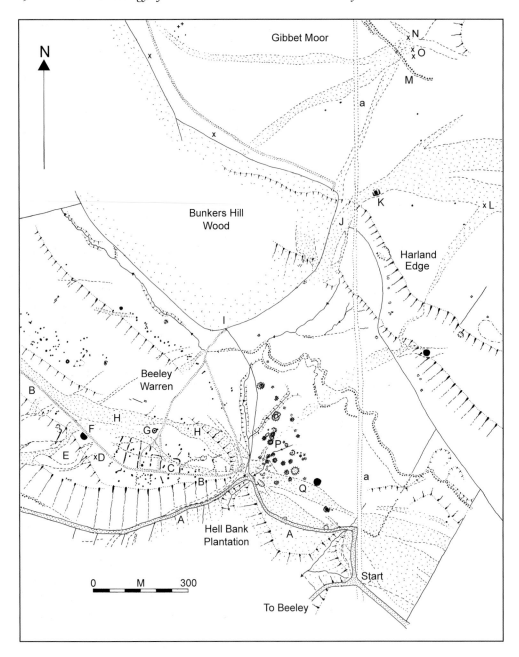

a firebreak next to the trackway. This is a prehistoric barrow closely associated with the prehistoric fields (pp. 25–9). A short distance to the east, but not visible in the tall grass until approached, is the Park Gate stone circle (G). This small Earlier Bronze Age monument, with its stones set in a bank, some standing and others fallen or robbed, and a low damaged central cairn, is typical of stone circles on the eastern moors built by local farming communities in prehistory

FIGURE 92. Walk 7: Beeley Warren and Harland Edge (A–Q see text) (for Key see Fig. 82, a: site of gas pipeline).

(pp. 30–33). The circle is lucky to have survived, as it is on an 'island' between braids of another major hollow-way (H), which ran from Chatsworth Bridge across the moors in the direction of Ashover (pp. 149–52).

A rough trackway leads up to just below Bunkers Hill Wood (I). This part of the impressive plantation, south of the old deer park, was created in the 1760s. Follow the plantation wall upslope, until near the top, when a braided hollow-way is just visible in the thick vegetation (J). This was part of the traditional route coming up the scarp behind to the cross and heading across the moor top in the direction of Chesterfield and Sheffield.

A short distance beyond the top of the steep slope is Hob Hurst's House (K). This is a highly unusual prehistoric barrow that is square in plan with a central stone setting, ditch and outer bank, and is carefully sited to overlook the extensive upland pastures to the north (pp. 25–9, 36–9). The site is named 'the house of the hobgoblin of the wood' and once must have had associated folklore.

From here a short walk due east from the barrow, using the old wire fence as a pointer, leads to a re-erected guide stoop (L) at the junction of roads from 'Bakewell' to 'Chesterfeild' and 'Sheaffeild' (p. 172). Going downhill to the north takes you to the head of the Umberley Brook Leat (M) dug in 1719 to supply water to Swiss Lake and the gardens at Chatsworth House (pp. 79–80). A short distance along this is a simple clapper bridge of slabs placed across the leat. Beyond there is a second guide stoop (N), on a different hollow-way to the last, going from 'Bakewell' (via Baslow) to 'Chesterfeild', placed here to reassure travellers on these featureless and somewhat intimidating moors (p. 158). Just 'upstream' there are two low boundary stones (O), one made in the 19th century, the other much older with a deeply inscribed cross and initials (pp. 126–7). These lay on the boundary between Beeley, Baslow and Walton.

From Hob Hurst's House go back down the scarp, retracing your route to the stile and then following the waymaked path to the high gate onto Beeley Warren. As you cross the stile note the uneven ground on the left over the wall next to the small stream (no access point through wall). Here there are many small upcast mounds and associated shaft hollows at the Beeley Colliery (P), which was last mined in the 19th century (pp. 139). However, the shallow workings you can see may well be at least as early as the 16th century and could be medieval in date. The major Chatsworth to Ashover hollow-way also passes here (Q).

Walk 8: Gardom's Edge (Figure 93)

This walk across moorland, some of which is Open Access Land, takes in extensive and varied prehistoric remains and important millstone quarries. Park at the pay and display Eric Byne Car Park at Robin Hood, just off the main road from Baslow to Chesterfield (SK 281 721). Please use gates and stiles at boundaries. Be aware of deep drops at the quarries along Gardom's Edge. The

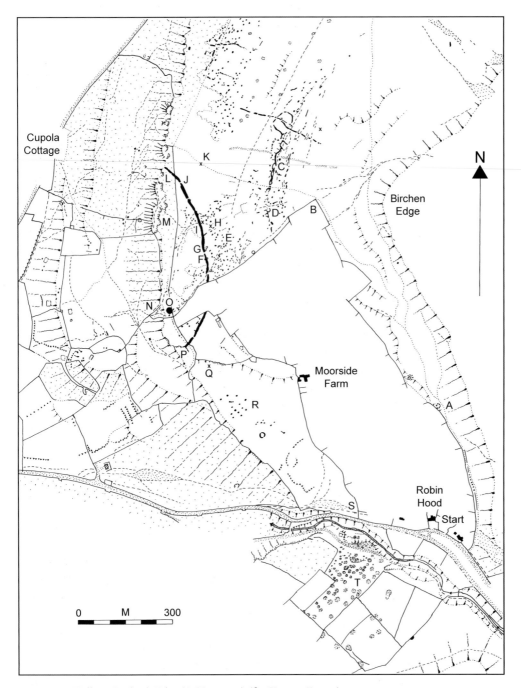

FIGURE 93. Walk 8: Gardom's Edge (A–T see text) (for Key see Fig. 82).

first and last parts of this walk are not on Core Estate land and archaeological detail has been included from other surveys undertaken by one of the authors (JB). The suggested route is about 3.5 miles (5.5 km) long and is moderate walking over rough ground. Route finding and site identification need map-reading skills.

From Robin Hood follow the footpath below Birchen Edge (take care on the road to reach this). A deep circular hollow (A) is at the site of one of the last shafts sunk in the northern half of Baslow Colliery (pp. 137–8). Further along, take the left branch of the footpath, which eventually takes you to the enclosure corner (B). This is a good point to take in the landscape differences between the moorland of the Gardom's Edge shelf to the north, which has not been intensively farmed since prehistory, and the fields on the south-facing land that you have passed, which may have been farmed for the last 4000 years, although much of what can be easily seen today dates to the last few hundred years.

Take the path running west which runs close to the top wall of the fields. The low ridge you cross has many prehistoric agricultural features (C) and the excavated site of a large circular house (D). There are further similar remains on the rocky ground further west (E). Together the prehistoric settlement and agricultural remains behind Gardom's Edge are amongst the most extensive and important in the region (pp. 20–3).

Where the birch scrub becomes denser, the main path passes through a broad but low, bracken-covered and hard to recognise bank of boulders and smaller stones (F). This is part of the Later Bronze Age scarp-edge enclosure (pp. 33–5). A narrow informal path follows its outer edge. Part way along the circuit a small post-medieval fold and sheep gathering wall has been added (G). A short distance beyond this, a detour to the right leads to a replica of a large horizontal slab with enigmatic prehistoric rock art (H). Against the enclosure bank is a domed millstone (I), of medieval or later date, which broke when it was being rolled over the bank on its way eastwards (p. 141). Further north, shortly before the enclosure bank is crossed by the post-medieval drystone wall, there is an excavated entrance (J). Take a moment to reflect on the amount of stone prehistoric people gathered from the surrounding area to build the monument.

Follow the drystone wall northwards for a short distance to where it ends and the cliff of Gardom's Edge can easily be accessed. Before crossing the fence onto Chatsworth Estate land it is possible to detour eastwards, following an obvious path into the trees, to a prehistoric standing stone that is just over head height (K). Once at the Edge a short walk leads to the northern end of the Gardom's Edge enclosure (L), where it has been robbed for walling stone but can still be found under the bracken ending at a large boulder at the scarp top.

A short way on, a disused trackway leads down into some of the Gardom's Edge millstone quarries (M), where with care millstone roughouts and abandoned stones can be inspected (pp. 142–3). It is easy in this evocative place, now overgrown with stunted oak trees, to imagine the hard labour needed to produce these vital products, which started in the medieval period and continued for several hundred years. When a stone accidentally broke or was found to be flawed this was the end of several weeks of wasted work.

Continuing along the top of the scarp, a deeply incised hollow-way (N) leads down from a blocked footgate in the scarp-top wall (p. 150). A short way on, just before the path goes through a narrow gateway in a high drystone wall, there are The Three Men (O). These three small but prominent post-medieval cairns commemorate deaths in a snowstorm (p. 160). What few people notice is that they are built on top of a low, vegetated and much larger cairn. This is one of the best-preserved prehistoric round barrows in the Peak (pp. 25–9).

On through the footgate leads to the badly robbed and difficult to recognise southern end of the Gardom's Edge enclosure (P). The rubble exposed in the footpath is nearly half a mile from the northern end of this thought-provoking site!

A well-used footpath takes you south back towards Robin Hood on Open Access Land owned by Moorside Farm. Cat Tor (Q) has a ruined quarryman's shelter at its base. There are fine examples of prehistoric clearance cairns in the larger grassy patches amongst the bracken (R). Just before the road is reached there is a flat linear terrace (S), which is the original course of the 1759 turnpike road from Baslow to Chesterfield.

Before returning to Robin Hood, an optional diversion leads, via a footpath from the south side of the main road after a short distance back towards Robin Hood, to a small area of Open Access Land on the south side of the stream (T). This ground was at the heart of the Baslow Colliery and has many early shaft hillocks, now mostly swathed in bracken, close to the outcrop of the coal (pp. 136–8).

CHAPTER ELEVEN

Postscript: Understanding Chatsworth

Our present understanding: Truth or truths

We hope that the preceding chapters have successfully illustrated the rich archaeological legacy to be 'read' in the Chatsworth landscape. This is an exceptional locale for its diversity of surviving archaeological features and contrasting historic landscapes, even when compared with other places in the upland zones with which Britain is richly endowed.

This book has attempted to outline our present understanding after several years of intensive research: the unpublished detailed archive reports have been responsible for the digital equivalent of the felling of several trees. What has been attempted here is an interwoven story of people and places, sites and landscapes, and archaeology and history. Hopefully the final text is all the more interesting as a result.

When starting the Chatsworth Project the great excitement was that there was so much to learn and new sites to find and describe. What we don't know is often more exciting than what we do; there is little point working on something where the answers are understood already. Conversely, often what seems simple at the beginning becomes more complex as alternative ways of viewing the evidence become apparent. Thoughtful enquiry is often about raising contrasting explanations and seeing which the evidence fits best, rather than strait-jacketing the evidence to fit preconceived ideas. Often constructive interpretations are best guesses and are open to alternative reconstruction. Equally common is acknowledgement that different interpretations are potentially valid because it is impossible to distinguish between them on available evidence. The best storyteller is the one who doesn't think they know 'The Truth' about the past, but who acknowledges multiple truths, weaves an explanation from them and guides others along this path. It is often difficult to get across this spirit of enquiry in an introductory book such as this on the Chatsworth Estate, as space does not permit in-depth discussion when there is so much ground to cover. But, this book is a starting point for your own investigations. Nothing would please us more than the reader taking our interpretations and questioning them, rising to this challenge by carrying out new and more in-depth study.

Readers should always remember that authors can never be 'Experts' who dole out 'Truth'. Rather, what is being written is inexorably bound up in the current ways in which authors and audience have learnt to understand the present and the past. Even description is interpretative, for it is governed by what authors include as important or omit as inconsequential. Deciding what 'facts' mean is currently governed by a healthy multiplicity of early 21st century perspectives on the world; these in themselves are complex with no agreement as to what are the most robust or valid. Archaeology has grown up and lost its naive certainty that single explanations are possible or even desirable. If this book had been written 100 years ago then early periods would have been interpreted in terms of invasions and very outdated viewpoints on what was civilised. These were influenced by the fact that Britain ruled an empire and justified this on the basis of very different prejudices about people, particularly in the developing world, to those of today. Much more would have been written about the world of the Dukes of Devonshire and their polite landscape, while the everyday details of farms, fields and industry, perceived as the preserve of the lower classes, would not have been deemed of interest.

Identifying the gaps

During the Chatsworth Project and in writing this volume the authors have always been aware that more could have been done. While the fieldwork was extensive, sites will have been missed which at the time of a visit were masked by undergrowth or thick heather. The cycle of controlled moorland burning demands that fieldwork should extend over 10 to 20 years before every spot was examined in favourable conditions. More significantly very little archaeological excavation has taken place. This technique would give us much detail about specific features and thus complement the extensive coverage provided by survey. In the Peak District, this approach has been limited because little of the known archaeology is ever threatened by destruction and thus evaluated at developers' expense, and because research excavations are prohibitively expensive. Even if the digging was done unpaid by volunteers, the cost of funding specialists to analyse the artefacts and environmental samples usually runs into thousands of pounds even on a relatively small excavation. Another limitation with the current output is that time did not permit comprehensive analysis of the voluminous detailed historical archives held by the Estate. While they were explored, it is several lifetimes' work to fully grasp and tease out all these have to offer.

Even with periods where locally there is voluminous physical evidence, and much research has been carried out, there is much to learn. In the case of earlier prehistory, and the Romano-British and earlier medieval periods, the problems are more profound; where do we start looking?

Future paradigms

While new insights can be gained by finding more information or looking at what is available in more depth, the biggest limitation with our understandings revolves around the questions it occurs to us to ask of the physical and written evidence left by past generations. New perspectives, which result from questions outside our current paradigms, are by definition unknowable. If a new book on Chatsworth is written in a hundred years time, it is hoped and anticipated that it will be significantly different to what is offered here.

Notes to the chapters

Chapter 1: Chatsworth in Context

1   Barnatt, J. and Williamson, T. (2005) *Chatsworth: A Landscape History*. Oxford: Windgather.

2   Barnatt, J. and Smith, K. (2004) *The Peak District; Landscapes Through Time*. Oxford: Windgather.

3   Barnatt and Williamson, *Chatsworth*.

4   Senior, W. (1617) *The mannor of Chatsworth belonging to the right honnrable William Lord Cavendish*. Bound volume of early-17th century surveys by William Senior, Chatsworth House.

5   Hicks, S. P. (1972) The impact of man on the East Moors of Derbyshire from Mesolithic times. *Derbyshire Archaeological Journal* 129, pp. 1–21; Long, D. J. (1994) *Prehistoric Field Systems and the Vegetational Development of the Gritstone Uplands of the Peak District*. Unpublished PhD thesis, University of Keele; Long, D. J., Chambers, F. M. and Barnatt, J. (1998) The palaeoenvironment and the vegetational history of a later prehistoric field system at Stoke Flat on the gritstone uplands of the Peak District. *Journal of Archaeological Science* 25, pp. 505–19.

6   Which covers about 5000 hectares, centred on Chatsworth and including Edensor, Calton, Beeley, Pilsley, Birchill, Cracknowl Pasture, Bubnell, Bramley and parts of Baslow, Brampton, South Darley and Walton.

7   Barnatt, J. (1997) *Chatsworth Park: Archaeological Survey 1996–7*. Bakewell: Unpublished report for the Trustees of the Chatsworth Settlement and English Heritage; Barnatt, J. (1998) *Chatsworth Moorlands: Archaeological Survey 1997–8*. Bakewell: Unpublished report for the Trustees of the Chatsworth Settlement and English Heritage; Barnatt, J. (2000) *Chatsworth Inbye Land: Archaeological Survey 1999–2000*. Bakewell: Unpublished report for the Trustees of the Chatsworth Settlement and English Heritage.

8   Bannister, N. R. (1997) *The Chatsworth Estate: Fields, Boundaries and Woodland Survey 1996–7* (Parkland). Unpublished report for the Trustees of the Chatsworth Settlement and English Heritage; Bannister, N. R. (1998) *The Chatsworth Estate: Fields, Boundaries & Woodland Survey 1997–1998* (Inbye land). Unpublished report for the Trustees of the Chatsworth Settlement and English Heritage; Bannister, N. R. (1998) *Chatsworth Buildings Survey 1997–1998* (Addendum). Unpublished report for the Trustees of the Chatsworth Settlement and English Heritage; Bannister, N. R. (1999) *The Chatsworth Estate: Fields, Boundaries & Woodland Survey 1998–1999* (Moorland) (2 vols). Unpublished report for the Trustees of the Chatsworth Settlement and English Heritage; Bannister, D. E. and Bannister N. R. (1997) *Chatsworth Buildings Survey 1996–1997*. Unpublished report for the Trustees of the Chatsworth Settlement and English Heritage.

9   Barnatt, J. and Bannister, N. (2002) Vestiges of a Rich and Varied Past: An Archaeological Assessment of the Earthworks, Field Boundaries and Buildings of the Chatsworth Landscape 1996–2000. Unpublished report for the Trustees of the Chatsworth Settlement and English Heritage.

10 Percifull, E and Thomas, S. (1998) Chatsworth Historic Landscape Survey, the Park and Gardens. Unpublished report for Chatsworth Estate; Percifull, E. and Thomas, S. (1998) Chatsworth Historic Landscape Survey, the Park and Gardens: a Notebook. Unpublished report for Chatsworth Estate; Williamson, T. (1998) Chatsworth Historic Landscape Survey, The Park and Gardens: A Brief History. Unpublished report for Chatsworth Estate.

11 This excluded Chatsworth House and buildings in the gardens and park, which were covered in the designed landscape survey.

12 Finch, J. and Giles, K. (eds) (2007) *Estate Landscapes: design, improvement and power in the post-medieval landscape*. Society for Post Medieval Archaeology Monograph 4; Boydell & Brewer.

Chapter 2: An Ancient Land: Farms and Monuments in Prehistory

1 Ainsworth, S. (2001) Prehistoric settlement remains on the Derbyshire gritstone moors. *Derbyshire Archaeological Journal* 121, pp. 19–69; Barnatt, J. (1986) Bronze Age remains on the East Moors of the Peak District. *Derbyshire Archaeological Journal* 106, pp. 18–100; Barnatt, J. (1990) *The Henges, Stone Circles and Ringcairns of the Peak District*. Sheffield: Sheffield Archaeological Monographs 1; Barnatt, J. (1996) Recent research at Peak District stone circles, including restoration work at Barbrook II and Hordron Edge, and new fieldwork elsewhere. *Derbyshire Archaeological Journal* 116, pp. 27–48; Barnatt, J. (1996) Barrows in the Peak District: a review and interpretation of extant sites and past excavations. In J. Barnatt and J. Collis (eds) *Barrows in the Peak District: Recent Research.* Sheffield: Sheffield Academic Press; Barnatt, *Chatsworth Moorlands*; Barnatt, J. (1999) Taming the Land: Peak District farming and ritual in the Bronze Age. *Derbyshire Archaeological Journal* 119, pp. 19–78; Barnatt, J. (2000) To each their own: later prehistoric farming communities and their monuments in the Peak. *Derbyshire Archaeological Journal* 120, pp. 1–86; Barnatt, J, (in prep.) From clearance plots to 'sustained' farming: Peak District fields in prehistory; Barnatt and Smith, *Peak District*, pp. 13–40; Barnatt and Bannister, *Vestiges*, pp. 33–61.

2 Bevan, B. (2005) Peaks Romana: the Peak District Romano-British rural upland settlement survey, 1998–2000. *Derbyshire Archaeological Journal* 125, pp. 26–58; Makepeace, G. A. (1998) Romano-British rural settlements in the Peak District and north-east Staffordshire. *Derbyshire Archaeological Journal* 118, pp. 95–138.

3 Radley, J. and Mellors, P. A. (1964) A Mesolithic structure at Deepcar, Yorkshire, England, and the affinities of its associated flint industry. *Proceedings of the Prehistoric Society* 30, pp. 1–24.

4 Barnatt, J. (1996) Moving between the monuments: Neolithic land use in the Peak District. In P. Frodsham (ed.) *Neolithic Studies in No-Man's Land: Papers on the Neolithic of Northern England, from the Trent to the Tweed.* Northern Archaeology, Vol. 13/14, pp. 45–62.

5 Barnatt, *Taming the land*; Barnatt, *To each their own*; Barnatt, *From clearance plots*.

6 Bradley, R. (2007) The Prehistory of Britain and Ireland. Cambridge University Press; Darvill, T. and Thomas, J. (eds) (1996) Neolithic Houses in North-West Europe and Beyond. Oxford: Oxbow; Grogan, E. (2004) The implications of the Irish Neolithic Houses. In I Shepherd and G, Barclay (eds) Scotland in Ancient Europe, pp. 103–14. Edinburgh: Societies of Antiquaries of Scotland.

7 Barnatt, *Moving between the monuments.*

8 Garton, D. (1991) Neolithic settlements in the Peak District: perspective and prospects. In: R. Hodges and K. Smith (eds) *Recent Developments in the Archaeology of the Peak District*. Sheffield: Sheffield Archaeological Monographs 2.

9 Barnatt, *The henges, stone circle and ringcairns*; Barnatt, *Moving between the monuments*; Barnatt and Collis; *Barrows*.

10 Barnatt, J., Bevan, B. and Edmonds, M. (1995–2000) *A Prehistoric landscape at Gardom's Edge, Baslow, Derbyshire: Excavations*. Bakewell: Five unpublished interim reports in the Peak District National Park Authority Cultural Heritage Team archive; Barnatt, J., Bevan, B. and Edmonds, M. (2002) Gardom's Edge: a landscape through time. *Antiquity* 76, no. 292, pp. 50–56.

11 Barnatt, *Chatsworth Moorlands*, 12.1, 13.3, 14.1, 19.10, 19.11, 19.14, 19.21, 25.2, 27.16, 27.17; Barnatt, *Chatsworth Inbye*, 54.2.

12 Radley, J. (1965) A ring bank on Beeley Moor. *Derbyshire Archaeological Journal* 85, pp. 126–131; Barnatt, *Chatsworth Moorlands*, 26.1.

13 Barnatt and Bannister, *Vestiges*, pp. 34–41; Barnatt, *Chatsworth Moorlands*, 12.1, 13.3, 14.1, 15.11, 19.3, 19.10, 19.11, 19.14, 19.21, 25.2, 26.1, 30.9; Barnatt, *Chatsworth Inbye*, 54.2. Possible sites – Barnatt, *Chatsworth Moorlands*, 14.19, 16.14, 17.11, 21.3, 23.8, 23.12, 26.19, 27.5, 27.16, 27.17, 29.7.

14 Barnatt, *Chatsworth Moorlands*, 13.3, 14.1; Barnatt, *Chatsworth Inbye*, 54.2; Barnatt, *Chatsworth Moorlands*, 19.3, 19.10, 19.11, 19.14, 19.21.

15 Barnatt, *Chatsworth Moorlands*, 12.1.

16 Barnatt, *To each their own.*

17 Groups of rectangular fields, side by side, with boundaries between each that have the same orientation.

18 Barnatt, *Chatsworth Moorlands*, 19.11, 19.14, 19.21.

19 Barnatt, *Chatsworth Moorlands*, 13.3/14.1/54.2.

20 Barnatt, *Chatsworth Moorlands*, 26.1. Possibly sites – Barnatt, *Chatsworth Moorlands*, 16.14, 23.8, 23.12, 30.9.

21 Barnatt, *Chatsworth Moorlands*, 15.11, 25.2. Possible sites – Barnatt, *Chatsworth Moorlands*, 14.19, 27.16, 27.17, 29.7.

22 Barnatt, *Chatsworth Moorlands*, 17.11, 21.3, 26.19, 27.5.

23 Barnatt, *Chatsworth Inbye*, 54.2.

24 Barnatt, *Chatsworth Inbye*, 53.4, 54.11.

25 Barnatt, *Chatsworth Inbye*, 38.58, 43.27, 44.2, 44.11, 44.15, 44.20, 44.25, 44.31, 44.32, 45.1.

26 Barnatt, *Chatsworth Inbye*, 36.12, 37.38, 41.18, 41.38, 41.69; Barnatt, *Chatsworth Park*, 7.22, 7.41, 8.15.

27 Barnatt, J. and Robinson, F. (1998) Excavations of a Bronze Age cremation burial and multi-period artefact scatters at Horse Pastures, Beeley, Derbyshire 1994. *Derbyshire Archaeological Journal* 118, pp. 24–64; Barnatt, *Chatsworth Inbye*, 48.28.

28 Burl, H. A. W. (2000) The Stone Circles of Britain, Ireland and Brittany. Yale; Barnatt, J. (1989) Stone Circles in Britain: Taxonomic and Distributional Analyses

and a Catalogue of Sites in England Scotland and Wales (2 vols.). Oxford: British Archaeological Reports, British Series, 215; Barnatt, *The henges, stone circle and ringcairns.*

29 Barnatt, Bronze Age remains; Barnatt, J. (1989) *The Peak District Barrow Survey* (8 volumes). Unpublished report for the Derbyshire Archaeological Advisory Committee. Bakewell: Peak District National Park Authority Archaeology Service archive. Barnatt and Collis, *Barrows.*

30 Barnatt and Bannister, *Vestiges*, pp. 41–50; Barnatt, *Chatsworth Park*, 7.22, 7.41. Barnatt, *Chatsworth Moorlands*, 12.11, 13.23a–c, 13.25a–b, 15.18, 18.1, 18.14, 18.15, 18.19, 19.2, 19.12, 19.19, 20.10, 20.11, 23.11, 26.15, 27.8a–c, 27.13, 27.14; Barnatt, *Chatsworth Inbye*, 37.38, 41.69, 43.27, 44.11, 44.15, 44.25, 44.31, 45.1. Possible sites – Barnatt, *Chatsworth Park*, 8.15; Barnatt, *Chatsworth Moorlands*, 13.8, 13.33, 14.4, 15.7, 18.23, 18.31, 29.14, 30.1; Barnatt, *Chatsworth Inbye*, 36.12, 38.58, 41.18, 41.38, 44.2, 44.20, 44.32.

31 Barnatt and Collis, *Barrows.*

32 Barnatt, *Chatsworth Moorlands*, 18.1.

33 Barnatt, J. (1996) A multi-phased barrow at Liffs Low, near Biggin, Derbyshire. In J. Barnatt and J. Collis, *Barrows*, pp. 124–26, 130–32.

34 Barnatt, *The henges, stone circle and ringcairns*, p. 87; Barnatt, *Barrows*, pp. 28, 92.

35 Beswick, P. and Wright, M. E. (1991) Iron Age burials from Winster. In Hodges, R. and Smith, K. (eds) *Recent Developments in the Archaeology of the Peak District*: pp. 45–56. Sheffield: Sheffield Archaeological Monographs 2; Barnatt, *Barrows*, p. 27.

36 Barnatt, *Chatsworth Moorlands*, 20.12, 20.11.

37 Barnatt, *Chatsworth Moorlands*, 18.19.

38 Barnatt, *Chatsworth Moorlands*, 27.8.

39 Barnatt, *Chatsworth Moorlands*, 13.23.

40 Barnatt, *Chatsworth Moorlands*, 27.13.

41 Barnatt, *Chatsworth Inbye*, 41.69.

42 Barnatt, Chatsworth Moorlands, 18.1; Bateman, T. (1861) Ten Years Diggings in Celtic and Saxon Grave Hills in the Counties of Derby, Stafford and York, p. 87.

43 Bateman, *Ten Years Diggings*, pp. 64–5; Likely to be Barnatt, *Barrows*, Sites 44.11, 44.31/44.39, 45.1, and possibly 43.27, 44.2, 44.15 or 44.20.

44 This is likely to be Barnatt, *Barrows*, Sites 44.31/44.39; Pegge, S. (1792) Derbeiesseira Romana. *Archaeologia* 10, pp. 17–36; Bateman, T. (1848) *Vestiges of the Antiquities of Derbyshire*. London, p. 22.

45 Riley, D. N. (1966) An Early Bronze Age cairn on Harland Edge, Beeley Moor, Derbyshire. *Derbyshire Archaeological Journal* 86, pp. 31–53; Barnatt, *Chatsworth Moorlands*, 18.15.

46 The charcoal produced a radiocarbon date of 2564–1696 Cal BC; Barnatt, J. (1995b) Neolithic and Bronze Age radiocarbon dates from the Peak District: a review. *Derbyshire Archaeological Journal* 115, pp. 5–19.

47 The charcoal produced a radiocarbon date of 2183–1420 Cal BC; Barnatt, *Radiocarbon dates.*

48 Further deposits included Scattered patches of cremated human bone, an inverted food vessel and sherds of others, sherds of collared and cordoned urns, a flint plano-convex knife, a flint scraper and flint flakes.

49 Barnatt, *Chatsworth Moorlands*, 27.8; Radley, J. (1969) A triple cairn and a rectangular cairn of the Bronze Age on Beeley Moor. *Derbyshire Archaeological Journal* 89, pp. 1–17; Barnatt, *The henges, stone circle and ringcairns*, p. 89–90.

50 Barnatt, *Chatsworth Moorlands*, 13.25, 27.8, Possible sites – Barnatt, *Chatsworth Moorlands*, 17.11, 21.3, 26.19, 27.5. Barnatt and Banister, *Vestiges*, pp. 51–2.

51 Barnatt, *Chatsworth Moorlands*, 13.25.

52 Barnatt, *Bronze Age remains*, Cairnfield 34; Barnatt, *Barrows*, Sites 29.23–24; Barnatt and Smith 2004, *Peak District*, Fig. 16.

53 Barnatt, *Chatsworth Moorlands*, 27.8; Barnatt, *Bronze Age remains*, Cairnfield 39; Barnatt and Smith *Peak District*, Fig. 16.

54 Radley, a triple cairn; Barnatt, J. (1991) The prehistoric cairnfield at Highlow Bank, Highlow, Derbyshire: a survey of all remains and excavation of one of the cairns, 1988. *Derbyshire Archaeological Journal* 111, pp. 5–30; Barnatt and Smith *Peak District*, Fig. 16.

55 Prehistoric faience is a form of opaque glass, usually blue in colour.

56 Barnatt, *Chatsworth Moorlands*, 27.13, 27.14, 27.12.

57 Barnatt, *Chatsworth Moorlands*, 14.19, 14.11, 14.22, 15.6, 18.7, 18.8, 18.9, 18.21, 18.28, 18.30, 18.44, 30.4.

58 Barnatt, *Chatsworth Moorlands*, 14.9, 14.18, 14.27, 16.2, 18.37, 18.42, 19.1, 20.11, 20.18, 25.14, 27.5, 27.14, 27.31, 29.7, 29.8, 30.1.

59 Barnatt, *Chatsworth Moorlands*, 19.15; Barnatt, *The henges, stone circle and ringcairns*, pp. 64–66.

60 Barnatt, *Chatsworth Moorlands*, 26.1; Radley, *A ring bank on Beeley Moor*; Barnatt *The henges, stone circle and ringcairns*, p. 66.

61 Barnatt, Bevan and Edmonds, *Gardom's Edge*; Barnatt, J., Bevan, B. and Edmonds, M. (2002) *A landscape through time.*

62 Barnatt, *Chatsworth Moorlands*, 19.9; Barnatt, *The henges, stone circle and ringcairns*, pp. 63–54.

63 Barnatt, *Chatsworth Moorlands*, 30.1; Barnatt, *Barrows*, pp. 42–3.

64 Barnatt, *To each their own.*

65 Barnatt, *Chatsworth Moorlands*, 13.21; Barnatt, *The henges, stone circle and ringcairns*, pp. 62, 64; Burl, A. (1988) *Four Posters: Bronze Age Stone Circles of Western Europe*. Oxford: British Archaeological Reports, British Series, 195. p. 73.

66 Barnatt, *Chatsworth Moorlands*, 13.6–8.

67 Barnatt, *Chatsworth Moorlands*, 14.11.

68 Barnatt, *Chatsworth Moorlands*, 13.6. Barnatt, *Chatsworth Inbye*, 54.3.

69 Barnatt, *Chatsworth Moorlands*, 14.8, 14.12.
70 Hart, C. R. (1981) *The North Derbyshire Archaeological Survey*. Chesterfield: North Derbyshire Archaeological Trust, pp. 73–75; Barnatt and Smith, *Peak District*, pp. 41–46.
71 Hart, C. R. and Makepeace, G. A. (1993) 'Cranes Fort', Conksbury, Youlgreave, Derbyshire: a newly discovered hillfort. *Derbyshire Archaeological Journal* 113, pp. 16–20.
72 Coombs, D. G. and Thompson, F. H. (1979) Excavations of the hill fort of Mam Tor, Derbyshire 1965–69. *Derbyshire Archaeological Journal* 99, pp. 7–51; Gerrish, E. J. S. (1983) The prehistoric pottery from Mam Tor: further considerations. *Derbyshire Archaeological Journal* 103, pp. 43–6; Barnatt, *radiocarbon dates*, Guilbert, G. G. and Vince, A. (1996) Petrology of some prehistoric pottery from Mam Tor. *Derbyshire Archaeological Journal* 116, 49–59; Barnatt, Bevan and Edmonds, *Gardom's Edge*.
73 Barnatt and Smith, *Peak District*, p. 46; Makepeace, G. A. (1999) Cratcliff Rocks – A Forgotten Hillfort. *Derbyshire Archaeological Journal* 119, pp. 12–18.
74 RCHME and PPJPB (1993) An Archaeological Survey and Catalogue of the Northern Halves of Gardom's and Birchen Edges, Baslow, Derbyshire. Unpublished report, NMR no: SK 27 SE 98, National Monuments Record,
Swindon; Barnatt, Chatsworth Moorlands, Site 12.10.
75 Ainsworth, S and Barnatt, J. (1998) A scarp edge enclosure at Gardom's Edge, Baslow, Derbyshire. Derbyshire Archaeological Journal 121, pp. 19–69; Barnatt, Bevan and Edmonds, *Gardom's Edge*; Barnatt, J., Bevan, B. and Edmonds, M. (2001) A time and place for enclosure: Gardom's Edge, Derbyshire. In T. Darvill and J. Thomas (eds) *Neolithic Enclosure*, pp. 111–131; Oswald, A., Dyer, C. and Barber, M. (2001) *The Creation of Monuments: Neolithic Causewayed Enclosures in the British Isles*. Swindon: English Heritage; Barnatt, Bevan and Edmonds, *A landscape through time*.
76 To perpetuate the traditional but increasingly anachronistic dichotomy.
77 Barnatt, *Chatsworth Inbye*, 43.14.
78 Stanley, J. (1954) An Iron Age fort at Ball Cross Farm, Bakewell. *Derbyshire Archaeological Journal* 74, pp. 85–99.
79 Barnatt, *Moving between the monuments*; Barnatt, *Taming the Land*; Barnatt, *To each their own*.
80 Wilson, A and Barnatt, J. (2004) Excavations of a prehistoric clearance cairn and ritual pits on Sir William's Hill, Eyam Moor, Derbyshire, 2000. *Derbyshire Archaeological Journal* 124, pp. 13–63.

Chapter 3: The Elusive Romans

1 Barnatt, Chatsworth Inbye 32.53–54, 33.8, 48.28; Barnatt and Robinson, *A Bronze Age cremation burial*.
2 Barnatt and Smith, *Peak District*, pp. 46–53; Wroe, P. (1982) Roman roads in the Peak District. *Derbyshire Archaeological Journal* 102, pp. 49–73.
3 Barnatt, J. (1999) Prehistoric and Roman mining in the Peak District: present knowledge and future research. *Mining History* 14.2, pp. 19–30.
4 This assumes that there were no specific ore deposits found at that time which were the exception to the rule. Most known ingots are marked 'Ex Arg' which may suggest silver was removed.
5 Roman lead ingots are usually known as 'pigs'.
6 Dearne, M. J., Anderson, S. and Branigan, K. (1995) Excavations at Brough Field, Carsington, 1980. *Derbyshire Archaeological Journal* 115, pp. 37–75; Ling, R. and Courtney, T. (1981) Excavations at Carsington, 1979–80. *Derbyshire Archaeological Journal* 101, pp. 58–87; Ling, R., Hunt, C. O., Manning, W. H., Wild, F. and Wild, J. P. (1990) Excavations at Carsington, 1983–84. *Derbyshire Archaeological Journal* 110, pp. 30–55.
7 Bevan, *Peaks Romana*; Makepeace, *Romano-British rural settlements*.

Chapter 4: Medieval Communities: Villages, Farms and Fields

1 Barnatt and Smith, *Peak District*, pp. 54–59.
2 Sometimes these were new constructions, but equally common was the reuse of prehistoric barrows. Some of the burials have high status grave goods such as swords and the well known Benty Grange helmet.
3 Sidebottom, P. C. (1999) Stone crosses in the Peak and 'the sons of Eadwulf'. *Derbyshire Archaeological Journal* 119, pp. 206–219.
4 Barnatt and Smith, *Peak District*, Fig. 27; Barnatt, *Chatsworth Moorland* 24.12; Sharpe, N. T. (2002) *Crosses of the Peak District*. Ashbourne: Landmark, pp. 40–41.
5 Bailey, M. (2002) *The English Manor c.1200–c.1500*. Manchester University Press; Faith, R (1997) *The English Peasantry and the Growth of Lordship*. Leicester; Lewis C, Dyer, C. C. and Mitchell, P. (2001) *Village, Hamlet and Field: Changing Medieval Settlements in Central England*. Oxford: Windgather.
6 Fealty is the acknowledgment of obligation to fidelity to the lord.
7 In the Peak District these are often reflected by the modern civil parishes.
8 Williams, A. and Martin, G. H. (1992) *Domesday Book:*

A Complete Translation. London: Penguin.

9   Barnatt, *Chatsworth Park* 9.26: Barnatt, *Chatsworth In bye* 48.26, 35.5, 35.6, 32.1, 32.15, 32.55, 39.16, 37.1.

10   Berewicks are outlying subsidiary settlements.

11   Barnatt and Smith, *Peak District*, p. 65.

12   The exact size of the royal manorial centres are difficult to assess as the given values in Domesday include the berewicks as well as the centres.

13   Hart, C. R. (1981) *The North Derbyshire Archaeological Survey*, pp. 154–62; Barnatt and Smith, *Peak District*, pp. 71–76.

14   Barnatt, *Chatsworth Inbye* 48.28.

15   Barnatt, *Chatsworth Park* 7.7; Sharpe, N. T. (2002) *Crosses of the Peak District*. Ashbourne: Landmark, p. 68.

16   Barnatt, *Chatsworth Inbye* 37.38.

17   Barnatt, *Chatsworth Moorland* 21.13.

18   Hart, C. R. and Robinson, C. (1993) Recent fieldwork on Beeley Warren, Beeley, Derbyshire. *Transactions of the Hunter Archaeological Society* 17, pp. 63–65; Barnatt, *Chatsworth Moorland* 19.13.

19   Sharpe, *Crosses*, p. 23–4.

20   Craven, M. and Stanley, M. (2001) *The Derbyshire Country House* (2 vols). Ashbourne: Landmark, pp. 107–09.

21   Whitlock, R. (1979) Historic Forests of England. London: Moonraker.

22   Barnatt and Smith, *Peak District*, pp. 92–93; Wiltshire, M., Woore, S., Crisp, B. and Rick. B. (2005) *Duffield Frith: History and Evolution of the Landscape of a Medieval Royal Forest*. Ashbourne: Landmark. Note: Duffield Frith later came to the Crown.

23   A pale is a term for a deer park 'fence', usually of wood, often with earthworks, and sometimes a wall.

24   Roffe, D. (1986) *The Derbyshire Domesday*. Darley Dale: Derbyshire Museums Service; Barnatt and Smith, *Peak District*, pp. 59–62.

25   Where a small number of large fields around settlements were farmed communally, each divided into many cultivation strips that were redistributed amongst individual farmers each year. Each farmer was given strips that were intermingled with other peoples. The lord of the manor also held some of this land, which was farmed for him by the local farmers.

26   Barnatt and Smith, *Peak District*, pp. 64–76.

27   Barnatt and Bannister, *Vestiges*, pp. 63–70.

28   Senior, W. (1617) *Lees and Edensore*. Bound volume of early-17th century surveys by William Senior, Chatsworth House. There are also later plans which show this layout – Barker, G. (1773) *A plan of Chatsworth Park and pleasure ground belonging to His Grace the Duke of Devonshire*, Chatsworth House, map 3330; Untitled and unfinished map of Edensor Village (1785), Chatsworth House, uncalendared map.

29   See Chapter 5.

30   The main road to the west is a late 18th or early 19th century addition.

31   Untitled and unfinished map of Edensor, Pilsley and Beeley (1785), Chatsworth House, map 2558 (20).

32   The road from the south-east is a 19th century addition.

33   1785 unfinished map of Edensor, Pilsley and Beeley.

34   Barnatt, *Chatsworth Inbye* 32.15, 32.55.

35   Senior, W. (n.d.) *Pilsley and Birchill*, Bound volume of early 17th century surveys by William Senior, Chatsworth House; Fowkes, D. V. and Potter, G. R. (eds) (1988) *William Senior's Survey of the Estates of the First and Second Earls of Devonshire c. 1600–28*. Chesterfield: Derbyshire Record Society, Volume 13, p. 134.

36   Barnatt, *Chatsworth Inbye* site 39.16.

37   Map of Birchill (1778). Chatsworth House, map 3020S.

38   Senior, *Lees and Edensore*.

39   Cameron, K. (1959) *The Place-Names of Derbyshire (3 Vols)*. Cambridge: Cambridge University Press, p. 91.

40   Barnatt and Bannister, *Vestiges*, pp. 63–70.

41   Senior, *Chatsworth*; Barnatt, *Chatsworth Park* 2.1, 2.4, 2.16.

42   Wightman, W. E. (1961) Open field agriculture in the Peak District. *Derbyshire Archaeological Journal* 81, pp. 111–125, p. 120.

43   Brighton, T. (1996) In search of medieval Chatsworth. *Bakewell and District Historical Society Journal* 23, pp. 21–35, p. 22.

44   Brighton, *Medieval Chatsworth*, p. 30.

45   Cameron, *Place-Names*, p. 73.

46   Barnatt, *Chatsworth Inbye* 50.1, 52.1/52.4; Cameron, *Place-Names*, pp. 44, 82.

47   Barnatt, *Chatsworth Moorland* 19.25.

48   Barnatt, *Chatsworth Inbye* 31.1; Cameron, *Place-Names*, p. 41.

49   Cameron, *Place-Names*, p. 41.

50   Cameron, *Place-Names*, p. 91.

51   It cannot be Calton Houses as this did not yet exist when Senior drew his 1617 map.

52   Barnatt, *Chatsworth Inbye* 44.34.

53   Chadwick, Rev. H. (1923) The Manor of Beeley. Derbyshire Archaeological Journal 45, pp. 24–41.

54   Chadwick, *Manor of Beeley*; Henstock, A. (1980) The course of Hereward Street; a reappraisal. *Derbyshire Archaeological Journal* 100, pp. 35–42; Robinson, F. (1993) *The Fields of Beeley: a Parish Survey*. Unpublished dissertation, University of Sheffield.

55   Frank Robinson *pers. comm.*

56   Chadwick, *Manor of Beeley*.

57   Cameron, *Place-Names*, p. 74.

58   Barnatt and Bannister, *Vestiges*, pp. 70–77.

59   Ridge and furrow comprises low linear ridges with shallow gullies between, which when broad often have origins as the cultivation strips used within medieval open fields. When these strips followed the contours of sloping ground they form narrow terraces with steep breaks of slope between and are termed strip lynchets.

60   Barnatt and Smith, *Peak District*, pp. 76–83.

61   The worst case of the Black Death hit in 1348 but there were subsequent outbreaks in later decades. The main period of civil unrest was during the Wars of the Roses between 1455 and 1485.

62   Barnatt, *Chatsworth Park* 7.1, 7.2, 7.4, 7.5, 8.1, 8.13, 8.16, 8.33, 9.7, 9.13 and possibly 7.3, 8.5, 9.12.

63   Barnatt, *Chatsworth Inbye* 38.5, 38.46 and possibly 36.21, 36.23, 36.39 (which may alternatively been in Pilsley's fields).

64   Senior, *Lees and Edensore*; Fowkes and Potter, *Senior's Survey*, pp. 134–6.

65   See Chapter 5.

66   Barnatt, *Chatsworth Inbye* 48.8, 48.13, 48.33, 49.1, 49.4, 52.26.

67   Jackson, J. C. (1962) Open field cultivation in Derbyshire. *Derbyshire Archaeological Journal* 82, pp. 54–72; Doe, V. S. (1973) The common fields of Beeley in the 17th century. *Derbyshire Archaeological Journal* 93, pp. 45–54; Robinson, *Fields of Beeley*.

68   Barnatt, *Chatsworth Inbye* 52.11.

69   1785 unfinished map of Edensor, Pilsley and Beeley.

70   Barnatt, *Chatsworth Inbye* 37.22, 37.35.

71   Untitled survey of Edensor and Pilsley (1785), Chatsworth archives, map 2581; Potter, P. (1805) Survey of the Hamlet of Pilsley and of the Liberty of Birchill, Chatsworth House, map 4083; Potter, P. (1805) Map of the Hamlet of Pilsley in the Parish of Edensor and of the Liberty of Birchill in the Parish of Bakewell, both being in the County of Derby, Chatsworth House, map 4084; Barnatt, Chatsworth Inbye 37.69.

72   Senior, *Pilsley and Birchill*.

73   Hart, *The North Derbyshire Archaeological Survey*, p. 134; Barnatt, J. (1993) *Greenwood Farm, Hathersage, Derbyshire: Archaeological Survey 1993*. Unpublished report. Bakewell: Peak District National Park Authority Cultural Heritage Team archive; Barnatt and Smith, *Peak District*, Fig. 38.

74   Herring, P. (2006) Medieval Fields at Brown Willy, Bodmin Moor. In: S. Turner (ed.) *Medieval Devon and Cornwall: Shaping an Ancient Countryside*. Oxford: Windgather.

75   Barnatt, *Chatsworth Park* 2.9, 4.14, 4.23, and possibly 2.16, 2.22, 2.24, 4.25.

76   1785 untitled survey of Edensor and Pilsley

77   Cameron, *Place-Names*, p. 42.

78   Barnatt, *Chatsworth Inbye* 31.30 and possibly 31.47.

79   Barnatt, *Chatsworth Inbye* 41.6, 41.25, 41.29, 41.40, 41.48, 41.50, 41.65; Senior, W. (1616) *Ashford and Holme*. Bound volume of early 17th century surveys by William Senior, Chatsworth House.

80   Barnatt, *Chatsworth Inbye* 46.46.

81   Barnatt, *Chatsworth Inbye* 44.12, 44.16.

82   Barnatt, *Chatsworth Moorland* 22.2–22.4, 22.18, 22.19, 22.21.

83   Respectively cut peat/soil and brushwood.

84   Barnatt and Bannister, *Vestiges*, pp. 77–79.

85   Barnatt, *Chatsworth Moorland* 21.4, 24.4.

86   Barnatt, *Chatsworth Moorland* 21.13.

87   Chadwick, *Manor of Beeley*; Henstock, *Hereward Street*; Robinson, *Fields of Beeley*.

88   See Chapter 6.

89   Barnatt, *Chatsworth Moorland* 19.13.

90   Senior, *Chatsworth*.

91   Barnatt, *Chatsworth Inbye* 54.10.

92   Barnatt and Bannister, *Vestiges*, pp. 77–79.

93   Boon work is the term for a manorial duty, for example seasonal work such as ploughing and harvesting done for the lord without cash payment.

94   Roberts, B. and Wrathmell, S. (2002) *Region and Place*. London: English Heritage; Williamson, T. (2003) Shaping Medieval Landscapes: Settlement, Society, Environment. Oxford: Windgather; Williamson, T. (2006) Mapping field patterns: a case study from Eastern England. *Landscapes* 7.1, pp. 55–67.

95   Barnatt and Smith, *Peak District*, Fig. 32.

96   In several places across the Peak, boundaries shown on Senior's early 17th century maps survive as banks and ditches. Here they were not later superseded by drystone walls as these boundaries fell out of use at an early date. Similarly, in some dispersed settlement areas the available evidence suggests that walls replace earlier hedges.

Chapter 5: The Cavendish Era: The Designed Landscape

1   Reviewed in Barnatt and Williamson, *Chatsworth*.

2   Senior surveys of *Ashford and Holme, Chatsworth, Lees and Edensore, Pilsley and Birchill*; Fowkes, and Potter, *Senior's Survey*.

3   Unwin, G. (1831) Untitled map of Devonshire holdings between Chatsworth/Beeley and Buxton. Chatsworth House, map 2661S.

4   Sheldon, J. (1975) *A Short History of Baslow and Bubnell*. Privately published.

5   Chadwick, *Manor of Beeley*.

6   These included the remainder of the present Cracknowl Pasture holding, which was acquired from the Arkwright family in the early 19th century, and land south-east of Birchill and in the Ballcross area, both of which lay within Bakewell Manor. The latter area had been owned by the Viscount of Melbourne in 1810 and was acquired by the Chatsworth Estate soon afterwards.

7   The exceptions are areas around the fringes, at the

Longside Moor area which were not acquired from the Arkwright Estate until after the late-1840s, and at Big and Little Bumper Pieces which were largely still held by the Duke of Rutland in 1831 and had been privatised at the Darley Enclosure Award of 1769.

8   Unwin's plan shows that the Beeley moors were seen as belong to the Estate several months before the Award was formalised.

9   Barnatt and Smith, *Peak District*, pp. 98–99; Craven and Stanley, *The Derbyshire Country House*.

10 Thompson, F. (1949) *A History of Chatsworth: being a supplement to the Sixth Duke of Devonshire's Handbook*. London: Country Life; Pevsner, N. (1978) *The Buildings of England: Derbyshire* (second edition). Harmondsworth: Penguin; Brighton, T. (1995) Chatsworth's sixteenth-century parks and gardens. *Garden History* 23.1, pp. 29–55; Duchess of Devonshire (1982) *The House. A portrait of Chatsworth*. London; Duchess of Devonshire (1987) *The Garden at Chatsworth*. Derby; Duchess of Devonshire (1990) *The Estate. A View from Chatsworth*. London; Pearson, J. (2002) Stags and Serpents: a History of the Cavendish Family and the Dukes of Devonshire (revised edition). Bakewell; Percifull and Thomas, *The Park and Gardens*; Percifull and Thomas, *A Notebook*; Williamson, *A Brief History*; Barnatt and Williamson, *Chatsworth*.

11 Barnatt, *Chatsworth Park* 2.47, 2.48; Barnatt and Williamson, *Chatsworth*, pp. 40–44, 116, 153–54, 161, 164.

12 Barnatt, *Chatsworth Park* 1.11; Barnatt and Williamson, *Chatsworth*, p. 76.

13 Barker, *A plan of Chatsworth Park*.

14 Barnatt, *Chatsworth Park* 1.7; Barnatt and Williamson, *Chatsworth*, pp. 137–42.

15 Barnatt, *Chatsworth Park* 1.8, 6.10.

16 Tom Williamson *pers. comm.*

17 Barnatt and Williamson, *Chatsworth*, pp. 44–49.

18 Barnatt and Williamson, *Chatsworth*, pp. 156–57.

19 Barnatt and Williamson, *Chatsworth*, pp. 98–100.

20 Barnatt and Bannister, *Vestiges*, pp. 103–05.

21 Barnatt and Williamson, *Chatsworth*, pp. 9, 45.

22 Barnatt and Williamson, *Chatsworth*, p. 48; Williamson, T. (2006) *The Archaeology of Rabbit Warrens*. Shire.

23 Barnatt, *Chatsworth Park* 9.17.

24 Brighton, T. (2004) *The Discovery of the Peak District*. Chichester: Phillimore, pp. 147–8, 151.

25 Pillow mounds are artificial mounds made for rabbits to inhabit, used to control and increase their breeding population. Barnatt, *Chatsworth Park* 9.14–9.16.

26 Chatsworth Archives, C/13, C/15, C/107, L91/1/1–4, L/91/3/1–4, L/94/56, AS/98, AS/1062, AS/1063, AS/1064, AS/1065.

27 Barnatt, *Chatsworth Park* 9.12.

28 Barnatt and Williamson, *Chatsworth*, p. 83.

29 Barnatt and Bannister, *Vestiges*, pp. 133–35.

30 Chatsworth Archives, C/107.

31 Even the old deer park has some indications of division

into fields in its lowermost part – see Barnatt and Williamson, *Chatsworth*, p. 83.

32 Chatsworth Archives, AS/1408.

33 Chatsworth Archives AS/98.

34 Barnatt and Williamson, *Chatsworth*, Fig. 34.

35 Barnatt and Williamson, *Chatsworth*, pp. 73–76, 201–02, Fig. 34.

36 Barnatt, *Chatsworth Park* 6.18.

37 Barnatt, *Chatsworth Park* 6.17.

38 Barnatt, *Chatsworth Park* 19.4, 19.28, 20.8, 21.1; Barnatt, *Chatsworth Inbye* 53.16, 54.32.

39 Barnatt, *Chatsworth Park* 14.5, 16.23, 54.20.

40 Barnatt and Williamson, *Chatsworth*, pp 143–48, 201–02, Fig. 34.

41 Barnatt, *Chatsworth Park* 6.16.

42 Barnatt, *Chatsworth Park* 6.15.

43 Barnatt, *Chatsworth Park* 5.11, 13.2, 15.2, 55.7.

44 Barnatt, *Chatsworth Inbye* 54.23; Barnatt and Williamson, *Chatsworth*, p. 201.

45 A rough map of roads from Chatsworth to Chesterfield (1824), Chatsworth House, map 3236; Unwin, Untitled map of Devonshire holdings.

46 Barnatt, *Chatsworth Inbye* 43.32.

47 Barnatt, *Chatsworth Park* 2.13, 2.14.

48 Barnatt, *Chatsworth Park* 2.43.

49 Barnatt, *Chatsworth Park* 2.35, 4.32, 7.16, 7.23.

50 This observation applies to both the 1760s park and enlargements to this made in the 1820s.

51 Barnatt and Williamson, *Chatsworth*, pp. 8–11, 121–125.

52 Barnatt and Williamson, *Chatsworth*, pp. 8–11, 180–81.

53 Barnatt and Williamson, *Chatsworth*, p. 164.

54 These spectacular wrought-iron gates were made in the late 17th century and originally stood outside the House, but were moved to their present position in about 1840.

55 Percifull, E and Thomas, *A Notebook*; Bannister and Bannister, *Chatsworth Buildings*, 2.15, 5.4, 5.5.

56 Bannister and Bannister, *Chatsworth Buildings*, 4.1, 4.7; Barbrook House unfortunately had to be demolished in the 1960s having succumbed to dry rot.

57 Bannister and Bannister, *Chatsworth Buildings*, 3.37.

58 Bannister and Bannister, *Chatsworth Buildings*, 2.33.

59 Bannister and Bannister, *Chatsworth Buildings*, 5.55, 7.1.

60 Bannister and Bannister, *Chatsworth Buildings*, 4.10.

61 Bannister and Bannister, *Chatsworth Buildings*, 5.42.

62 Barnatt and Williamson, *Chatsworth*, pp. 157–69; Barnatt and Bannister, *Vestiges*, pp. 98–103.

63 Bannister and Bannister, *Chatsworth Buildings*, 5.6.

64 Bannister and Bannister, *Chatsworth Buildings*, 5.28, 5.29; Read, H. (1995) *Edensor 1760–1860: A Century of Change*. Unpublished typescript, Chatsworth House.

65 Barnatt, J. with Rieuwerts, J. H. and Roberts, J. G. (1996) *The Lead Mine Related Landscape of the Peak District: Part 1 – Smelting Sites, Fuel Sources and Communications*. Unpublished Report for English Heritage. Bakewell: Peak District National Park Authority Cultural Heritage Team

archive; Bevan, B. (2004) *The Upper Derwent: 10.000 Years in a Peak District Valley.* Port Stroud: Tempus, pp. 131–34; Barnatt and Williamson, Chatsworth, pp. 45–6.

66 Such coppices also commonly included standards spaced within the wood, which were left unfelled.

67 Farey, J. (1813) *General View of the Agriculture and Minerals of Derbyshire* (Vol. 2). London.

68 Barnatt and Bannister, *Vestiges*, pp. 91–96.

69 Barnatt and Williamson, *Chatsworth,* pp. 98–100.

70 Barnatt, *Chatsworth Park* 9.8, 9.10.

71 Barnatt, *Chatsworth Inbye* 43.28.

72 Barnatt and Bannister, *Vestiges*, pp. 91–96.

73 Senior, *Lees and Edensore*; Lindop Wood has been extensively replanted and now is mostly conifers.

74 Ordnance Survey (1879) 25 inch to a mile map.

75 Campbell, E. (1855) Plan of lands in Edensor, Pilsley, Birchill and Bakewell belonging to His Grace the Duke of Devonshire, Chatsworth House, map 2520; Map of Edensor and Pilsley (1867) Chatsworth House, uncalendared map; 1879 Ordnance Survey.

76 1785 untitled survey of Edensor and Pilsley.

77 Earthworks associated with this survive over much of the length except the Edensor end. Barnatt, *Chatsworth Inbye* 38:60.

78 Barnatt, *Chatsworth Inbye* 38.2.

79 Barnatt, *Chatsworth Inbye* 36.22.

80 1785 untitled survey of Edensor and Pilsley.

81 Barnatt and Williamson, *Chatsworth,* pp. 156–57.

82 Barnatt, *Chatsworth Inbye* 53.10, 54.21.

Chapter 6: The Cavendish Era: The Farmed Landscape

1 Barnatt and Bannister, *Vestiges*, pp. 64–66, 115–16.

2 Bannister and Bannister, *Chatsworth Buildings,* 2.21; Barnatt, *Chatsworth Inbye* 34.6, Bannister, *Chatsworth Buildings,* 2.22a; Barnatt, *Chatsworth Moorland* 12.37

3 Ward, G. H. B. (1926) Transcription of Baslow Boundary. *Sheffield Clarion Ramblers 1925–26*, pp. 140–143; Barnatt, *Chatsworth Inbye* 55.1, 53.1.

4 Bannister and Bannister, *Chatsworth Buildings,* 6.1; Barnatt, *Chatsworth Inbye* 40.6.

5 Bannister and Bannister, *Chatsworth Buildings,* 2.4; Barnatt, *Chatsworth Inbye* 33.11.

6 Bannister and Bannister, *Chatsworth Buildings;* Bannister, *Chatsworth Buildings*; Barnatt and Bannister, *Vestiges*, pp. 116–32.

7 Bannister and Bannister, *Chatsworth Buildings,* 7.15, 7.25, 7.35, 7.36, Bannister, *Chatsworth Buildings,* 7.31; Barnatt, *Chatsworth Inbye* 37.1.

8 Bannister and Bannister, *Chatsworth Buildings,* 7.41; Barnatt, *Chatsworth Inbye* 37.1.

9 Bannister and Bannister, *Chatsworth Buildings,* 7.1; Barnatt, *Chatsworth Inbye* 36.51.

10 Bannister and Bannister, *Chatsworth Buildings,* 7.46; Barnatt, *Chatsworth Inbye* 37.1.

11 Plans of the Houses, Buildings, Gardens in Beeley (1850) Chatsworth House. Uncalendared plans; Barnatt and Bannister, *Vestiges*, pp. 118–23.

12 Bannister and Bannister, *Chatsworth Buildings,* 3.19; Barnatt, *Chatsworth Inbye* 48.26.

13 Existing buildings that were formerly thatched include 5 Brookside, the cottage east of Club Cottage, Rose Cottage, Last Cottage and Chapel Terrace; Bannister and Bannister, *Chatsworth Buildings,* 3.5, 3.6, 3.18, 3.27, 3.28; Barnatt, *Chatsworth Inbye* 48.26.

14 Bannister and Bannister, *Chatsworth Buildings,* 2.12, 7.50.

15 Bannister and Bannister, *Chatsworth Buildings,* 3.31;

Barnatt, *Chatsworth Inbye* 48.26.

16 Bannister and Bannister, *Chatsworth Buildings,* 3.6; Barnatt, *Chatsworth Inbye* 48.26.

17 Frank Robinson *pers comm.*

18 Bannister and Bannister, *Chatsworth Buildings,* 3.3, 3.4; Barnatt, *Chatsworth Inbye* 48.26.

19 Bannister and Bannister, *Chatsworth Buildings,* 3.2; Barnatt, *Chatsworth Inbye* 48.26.

20 Bannister and Bannister, *Chatsworth Buildings,* 2.12.

21 Bannister and Bannister, *Chatsworth Buildings,* 2.11; Barnatt, *Chatsworth Inbye* 35.5, 35.6.

22 Bannister and Bannister, *Chatsworth Buildings,* 5.33; Barnatt, *Chatsworth Inbye* 46.35.

23 Bannister and Bannister, *Chatsworth Buildings,* 5.38; Barnatt, *Chatsworth Inbye* 46.35.

24 Bannister and Bannister, *Chatsworth Buildings,* 6.2; Barnatt, *Chatsworth Inbye* 39.16.

25 This was demolished sometime after 1871; Tithe Appointment Plan of Bubnell Township in the Parish of Bakewell in the County of Derby (1847), Derbyshire Record Office D2057A/PI41/2a; Map of Bubnell & Baslow (1871), Chatsworth Estate Office map 2553; Bannister and Bannister, *Chatsworth Buildings,* 2.5; Barnatt, *Chatsworth Inbye* 31.1.

26 Bannister and Bannister, *Chatsworth Buildings,* 3.34; Barnatt, *Chatsworth Inbye* 50.1.

27 Bannister, *Chatsworth Buildings,* 3.26; Barnatt, *Chatsworth Inbye* 52.1, 52.4; Chadwick, *Manor of Beeley.*

28 Barnatt, *Chatsworth Inbye* 52.2.

29 Wade Martins, S. (2002) *The English Model Farm, Building the Agricultural Ideal, 1700–1914.* Wade Martins, S. (2004) *Farmers, Landlords and Landscapes: Rural Britain 1720 to 1870.* Oxford: Windgather.

30 Bannister, *Chatsworth Buildings,* 4.4; Barnatt, *Chatsworth Inbye* 35.14.

31 Bannister and Bannister, *Chatsworth Buildings,* 4.2;

32 Duchess of Devonshire, *The House.*

33 Bannister and Bannister, *Chatsworth Buildings,* 5.56, 5.57; Barnatt, *Chatsworth Inbye* 36.64, 36.63.

34 Bannister and Bannister, *Chatsworth Buildings,* 7.2; Barnatt, *Chatsworth Inbye* 36.52.

35 Bannister and Bannister, *Chatsworth Buildings,* 2.25; Barnatt, *Chatsworth Inbye* 55.1.

36 This was here by 1824 at the latest as it is shown on the 1824 'A rough map of roads from Chatsworth to Chesterfield'; Bannister and Bannister, *Chatsworth Buildings,* 4.11; Barnatt, *Chatsworth Inbye* 53.1.

37 Bannister and Bannister, *Chatsworth Buildings,* 2.20; Barnatt, *Chatsworth Inbye* 34.1.

38 Bannister and Bannister, *Chatsworth Buildings,* 2.22; Barnatt, *Chatsworth Moorland* 12.49.

39 Tithe Appointment Plan of the Township of Baslow in the Parish of Bakewell in the County of Derby (1848) Matlock: Derbyshire Record Office, D2360/DL93a; Ordnance Survey (1879).

40 Barnatt and Bannister, *Vestiges,* pp. 133–65, 235–92.

41 Senior, *Chatsworth;* Senior, *Lees and Edensore.*

42 Barnatt, *Chatsworth Park* 2.1, 2.31, 2.37, 3.1.

43 Barnatt, *Chatsworth Park* 2.4.

44 Barnatt, *Chatsworth Park* 4.13, 4.15, 4.22, 4.24, 4.27.

45 Barnatt, *Chatsworth Park* 7.1, 7.2, 7.3, 7.4, 7.5, 8.1, 8.5, 8.13, 8.16, 8.33, 9.12, 9.13, 9. 22.

46 Barnatt, *Chatsworth Inbye* 43.30, 44.4, 44.9, 44.19, 44.24.

47 Doe, *The common fields of Beeley.*

48 Enclosure Award Map of the Township of Beeley in the County of Derby (1832), Matlock: Derbyshire Record Office, Q/RI 16.; anon. 1836 Two maps entitled *'Beeley'.* Chatsworth House, uncalendared maps.

49 Barnatt and Bannister, *Vestiges,* pp. 142–48.

50 Farey, *General View,* Vol. 2, p. 84.

51 Hodges, R. (1991) Wall-to-Wall History: the Story of Roystone Grange. London: Duckworth.

52 Campbell, E. (1855) *Plan of the Duke of Devonshire's Estate in the township of Beeley in the County of Derbyshire, Revised by Ed. Campbell,* Chatsworth Estate Office, map 2526.

53 Barnatt and Bannister, *Vestiges,* pp. 179–89.

54 Bannister and Bannister, *Chatsworth Buildings,* 5.51, 5.65, 5.82, 5.83; Barnatt, *Chatsworth Inbye* 38.10, 38.38, 36.28, 36.27.

55 Bannister and Bannister, *Chatsworth Buildings,* 5.74, 5.71, 5.70, 5.69, 5.68, 5.66, 5.65, 5.64, 5.63, 5.62; Barnatt, *Chatsworth Inbye* 38.26, 38.29–30, 38.33, 38.36–38, 38.43, 38.54, 38.57.

56 Bannister, *Chatsworth Buildings,* 5.81; Barnatt, *Chatsworth Inbye* 36.24.

57 Bannister, *Chatsworth Buildings,* 6.5; Barnatt, *Chatsworth Inbye* 41.68.

58 Bannister, *Chatsworth Buildings,* 5.36; Barnatt, *Chatsworth Inbye* 46.43.

59 Although other examples are known, as near Greenwood Farm south of Hathersage, see Barnatt, *Greenwood Farm.*

60 Barnatt and Bannister, *Vestiges,* pp. 165–71.

61 They are relatively frequent at Yeld Farm, Bramley Farm, Bubnell Farm, Bubnell Cliff Farm and Harewood Grange, with fewer examples at Calton Lees, Beeley, Cracknowl Pasture and Pilsley. Areas where these posts do not occur are Birchill, Edensor, Handley Bottom and Fallinge.

62 Farey, Vol. 2, *General View.*

63 Farey, Vol. 2, *General View,* p. 84.

64 Barnatt and Bannister, *Vestiges,* pp. 175–79.

65 Barnatt, *Chatsworth Inbye* 41.8, 41.9, 41.10, 41.16, 41.21, 41.22, 41.37, 41.44, 41.53, 41.55, 41.61, 41.64, 41.82, 41.83.

66 Barnatt, *Chatsworth Inbye* 43.11, 43.13, 44.28.

67 These occur next to Edensor Village, at Bramley, Bubnell Cliff, west of Pilsley, Birchill, Birchill Flatt and possibly near Pilsley and on Harewood Moor; Barnatt, *Chatsworth Park* 7.8; Barnatt, *Chatsworth Inbye* 31.20, 32.62, 37.43, 39.5, 40.10, 40.14 and possibly 24.8, 36.16, 37.30.

68 Barnatt, *Chatsworth Inbye* 36.54.

69 Barnatt, *Chatsworth Moorland* 13.24, 19.6, 19.8, 27.27.

70 Barnatt, *Chatsworth Moorland* A12.26, 12.29,13.25, 15.7, 15.9, 18.51, 19.33.

71 Hey, D. (2007) The Grouse Moors of the Peak District. In P. S. Barnwell and M. Palmer (eds) *Post-Medieval Landscapes.* Oxford: Windgather.

72 Enclosure Award Map of the Commons and Waste lands in the Township of Baslow, Hamlets of Bubnell, Curbar and Froggatt all in the Manor of Bakewell (1826) Matlock: Derbyshire Record Office, Q/RI 15; *Enclosure Award Map of the Township of 1832.*

73 Barnatt, *Chatsworth Moorland* 13.13, 13.22, 14.20, 16.10, 16.20, 17.6, 17.10, 18.12, 18.22, 20.4, 20.16, 25.6, 26.7, 26.23.

74 Barnatt, *Chatsworth Moorland* 12.6.

75 Barnatt, *Chatsworth Moorland* 25.3.

76 Barnatt, J. (1993) *Edale Valley: Archaeological Survey 1993.* Unpublished report. Bakewell: Peak District National Park Authority Cultural Heritage Team archive; Barnatt and Smith, *Peak District,* Fig. 58; Bevan, *The Upper Derwent,* pp. 103; Barnatt, J. (1987) *A preliminary survey of Archaeological Remains within the Warslow Moors Estate, Staffordshire.* Unpublished report. Bakewell: Peak District National Park Authority Cultural Heritage Team archive.

77 Formerly the Manor and Township of Beeley.

78 Barnatt, *Chatsworth Moorland* 14.24, 17.15, 17.16, 17.17.

79 Sheldon, *Baslow and Bubnell.*

80 Barnatt, *Chatsworth Moorland* 14.24, 17.14.

81 This was part of Brampton by 1831 at the latest.

82 Barnatt, *Chatsworth Moorland* 14.13.

83 Barnatt, *Chatsworth Moorland* 25.9–12.

84 RCHME (1990) *Gibbet Moor, Derbyshire.* Unpublished

report, NMR no: SK 27 SE 22, National Monuments Record, Swindon.

85 RCHME and PPJPB, *An Archaeological Survey and Catalogue of the Northern Halves of Gardom's and Birchen Edge*; Ainsworth, S. and Barnatt, J. (1998) An Archaeological Survey of the Landscape on Big Moor and Ramsley Moor, Baslow and Holmesfield, Derbyshire

(Scheduled Ancient Monument 136). Unpublished report for the National Monuments Record, Swindon.

86 Bill Bevan *pers. comm.*

87 Barnatt, *Chatsworth Moorland* 13.16–17, 16.28; Barnatt, *Chatsworth Inbye* 54.6.

88 Barnatt, *Chatsworth Moorland* 12.28.

89 Sheldon, *Baslow and Bubnell.*

Chapter 7: Wealth from the Earth: Two Thousand Years of Industry

1 Barnatt and Smith, *Peak District*, pp. 111–131.

2 Barnatt, *Prehistoric and Roman mining*; Barnatt, J. and Penny, R. (2004) *The Lead Legacy: The Prospects for the Peak District's Lead Mining Heritage.* Bakewell: Peak District National Park Authority; Barnatt, J. with Rieuwerts, J. (1995) *The Lead Mine Affected Landscape of the Peak District.* Unpublished report. Bakewell: Peak District National Park Authority Cultural Heritage Team archive; Barnatt and Smith, *Peak District*, pp. 111–117; Ford, T. D. and Rieuwerts, J. H. (eds) (2000) *Lead Mining in the Peak District* (4th Edition). Ashbourne: Landmark; Kiernan, D. (1989) *The Derbyshire Lead Industry in the Sixteenth Century.* Chesterfield: Derbyshire Record Society, Vol. 14; Rieuwerts, J. H. (1998) *Glossary of Derbyshire Lead Mining Terms.* Matlock Bath: Peak District Mines Historical Society; Wood, A. (1999) *The Politics of Social Conflict: The Peak Country 1520–1770.* Cambridge: Cambridge University Press.

3 Robey, J. and Porter, L. (1972) *The Copper and Lead Mines of Ecton Hill, Staffordshire.* Ashbourne: Moorland; Porter, L. and Robey, J. (2000) *The Copper and Lead Mines around the Manifold Valley.* Ashbourne: Landmark; Barnatt, J. (2002) The Development of Deep Ecton Mine, Staffordshire, 1723–1760. *Mining History* 15.1, pp. 10–23; Porter, L. (2004) *Ecton Copper Mines under the Dukes of Devonshire: 1760–1790.* Ashbourne: Landmark.

4 Barnatt and Penny, *Lead Legacy.*

5 A pipe is an irregular mineral deposit, rather than one within a vein; Barnatt, J. and Rieuwerts, J. (1998) The Upper Nestus Pipes: an ancient lead mine in the Peak District of Derbyshire. *Mining History* 13.5, pp. 51–64.

6 The water table is the point below which any mine workings would quickly flood unless effective ways of pumping or draining the water were employed.

7 Rieuwerts, J. H. (1987) *History and Gazetteer of the Lead Mine Soughs of Derbyshire.* Sheffield: Privately published; Rieuwerts, J. H. (2007) *Lead Mining in Derbyshire: History, Development & Drainage. Vol. 1: Castleton to the River Wye.* Ashbourne: Landmark.

8 Barnatt, J., Rieuwerts, J. and Thomas, G. H. (1997) Early use of gunpowder in the Peak District: Stone Quarry Mine and Dutchman's Level, Ecton. *Mining History,* 13.4, pp. 24–43; Rieuwerts, J. H. (1998) Early gunpowder work in Longe or Cromford Sough, 1662–3 and 1676–1680.

Mining History 13.6, pp. 1–5; Barnatt, J. and Worthington, T. (2006) Using Coal to Mine Lead: Firesetting at Peak District Mines. *Mining History* 16.3, pp. 1–94.

9 Before this time the only way limestone could be removed was by lighting fires against the rock. This technique, known as firesetting, was a slow process and there was a danger of suffocation from the smoke in the workings; Barnatt and Worthington, *Using Coal to Mine Lead.*

10 The term used for the processing of the ore, by removing unwanted gangue minerals with which the ore was mixed as it came out of the mine, to produce a concentrate ready for sale to the lead smelters.

11 Barnatt, *Chatsworth Inbye* 41.28, 41,32, 41.35, 41.66.

12 Sheffield Archives, Bagshaw Collection, 473.

13 Kiernan *The Derbyshire Lead Industry*; Willies, L. (1990) Derbyshire lead smelting in the eighteenth and nineteenth centuries. *Bulletin of the Peak District Mines Historical Society* 11.1, pp. 1–19; Barnatt, J. with Rieuwerts, J. and Roberts, J. (1996) *The Lead Mine Related Landscape of the Peak District: Part 1 – Smelting Sites, Fuel Sources and Communications.* Unpublished report. Bakewell: Peak District National Park Authority Cultural Heritage Team archive, pp. 25–28.

14 Kiernan, *The Derbyshire Lead Industry*; Barnatt with Rieuwerts and Roberts, *The Lead Mine Related Landscape.*

15 Kiernan, D. and Van de Noort, R. (1992) Bole smelting in Derbyshire. In Willies, L. and Cranstone, D (eds) *Boles and Smeltmills: Report of a Seminar on the History and Archaeology of Lead Smelting held at Reath, Yorkshire, 15–17 May 1992.* Historical Metallurgy Society.

16 Barnatt, *Chatsworth Moorland* 18.41, 18.45, 26.5, 27.20, 27.21, 27.34.

17 Radley, *A triple cairn*; Barnatt, *Chatsworth Moorland* 27.8.

18 Bateman, *Ten Years Diggings*, p. 65; Barnatt, *Chatsworth Inbye* 44.11, 45.1.

19 Barnatt, *Chatsworth Moorland* 27.21.

20 Kiernan, *The Derbyshire Lead Industry*, pp. 170–72; Barnatt and Williamson, *Chatsworth*, pp. 45–6.

21 Crossley, D. and Kiernan, D. (1992) The lead smelting mills of Derbyshire. *Derbyshire Archaeological Journal* 112, pp. 6–47, site 1.4.

22 Crossley and Kiernan, *The lead smelting mills*, site 1.1; Barnatt, *Chatsworth Inbye* 55.37.

23 Barnatt, *Chatsworth Moorland* 17.13.

24 Willies, L. (1969) Cupola lead smelting sites in Derbyshire, 1737–1900. *Bulletin of the Peak District Mines Historical Society* 4.1, 97–115, p. 103; Barnatt with Rieuwerts and Roberts, *The Lead Mine Related Landscape*, p. 46.

25 Barnatt, *Chatsworth Moorland* 22.8, 23.1.

26 Red lead is an oxide of lead which was produced in a furnace from lead ores and used as a pigment for paint and dyeing.

27 Willies, L. (1973) The Barker family and the eighteenth century lead business. *Derbyshire Archaeological Journal* 93, pp. 55–74; Crossley and Kiernan, *The lead smelting mills*, p. 34; Barnatt with Rieuwerts and Roberts, *The Lead Mine Related Landscape*, p. 39.

28 Barnatt and Smith, *Peak District*, pp. 112, 117–19.

29 Hopkinson, G. G. (1957) The development of the South Yorkshire and North Derbyshire coalfield, 1500–1775. *Transactions of the Hunter Archaeological Society* 7.6, pp. 295–319.

30 Farey, J. (1811) General View of the Agriculture and Minerals of Derbyshire, Vol. 1. London; Lund, J. (1998) *An Archaeological Survey of the Surface Coal Mine Remains on the Eastern Moors of the Peak District.* Unpublished report. Bakewell: Peak District National Park Authority Cultural Heritage Team archive.

31 Barnatt, *Chatsworth Moorland* 13.1; Barnatt, *Chatsworth Inbye* 55.6, 55.34; Barnatt and Bannister, *Vestiges*, pp. 199–203; Barnatt and Smith, *Peak District*, p. 9.

32 The core area of the mining, near the outcrop is now Open Access land, whereas the deeper shaft sites are on private Chatsworth Estate farmland.

33 Chatsworth Archive AS/948.

34 Untitled map of the southern half of the Baslow Colliery (1832), Coal Authority Archives, plan EM 817; Barnatt and Williamson, *Chatsworth*, pp. 154–6.

35 Ward, G. H. B. (1935) Facts about Robin Hood (Baslow) and Millstone Bridge Toll Bar. *Sheffield Clarion Ramblers 1934–35*, pp. 133–150.

36 Barnatt, *Chatsworth Inbye* 53.8, 53.9.

37 Chatsworth archives, Hardwick Manuscripts 27.

38 Chatsworth archives, Hardwick Manuscripts, book of disbursements 1656–1668.

39 Chatsworth archives AS/1064.

40 Barnatt and Bannister, *Vestiges*, pp. 201–03; Barnatt and Williamson, *Chatsworth*, pp. 154–56.

41 This was part of the agreement drawn up to work the coal under the park.

42 Untitled map of the southern half of the Baslow Colliery; Farey, *General View, Vol. 1*, p 193.

43 Barnatt, *Chatsworth Moorland* 20.7.

44 Barnatt, *Chatsworth Moorland* 20.7; Barnatt and Bannister, *Vestiges*, pp. 203–04.

45 Chadwick, *The Manor of Beeley*; Hopkinson, *South Yorkshire and North Derbyshire coalfield*, p. 297.

46 Farey, *General View, Vol. 1*, p. 190.

47 The very variable 'seat-earths' below coal seams are known today as ganister and fire clay, and range from extremely hard and fine grained silica-rich rock to soft clays. Several had refractory qualities and historically were useful in making firebricks and for iron/steel smelting.

48 Records exist within Chatsworth archives (L 94/77 blue) of an assessment of the Beeley Colliery made in 1835, written by J. A. Twigg and deposited in the Chatsworth Archives in 1886, appended to a second report written in that year by R. G. Coke. Exploration for coal somewhere on Beeley Moor is noted in 1864–65 in Burdekin, T. A. (ed.) (2003) *A Victorian Farmers Diary. William Hodkin's Diary 1864–66. Life in and around Beeley on the Chatsworth Estate.* Matlock: Derbyshire County Council. Assessed in: Webster, R. (2006) Coal Mining on Beeley Moor, Peak District Mines Historical Society Newsletter 119, pp. 6–7.

49 Barnatt, *Chatsworth Moorland* 14.15, 14.17.

50 Farey, *General View, Vol. 1*, pp. 188–215; Barnatt with Rieuwerts and Roberts, *The Lead Mine Related Landscape*.

51 Barnatt and Smith, *Peak District*, pp. 121–27.

52 Radley, J. (1963–4) Peak millstones and Hallamshire grindstones. *Transactions of the Newcomen Society* 36, pp. 165–173; Tucker, G. (1985) Millstone making in the Peak District of Derbyshire: the quarries and the technology. *Industrial Archaeology Review* 8.1, pp. 42–58; Polak, J. P. (1987) The production and distribution of Peak millstones from the sixteenth to the eighteenth centuries. *Derbyshire Archaeological Journal* 107, pp. 55–72.

53 Kerry, Rev. C. (1900) The court rolls of Baslow, Derbyshire, commencing anno 13 Ed. II (1319–20). *Derbyshire Archaeological Journal* 22, pp. 52–90; Kerry, Rev. C. (1901) The court rolls of Baslow, Derbyshire, (continued). *Derbyshire Archaeological Journal* 23, pp. 1–39; Polak, *Peak millstones*.

54 Masser, A. P. (1996) *The Peak Millstone Quarries of Gardom's Edge, Baslow: a Survey.* Unpublished M.A. thesis, University of Sheffield; Barnatt and Williamson, *Chatsworth*, p. 84.

55 Chatsworth archives L91/1/1.

56 Chatsworth Archives AS/948.

57 Radley, *Peak millstones and Hallamshire grindstones*; Tucker, *Millstone making*; Masser, *The Peak Millstone Quarries*.

58 Barnatt, *Chatsworth Moorland – scarp* 12.2, 12.3, 12.7, 12.8, 12.9, 12.61 and below 12.5, 12.16, 12.17.

59 Barnatt, *Chatsworth Moorland* 12.4, 12.13, 12.19, 12.31.

60 Barnatt, *Chatsworth Moorland* 12.7, 12.13, 12.61.

61 Radley, J. (1964) A millstone maker's smithy on Gardom's Edge, Baslow. *Derbyshire Archaeological Journal* 84, pp. 123–127.

62 Barnatt, *Chatsworth Moorland* 12.16.

63 Barnatt, *Chatsworth Moorland* 12.17.

64 Barnatt, *Chatsworth Park* 3.21; Barnatt, *Chatsworth Inbye* 55.40, 55.41.

65 Barnatt, *Chatsworth Park* 3.16, Barnatt, *Chatsworth Inbye* 55.15.

66 Main sites: Barnatt, *Chatsworth Moorland* 27.3, 27.9, 27.18, 27.19, 27.22, 27.23, 29.10, 30.11. Peripheral workings: Barnatt, *Chatsworth Moorland* 26.16, 26.18, 26.25, 27.7, 27.30, 27.31, 27.35, 30.5, 30.6; Barnatt and Bannister, *Vestiges*, pp. 209–12.

67 Barnatt, *Chatsworth Inbye* 50.8, 50.15.

68 Barnatt, *Chatsworth Moorland* 27.9, 27.22, 27.23.

69 Barnatt, *Chatsworth Moorland* 27.9 or 27.3, 27.19.

70 Earlier quarries: Barnatt, *Chatsworth Moorland* 27.3, 27.9, 27.18, 27.19; later quarries: Barnatt, *Chatsworth Moorland* 27.22, 27.23, 29.10, 30.11; Barnatt, *Chatsworth Inbye*, 50.8, 50.15.

71 Cooper, N. (1991) *Transformation of a Valley: the Derbyshire Derwent.* Cromford: Scarthin; Derwent Valley Mills Partnership (2001) *The Derwent Valley Mills and their Communities.* Matlock; Barnatt and Smith, *Peak District*, pp. 119–21.

72 Barnatt, *Chatsworth Park* 8.20; Barnatt and Williamson, *Chatsworth*, pp. 107–08.

73 Naylor, D. (2005) *The Chatsworth Villages: Beeley, Edensor & Pilsley.* Ashbourne: Landmark, p. 36.

74 Senior, *Lees and Edensore;* 1785 unfinished map of Edensor, Pilsley and Beeley.

75 Bannister and Bannister, *Chatsworth Buildings*, 2.24; Barnatt, *Chatsworth Inbye* 55.35–37.

Chapter 8: Lines Between Places: From Packhorse Routes to Tarmac Roads

1 Hey, D. (1980) *Packmen, Carriers and Packhorse Roads.* Leicester: Leicester University Press; Dodd, A. E. and Dodd, E. M. (1980) *Peakland Roads and Trackways.* Ashbourne: Moorland. 2nd ed.

2 Radley, J. (1963) Peak District roads prior to the turnpike era. *Derbyshire Archaeological Journal* 83, pp. 39–50; Dodd and Dodd, *Peakland Roads*; Barnatt and Smith, *Peak District*, pp. 103–07.

3 Barnatt, *Chatsworth Moorland* 20.9/21.7.

4 Barnatt, *Chatsworth Moorland* 12.12, 12.24.

5 Radley, *Peak District roads.*

6 Barnatt and Bannister, *Vestiges*, pp. 219–22.

7 Barnatt and Smith, *Peak District*, Fig. 56; Barnatt, *Chatsworth Inbye* 34.2.

8 Barnatt, *Chatsworth Park* 3.8, 3.16, 13.10, 13.14, 13.19–20, 14.6, 15.1, 16.18, 17.1; Barnatt, *Chatsworth Inbye* 54.1, 54.5, 54.9, 54.14, 55.3–4, 55.10, 55.15, 55.43.

9 Barnatt, *Chatsworth Moorland* 14.23.

10 Barnatt, *Chatsworth Inbye* 54.9, 54.14.

11 Dodd and Dodd, *Peakland Roads*, p. 124.

12 Barnatt, *Chatsworth Moorland* 12.12, 12.24, 12.31, 12.40, 12.58; Barnatt, *Chatsworth Inbye* 55.39.

13 Barnatt, *Chatsworth Inbye* 55.39, 55.6.

14 Barnatt, *Chatsworth Park* 2.36, 5.1; Barnatt, *Chatsworth Moorland* 14.21, 16.1, 16.11, 16.15; Barnatt, *Chatsworth Inbye* 54.9.

15 Barnatt, *Chatsworth Park* 6.8.

16 Barnatt, *Chatsworth Park* 6.13, Barnatt, *Chatsworth Moorland* 19.17, 19.26, 20.9, 21.2, 21.5, 21.7, 21.11, 24.3, 26.4, 26.21; Barnatt, *Chatsworth Inbye* 51.5.

17 Barnatt, *Chatsworth Moorland* 21.13, 21.8, 20.7, 26.5.

18 Barnatt, *Chatsworth Moorland* 19.13, 19.17; Barnatt, *Chatsworth Inbye* 52.14.

19 Barnatt, *Chatsworth Moorland* 16.19, 16.21, 16.29, 16.16, 16.29, 18.3, 19.5, 19.29, 20.1; Barnatt, *Chatsworth Inbye* 50.20, 50.21, 50.23.

20 Barnatt, *Chatsworth Moorland* 18.6.

21 Barnatt, *Chatsworth Inbye* 48.30, 52,12 and Barnatt, *Chatsworth Moorland* 18.5, 18.16, 20.12, 52.17, 19.20.

22 Barnatt, *Chatsworth Moorland* 27.9; Barnatt, *Chatsworth Inbye* 49.7, 50.14, 50.24.

23 Barnatt, *Chatsworth Inbye* 48.6, 49.2.

24 Barnatt, *Chatsworth Moorland* 15.4, 15.6, 16.13, 17.2, 17.5–6, 17.8–9, 18.38, 18.46, 21.12, 21.14, 22.1, 22.5, 23.3–4, 23.7, 25.4, 26.17, 26.20, 27.4, 27.6, 27.15, 27.32, 28.4, 28.7, 29.2, 29.9, 29.12, 29.15, 30.2–3, 30.7.

25 Barnatt, *Chatsworth Moorland* 18.41, 18.45, 27.8, 27.20, 27.21.

26 Barnatt, *Chatsworth Moorland* 21.8, 18.48.

27 Barnatt, *Chatsworth Moorland* 21.12, 21.13.

28 Barnatt and Bannister, *Vestiges*, pp. 222–23.

29 Barnatt, *Chatsworth Moorland* 11.1; Barnatt, *Chatsworth Inbye* 37.62, 37.65, 37.72, 38.18, 40.17.

30 *1778 Map of Birchill.*

31 Barnatt, *Chatsworth Inbye* 38.23.

32 Barnatt, *Chatsworth Inbye* 38.22.

33 Barnatt, *Chatsworth Inbye* 43.6, 43.9, 43.12.

34 Barnatt, *Chatsworth Park* 7.42, 7.47, 8.10, 11.5.

35 Barnatt, *Chatsworth Park* 9.30.

36 Barnatt and Williamson, *Chatsworth*, pp. 105–06.

37 Barnatt, *Chatsworth Park* 8.32; Senior, *Lees and Edensore.*

38 Barnatt, *Chatsworth Inbye* 44.23, 44.36; Barker, *A plan of Chatsworth Park.*

39 Radley, J. and Penny, S. R. (1972) The turnpike roads of the Peak District. *Derbyshire Archaeological Journal* 92, 93–109; Hey, *Packmen*; Dodd, and Dodd, *Peakland Roads*; Barnatt and Smith, *Peak District*, pp. 107–110.

40 Radley and Penny, *The turnpike roads*; Dodd, and Dodd, *Peakland Roads.*

41 The East Moor to Wardlow (via Baslow and Hassop) Turnpike of 1759.

42 The Rowsley Bridge to Stone Edge Turnpike and the Stone Edge to Wensley (Cross Green via Darley Bridge) Turnpike, both of 1760.

43 The Grindleford Bridge to Newhaven (via Calver and Bakewell) Turnpike of 1759.

44 The Baslow to Owler Bar (via Bar Brook) Turnpike of 1803, and the Baslow to Chesterfield (via Wadshelf) Turnpike of 1812.

45 The Bakewell to Baslow (via Birchill) Turnpike of 1801 and the Ashford (Churchdale) to Edensor Turnpike of 1812.

46 Barnatt and Bannister, *Vestiges*, pp. 226–31.

47 Barnatt and Williamson *Chatsworth*, p. 88.

48 Barnatt and Williamson *Chatsworth*, pp. 106, 112; Barnatt, *Chatsworth Moorland* 24.2.

49 Although the route could have still been followed after 1759–60 down as far as the park and then to Edensor via the new One Arch Bridge, the new turnpike must have provided a better route.

50 The visual effect was perhaps never good, as the trees would probably have grown poorly and been stunted.

51 Unwin, *Untitled map of Devonshire holdings*; Unwin, G. (1831) Untitled map of Edensor, Pilsley and Birchill. Chatsworth House, bound volume of maps; Enclosure Award Map for Ashover (1783) Matlock: Derbyshire Record Office, D59A.

52 Barnatt, *Chatsworth Park* 3.9; Barnatt, *Chatsworth Inbye* 55.33, A55.38.

53 Barnatt, *Chatsworth Inbye* 55.55.

54 Barnatt, *Chatsworth Inbye* 41.54.

55 An 18th century turnpike between these two places ran further north and does not impinge of the Core Estate.

56 Unwin, *Untitled map of Devonshire holdings*.

57 Barnatt, *Chatsworth Inbye* 37.18, 37.39, 37.41, 37.70.

58 Barnatt and Williamson, *Chatsworth*, p. 161; Barnatt, *Chatsworth Park* 9.21.

59 *1824 rough map of roads from Chatsworth to Chesterfield*.

60 Whether this was part of the same scheme or somewhat earlier is not known; Plan of the Road from Chesterfield to the Turnpike Road at Hernstone Lane Head with different branches, etc. (1791) Nottingham University, BAG600; A map of Beeley in the County of Derbyshire (1814) Chatsworth Estate Office, map 2687.

61 Barnatt and Williamson, *Chatsworth*, pp. 172–74.

62 Barnatt and Williamson, *Chatsworth*, pp. 79–80, 174.

63 Unwin, *Untitled map of Devonshire holdings*; Ordnance Survey (1839) One inch to a mile map, first edition, sheets 81 SE and 82 SW (unpublished two inch to a mile versions without hachures – dated 1839); Barnatt, *Chatsworth Inbye* 39.9.

64 Barnatt and Williamson, *Chatsworth*, pp. 172–180.

65 Barnatt, *Chatsworth Moorland* 14.23, 18.6, 18.48, 21.8.

66 Radley, *Peak District roads*, p. 43; Dodd, and Dodd, *Peakland Roads*, p. 84; Hey, *Packmen*, pp. 35–47; Smith, H. (1996) *The Guide Stoops of Derbyshire*. Privately published, pp. 4–7.

67 Barnatt, *Chatsworth Inbye* 38.23.

68 Barnatt, *Chatsworth Moorland* 14.5.

69 Barnatt, *Chatsworth Moorland* 12.11, 12.12.

70 Ward, G. H. B. (1927) The Three Men, ancient bridle way and Clod Hall. *Sheffield Clarion Ramblers 1926–27*, pp. 59–64.

71 Ward, G. H. B. (1929) The Three Men on Gardom's Edge. *Sheffield Clarion Ramblers 1928–29*, p. 176.

72 Barnatt, *Chatsworth Moorland* 30.12.

73 Barnatt, *Chatsworth Moorland* 15.14; Barnatt, *Chatsworth Inbye* 36.71, 37.47, 40.20, 41.84, 55.54.

74 Barnatt, *Chatsworth Inbye* 55.33.

75 Barnatt, *Chatsworth Inbye* 34.17.

Chapter 9: The Woven Strands: The Past in the Present

1 Barnatt and Smith, *Peak District*.

2 For a more detailed summary of these and later garden and parkland features see Barnatt and Williamson, *Chatsworth*, pp. 193–222.

Peak District Archaeology: General Reading

Ainsworth, S. (2001) Prehistoric settlement remains on the Derbyshire gritstone moors. *Derbyshire Archaeological Journal* 121, pp. 19–69.

Barnatt, J. (1986) Bronze Age remains on the East Moors of the Peak District. *Derbyshire Archaeological Journal* 106, pp. 18–100.

Barnatt, J. (1990) *The Henges, Stone Circles and Ringcairns of the Peak District*. Sheffield: Sheffield Archaeological Monographs 1.

Barnatt, J. (1996) Moving between the monuments: Neolithic land use in the Peak District. In P. Frodsham (ed.) *Neolithic Studies in No-Man's Land: Papers on the Neolithic of Northern England, from the Trent to the Tweed*. Northern Archaeology, Volume 13/14, pp. 45–62.

Barnatt, J. (1996) Recent research at Peak District stone circles, including restoration work at Barbrook II and Hordron Edge, and new fieldwork elsewhere. *Derbyshire Archaeological Journal* 116, pp. 27–48.

Barnatt, J. (1999) Taming the Land: Peak District farming and ritual in the Bronze Age. *Derbyshire Archaeological Journal* 119, pp. 19–78.

Barnatt, J. (2000) To each their own: later prehistoric farming communities and their monuments in the Peak. *Derbyshire Archaeological Journal* 120, pp. 1–86.

Barnatt, J. and Collis, J. (eds) (1996) *Barrows in the Peak District: Recent Research*. Sheffield: Sheffield Academic Press.

Barnatt, J. and Manley, R. (2006) *In the Footsteps of the Ancestors: Heritage Walks*. Bakewell: Peak District National Park Authority.

Barnatt, J. and Penny, R. (2004) *The Lead Legacy: The Prospects for the Peak District's Lead Mining Heritage*. Bakewell: Peak District National Park Authority.

Barnatt, J. and Smith, K. (2004) *The Peak District; Landscapes Through Time*. Oxford: Windgather.

Barnatt, J. and Williamson, T. (2005) *Chatsworth: A Landscape History*. Oxford: Windgather.

Barnatt, J. and Worthington, T. (2006) Using coal to mine lead: firesetting at Peak District mines. *Mining History* 16.3, pp. 1–94.

Bateman, T. (1848) *Vestiges of the Antiquities of Derbyshire*. London.

Bateman, T. (1861) *Ten Years Diggings in Celtic and Saxon Grave Hills in the Counties of Derby, Stafford and York*. London and Derby.

Bevan, B. (2004) *The Upper Derwent: 10.000 Years in a Peak District Valley*. Port Stroud: Tempus.

Bevan, B. (2005) Peaks Romana: the Peak District Romano-British rural upland settlement survey, 1998–2000. *Derbyshire Archaeological Journal* 125, pp. 26–58;

Brighton, T. (2004) *The Discovery of the Peak District*. Chichester: Phillimore

Cameron, K. (1959) *The Place-Names of Derbyshire (3 Vols.)*. Cambridge: Cambridge University Press.

Cooper, N. (1991) *Transformation of a Valley: the Derbyshire Derwent*. Cromford: Scarthin.

Craven, M. and Stanley, M. (2001) *The Derbyshire Country House (2 vols)*. Ashbourne: Landmark.

Derwent Valley Mills Partnership (2001) *The Derwent Valley Mills and their Communities*. Matlock.

Dodd, A. E. and Dodd, E. M. (1980) *Peakland Roads and Trackways*. Ashbourne: Moorland. 2nd ed.

Dowager Duchess of Devonshire (2005) *Round About Chatsworth*. London: Francis Lincoln.

Duchess of Devonshire (1982) *The House. A portrait of Chatsworth*. London.

Duchess of Devonshire (1987) *The Garden at Chatsworth*. Derby

Duchess of Devonshire (1990) *The Estate. A View from Chatsworth*. London.

Edmonds, M. and Seaborne, T. (2001) *Prehistory in the Peak*. Port Stroud: Tempus.

Ford, T. D. (2002) *Rocks and Scenery of the Peak District*. Ashbourne: Landmark.

Ford, T. D. and Rieuwerts, J. H. (eds) (2000) *Lead

Mining in the Peak District (4th Edition). Ashbourne: Landmark.

Harris, H. (1971) *Industrial Archaeology of the Peak District.* Newton Abbot: David and Charles.

Hart, C. R. (1981) *The North Derbyshire Archaeological Survey.* Chesterfield: North Derbyshire Archaeological Trust.

Heath, J. (1993) *An Illustrated History of Derbyshire.* Derby: Breedon Books.

Hey, D. (1980) *Packmen, Carriers and Packhorse Roads.* Leicester: Leicester University Press.

Hodges, R. (1991) *Wall-to-Wall History: the Story of Royston Grange.* London: Duckworth.

Hopkinson, G. G. (1957) The development of the South Yorkshire and North Derbyshire coalfield, 1500–1775. *Transactions of the Hunter Archaeological Society* 7.6, pp. 295–319.

Joyce, B., Michell, G. and Williams, M. (1996) *Derbyshire. Detail and Character.* Alan Sutton Publishing Ltd.

Kiernan, D. (1989) *The Derbyshire Lead Industry in the Sixteenth Century.* Chesterfield: Derbyshire Record Society, Vol. 14.

Makepeace, G. A. (1998) Romano-British rural settlements in the Peak District and north-east Staffordshire. *Derbyshire Archaeological Journal* 118, pp. 95–138.

Naylor, D. (2005) *The Chatsworth Villages: Beeley, Edensor & Pilsley.* Ashbourne: Landmark.

Pearson, J. (2002) Stags and Serpents: a History of the Cavendish Family and the Dukes of Devonshire (revised edition). Bakewell.

Pevsner, N. (1978) *The Buildings of England: Derbyshire* (second edition). Harmondsworth: Penguin.

Polak, J. P. (1987) The production and distribution of Peak millstones from the sixteenth to the eighteenth centuries. *Derbyshire Archaeological Journal* 107, pp. 55–72.

Radley, J. and Penny, S. R. (1972) The turnpike roads of the Peak District. *Derbyshire Archaeological Journal* 92, pp. 93–109.

Rieuwerts, J. H. (1998) *Glossary of Derbyshire Lead Mining Terms.* Matlock Bath: Peak District Mines Historical Society.

Rieuwerts, J. H. (2007) Lead Mining in Derbyshire: History, Development & Drainage. Vol. 1: Castleton to the River Wye. Ashbourne: Landmark.

Roffe, D. (1986) *The Derbyshire Domesday.* Darley Dale: Derbyshire Museums Service.

Sharpe, N. T. (2002) *Crosses of the Peak District.* Ashbourne: Landmark.

Sidebottom, P. C. (1999) Stone crosses in the Peak and 'the sons of Eadwulf'. *Derbyshire Archaeological Journal* 119, pp. 206–219.

Smith, H. (1996) *The Guide Stoops of Derbyshire.* Privately published.

Thompson, F. (1949) *A History of Chatsworth: being a supplement to the Sixth Duke of Devonshire's Handbook.* London: Country Life.

Tucker, G. (1985) Millstone making in the Peak District of Derbyshire: the quarries and the technology. *Industrial Archaeology Review* 8.1, pp. 42–58.

Williams, A. and Martin, G. H. (1992) *Domesday Book: A Complete Translation.* London: Penguin.

Wood, A. (1999) *The Politics of Social Conflict: The Peak Country 1520–1770.* Cambridge: Cambridge University Press.

Index